D0084905

AMERICAN E
AND CORPOR

PEDAGOGY A
SHIRLEY R. ST

AMERICAN
AND CORPO
The Free M
by Deron B

PEDAGOGY AND POPULAR
VOLUME I
GARLAND REFERENCE LIB
VOLUME 1159

AMERICAN EDUCATION
AND CORPORATIONS
THE FREE MARKET GOES TO SCHOOL

DERON BOYLES

GARLAND PUBLISHING, INC.
A MEMBER OF THE TAYLOR & FRANCIS GROUP
NEW YORK AND LONDON
1998

Copyright © 1998 by Deron Boyles

Library of Congress Cataloging-in-Publication Data

Boyles, Deron.
    American education and corporations : the free market goes to school /
  by Deron Boyles.
        p.   cm. — (Garland reference library of social science ; v. 1159.
  Pedagogy and popular culture ; v. 1)
    Includes bibliographical references and index.
    ISBN 0-8153-2822-2 (alk. paper)
    1. Industry and education—United States.   2. Commercialism in
  schools—United States.   I. Title.   II. Series: Garland reference library of
  social science ; v. 1159.   III. Series: Garland reference library of social
  science.   Pedagogy and popular culture ; v. 1.
  LC1085.2.B69   1998
  371.19'5'0973—dc21   98-4443
                                                                              CIP

Printed on acid-free, 250-year-life paper
Manufactured in the United States of America

To Jeremy Thomas Wilson
and Sandra Herman

Contents

Illustrations

Acknowledgments

A work of this kind does not emerge without the help and support of very special people. I am most appreciative of a supportive family: my parents, Robert and Mary Boyles; my sister, Beth Carraway and her family—Steve, Jason, and Christi; and a grandmother, Mary Tribbett, who unknowingly has been an inspiration. Other very special people who either directly or indirectly influenced this work include my most influential teachers: Jack Conrad Willers, John Lachs, Henry Giroux, Ron Shomo, Phyllis Levitt, and Jim Orth.

Additionally, it is rare when a professor is fortunate enough to have a graduate assistant who surpasses all expectations. It is even more rare when the professor recognizes it at the time. However, I can't help but recognize the intellect and insight of Greg Seals, my graduate research assistant. I have learned from him and have benefitted greatly from our interaction. This work would not have been possible without his very able assistance.

Other friends, colleagues, and students (both past and present) continue to impress me with their wisdom and I am grateful to those who were positively fastidious in their review of my work, especially Darren Pascavage, Demetrios J. Stavropoulos, Dorothy Huenecke, and Wayne Urban. I also thank Diane Ginsberg and her son Brian for their help with the Six Flags "Read to Succeed" program.

The tireless technical support of Toni Marchiveccio, Meredith Lester, and Lauren Clendenen made this project possible. Without Toni's computer expertise, Meredith's patience with the formatting gremlins and willingness to revise and correct my work, and Lauren's unerring confidence that the work would be completed, it would not be finished. I appreciate their encouragement and support.

A small section of chapter 2 appeared in *The Humanist* (July/August 1995): 20-24, and another small section of chapter 3 appeared in *Journal of Thought* 28, nos. 1 & 2 (Spring/Summer 1993): 95-100. Permission to use copyrighted material was granted by the American Federation of Teachers. Permission was also granted to reprint material from Kroger and the Conference Board and I am grateful to these organizations.

Two very special people, Joe Kincheloe and Shirley Steinberg, provided me this opportunity and it is to them that I am most thankful.

Introduction

An assembly takes place at the local high school. Students file in and take their seats. Some are raucous, some quiet. While teachers stand guard at the ends of rows of seats and point to disruptive students in an effort to reduce chaos, the lights dim in the auditorium. Catcalls and whistling are "shhushh-ed" as the curtain opens. Spotlights appear on the stage and a band comes forward playing electric guitars, synthesizers, and drums. They sing, too, but something seems a bit out of place. The band, it turns out, is not singing popular rock-and-roll music or their own lyrics. The band isn't even from the high school. The band performing is, instead, part of "Chemipalooza," the Dow Chemical Company "spin-off" on the Generation X rock music Lollapalooza tours of the 1990s. The assembly is sponsored by Dow Chemical and the performance is a celebration of plastics and other chemistry-oriented products Dow produces. The "tour," it turns out, is a celebration of science, the chemical industry, and careerism. Dow is promoting itself and its interests by linking chemistry and schools as a way to encourage students to become future scientists and, in not-so-concealed ways, Dow consumers. The free market comes to school.

Dow isn't alone. Scholastic, Inc., provides schools with instructional packages including *Teenage Mutant Ninja Turtles II: The Secrets of the Ooze* and *Jetsons: The Movie* as courses on the environment.[1] Nike supplies shoe-making kits; Sprite advertises on the sides of school buses; and Campbell Soup Company does "science experiments" comparing the "thickness" of its sauce to that of its competitor Prego.[2] Writing in *Business Week*, Pat Wechsler notes, "The National Soft Drink Association offers teachers a poster called. . . 'Soft Drinks and Nutrition,' which... compares the heavily sweetened products of its member companies to milk and fruit."[3] Each of these initiatives differ, but they share a common purpose–increasing corporate influences on and in schools.

Is there any problem with such free-market entrepreneurship? In a capitalist society, such initiatives are applauded and encouraged by those who see nothing wrong with using schools as sites for product promotion.[4] There are "educational outcomes," so the consumer-materialist argument goes, and since schools are in need of funding and corporations have plenty of money, why shouldn't corporations get some return on their investment? Schools, after all, are not separate from the societies they inhabit. Since students (and teachers) are constantly subjected to advertising—as is the rest of America—it would be unrealistic to think schools could keep advertising out of their buildings or their curriculum. True.

Yet what follows is a different perspective. The text suggests that "Chemipalooza" tours and *Ninja Turtles* marketing further reinforce schools as places for corporate training and corporate profiteering instead of critical discernment and education. To be clear, the problem with schools as sites for corporate influences is at least threefold. First, they limit and reduce the capacities of students and teachers to be critical citizens (and critical consumers) by structuring the school sphere–organizationally, in terms of the curriculum, etcetera—so that marketing strategies such as quasi rock concerts and Hollywood-hyped cartoons, etcetera hegemonically influence many, though fortunately not all, young minds into accepting the product connection between the programs, curriculum, and specific texts.

The second problem with schools as sites for corporate influence is that it restricts teachers to those programs that have corporate support (tacit or explicit) by highlighting corporate needs for certain kinds of workers who possess specific kinds of "skills"—all codified by corporations and reflected in state curriculum objectives. Ironically, businesses assert that their involvement reduces bureaucracy and increases teacher autonomy. Even if this is initially true and teachers find themselves free from much of the "red tape" of current public institutions, teachers nonetheless face a different master: businesses that take accountability to mean quantified, reductionistic measures in terms of "outputs" and "products."

The third problem with schools as sites for corporate influence is that it reinforces the assumption that schools primarily exist for workforce preparation. "Chemipalooza," for example, shows students possible occupations in chemistry. On this assumption, corporations are doing the equivalent of a public service and are to be applauded for their involvement. This book encourages that we carefully consider who benefits from corporate involvement and argues that surface acceptance of capitalist realities glosses over serious consequences of class, culture, and gender disparities.

On a broader scale, this work argues that corporate involvement in American public schools represents a growing threat to democratic citizenship. When corporations are in control, profit interests perpetually risk undermining curriculum programs that are expensive and for-profit agendas overtly intimidate faculty who disagree with company policy. Corporations promote schools as sites for technorationality, consumer materialism, and intransitive consciousness when, instead, as this book offers, schools should be sites for multirational investigation, economic discernment, and critical transitivity. Technorationality, or technical rationality, is a way of thinking that reduces theories and ideas to empirical explanations and "overhead projector" charts and listings. Technorationality operates on "givens" such as "real-world" "facts" that are immutable and unchangeable, thus restricting divergent positions or critical questions. It is linked to consumer materialism in that the "givens" and the reductions that are characteristic of technorationality are necessary conditions for consumer materialism.

Consumer materialism commodifies existence by reducing searching, being, and thinking to objectified and reductionistic particulars. For schooling, it means, in part, that students see their roles as "getting" right answers to questions instead of searching for meaning and understanding by contesting standardized curricula. The "right answers" are material goods, "getting" is what consumers do. As Steinberg and Kincheloe argued in *Kinder-Culture: The Corporate Construction of Childhood*, "patterns of consumption shaped by corporate advertising empower commercial institutions as the teachers of the new millenium. Corporate culture pedagogy has 'done its homework'—it has produced educational forms that are wildly successful when judged on the basis of their capitalist intent."[5] Similarly teachers see their roles as "getting" preordained procedures that will allow the efficient transfer of information from them (or the adopted texts/curriculum) to their students. The content are the goods, "getting" is, again, what consumers do. "Hooked on Phonics" is an illustration of technorationality and consumer materialism taken together. Literacy is reduced to tapes, booklets, charts, and graphs (technorationality) and sold to consumers who operate from the materialist assumptions that purchasing or *having* the goods means they are one step closer to *being* literate (consumer materialism). This is barely different from textbook adoptions and standardized testing. The technorational value attached to standardized test scores has people buying houses in certain districts and not others, all on the consumer-materialist assumption that teaching and learning are commodifiable goods that *are* represented by standardized tests. Teachers and students are part of this problem but, as chapter 1 points out, students and teachers are not to blame. Their *roles* are constructed to fit consumer-materialist expectations, partly via technorational means, and all with an ironic benefit to corporations in the form of educational goals touting economic competitiveness, international rankings, and businesses' valuation of accountability and efficiency models ("givens" of "the real world"?).

Technorationality and consumer materialism represent, in part, the "givens" that reinforce intransitive consciousness (or intransitivity). Intransitivity comes from Freire and means "noncritical (in)action." He clarifies that intransitiveness repudiates the power of individuals to change their existences, for example, "I can't speak out about teaching-to-the-test because I might lose my job . . . that's the 'real world' and I can't do anything about it."[6] Differently, semitransitiveness is characterized by individuals who see the world as changeable, but see the world in unrelated segments such that semitransitiveness is two-dimensional and short term. For example, groups may feed the hungry but never ask why hungry people exist in a society with yearly food surpluses.[7] While intransitiveness and semitransitiveness are visible in schools, Freire's ultimate achievement—critical transitivity—is rarely evidenced. Critical transitiveness is demonstrated when individuals make, according to Shor, "broad connections between individual experience and social issues. . . . In education, critically conscious teachers and students synthesize personal and social meanings with a specific theme, text, or issue."[8] Said differently, student and teacher experiences are vital components of the critique of topics. This does not mean that any perspective carries the same weight as any other perspective, but it does mean that student and teacher viewpoints are encouraged and utilized in a process of investigation that does not accept the impervious realities of science, mathematics, literature, and history, etcetera.

School-business partnerships and privatization efforts are the primary means through which corporations thwart critical transitivity and this text offers evidence and arguments to support the claim. Chapter 1, "Schools as Sites for Consumer Materialism," offers conceptual distinctions among "education," "schooling," and "training" in order to distinguish between what schools *are* doing and what schools *ought* to be doing. In this light, readers should be clear from the beginning that this chapter, indeed the entire text, is philosophically normative. That is, it represents an argument for schools to change from what they currently are—arguably training-oriented sites hegemonically producing intransitive workers for corporate interests—to something different; something akin to education-oriented sites for critical citizenship. In this vein, the polemics of the book are to be taken as stylistic liberties, not universal condemnations. Extensive citations are noted in order to provide as broad a base of evidence as is possible, given the limits of this project, such that temporal conclusions might be seen or drawn. The brief history given in chapter 1 is too brief and readers are encouraged to see the endnotes for further reading and clarification. In fact, entire texts have been written on each of the subthemes in chapter 1: conceptual analysis in education, history of education, politics of the textbook, curriculum and curriculum theory, and the proletarianization of teachers. Each of these subthemes is nonetheless connected to consumer materialism and taken together, set up a background perspective through which the subsequent chapters should be viewed.

Chapter 2, "Corporate Culture and Schools: Consultants in Search of New Markets," explores the infusion of corporate culture into U.S. schools. The chapter highlights corporate calls for schools to fall in line when it comes to seeing the purpose of schools as training for economic competitiveness. A mini-industry of consultants has sprung up in and around schools whereby professional or in-service days are spent looking and listening to human-resource pep talks by those who have literally bought into corporate culture's ontology and are reaping profits as a result.

Chapter 3, "The Kroger Connection," focuses attention on school-business partnerships. The chapter provides illustrations of actual partnerships as well as those programs that reflect the school-business partnership ethos. In other words, in addition to Kroger, Honeywell, Burger King, Pizza Hut, Six Flags, etcetera, the chapter includes initiatives such as Junior Achievement and KAPOW. These are programs intended to have students, as early as fourth grade, consider vocational and job opportunities for their future. Somewhat distinct from traditional school-business partnerships, these initiatives are included because businesses fund the programs and unashamedly urge elementary and middle-school students to pick a career. They "fit"with school-business partnerships, such as the one between Honeywell and Minneapolis schools, insofar as they seek workers for their industries. Chapter 3 asks whether such programs represent conflicts of interest or not. Further, chapter 3 explores the "philanthropy" of corporations in their school-business relationships and asks whether the "philanthropic" effort is actually marketing in disguise.

Chapter 4, "Privatization and the Future of Public Schooling," explores efforts at privatizing American public schools. The chapter begins by asserting that, at root, the privatization initiative is one grounded in capitalist hegemony and that the notion of correspondence (strict and otherwise) is vital to understanding the push for privatizing public schools. Corporations and their allies, along with cultural and economic conservatives, are joining forces with disgruntled parents in lodging a marketing campaign targeted at pitting school against school in a free-market free-for-all. Privatization is carefully defined in order to distinguish between religious, nonprofit private, and other kinds of private schools. Where school-business partnerships are exploited by different markets, privatization intends to make schools distinct markets themselves. The consequences are intriguing and will be considered in terms of choice, control and power, testing, and profits. Baltimore, Chelsea, Milwaukee, and Dade County provide illustrations of the point and highlight the problems.

Finally, chapter 5, "Critically Transitive Teachers," offers arguments and illustrations for making schools democratic spaces that spurn oligopolistic influence and consumer materialism. The chapter envisions schools achieving their latent potential as education-oriented sites for critical transitivity by extending and developing foregoing arguments in the text. Specifically, education-oriented schooling, critical transitivity, and multiple ways of knowing will be used to make the case that *public* school should be revised by changing the nature and role of teaching. The chapter explores the potential of teachers as intellectuals and as collectively autonomous people engaged in experiential, education-oriented schooling in the context of pluralist democracy. As if this is not enough of a task, the chapter also argues for a different role for colleges of education—one that fosters critical questioning by reducing the very consumer-materialist expectations they often perpetuate.

NOTES

1. George Kaplan, "Profits R Us: Notes on the Commercialization of America's Schools," *Phi Delta Kappan* (November 1996): K6.

2. Pat Wechsler, "This Lesson Brought To You By...," *Business Week* (30 June 1997): 68-69.

3. Ibid.

4. Ronald E. Berembeim, "Preparing Students for Health Services Occupations," *Corporate Support of Dropout Prevention and Workforce Readiness* (New York: The Conference Board, 1993), 34-36. See also, John A. Nidds and James McGerald, "Corporate America Looks at Public Education," *Principal* (March 1995): 22-23; and Andrew Ashwell and Frank Caropreso, eds., *Business Leadership: The Third Wave of Education Reform* (New York: The Conference Board, 1989).

5. Shirley R. Steinberg and Joe L. Kincheloe, *Kinder-Culture: The Corporate Construction of Childhood* (Boulder, CO: Westview Press, 1997), 4.

6. See Paulo Freire, *Education for Critical Consciousness* (New York: Seabury, 1973); and Ira Shor, *Empowering Education* (Chicago: University of Chicago Press, 1992), 127-128.

7. Ibid.

8. Shor, op. cit.

AMERICAN EDUCATION AND CORPORATIONS

CHAPTER 1

Schools as Sites for Consumer Materialism

"The aim of totalitarian education has never been to instill convictions but to destroy the capacity to form any."[1]

Both teachers and students are the primary targets of consumer materialism in American schools and both groups hegemonically contribute to the successful replication of consumer materialism in schools.[2] Not an exercise in placing blame on either teachers or students, they nonetheless (perhaps unwittingly) perpetuate non criticality. Teachers seek, as Roger Simon puts it, a language of technique: "how-to" methods for the complex problems they face, both interpersonally and pedagogically in schools.[3] What Simon means is that teachers want doable procedures they can apply the next day. Without critical thought on their part, they quest for the kind of certainty that privileges consumer materialism and reductionism because certainty is viewed as a commodified endpoint. Not surprisingly, maybe consequently, students also seek easy paths to "getting" "correct" "answers." They see teachers pointing to finite objectives and outlining the steps one takes to achieve those objectives. Learning becomes a particularized process of acquisition and for those students willing to play the game, "success" is defined by Cartesian foundations: logical, sequential, objective means to an end. External procedures are linked with pre-defined goals, not unlike consumer materialism, which posits pre-defined ends such as products and goods. Once persuaded of the value (image-bound?) of the goods, working becomes the external procedure to acquire the goods.

One reason teachers and students are in such positions is because the organization of the school, as it is presently constructed, institutionalizes consumer materialism. With schools firmly entrenched in management hierarchies, they emphasize consumer-materialist expectations: efficiency, authority, and good "end-products." Facing societal appeals to scientism, schools view their role as transmitting (efficiency) necessary information from curriculum guidelines (authority) via teachers to students, who become testable objects for school-by-school or county-by-county comparison (end products). Schools also face constrained budgets and limited resources, making them increasingly vulnerable to business "partnerships," typically entered into in order to buy technology and to have corporate "mentors" assigned to them. In specific instances, business programs such as candle sales, flea markets, and candy drives fund curriculum-linked clubs and organizations with only 50 percent or so of the proceeds going to the clubs and organizations.

Symptomatic of the larger problem are the terms used to talk about schools: "standards," "objectives," "outcomes," "skills," and "goals" are part of discussions comparing American schools to other countries. *America 2000*,[4] *What Work Requires of Schools*,[5] *Learning a Living*,[6] and others, are government committee-processed, reports each linking the purpose of American schools inextricably to business interests. In addition to government reports, corporate reports such as *The Fourth R: Workforce Readiness*,[7] *Labor Force 2000: Corporate America Responds*,[8] *Business Leadership: The Third Wave of Education Reform*,[9] and many more, reinforce assumptions about the nature, role, and purposes of American schools. By sheer saturation via corporate advocates, the last fifteen years have seen a continuous stream of "Allstate Forum" reports using reductionist language to mold the ethos and expectations of the general population even more fully into the fold of business-speak and training. When President Bill Clinton talks about education, he links it to job training.[10] When governors in states such as South Carolina, Alabama, and Georgia talk about education, they link it to state economic-growth strategies for enticing Mercedes-Benz and BMW plants to relocate to their areas. Schools become hyperparticularized social institutions to attract big business and to narrowly train students for those businesses. One consequence of this is that education and training are confused as being synonymous. Such confusion sets the tone for "education" discourse. When conversations about "education" are consistently connected to jobs, international competition, and the materialist logic of "getting ahead," Whitman's "powerful play" may go on, but it does so with constrained, minimal, and abridged verses for women, people of color, and other (current) minority status groups.

To assert a different case from that which is currently entrenched means outlining a narrative other than that which is popular with policymakers, administrators, parents, and in many cases (sadly), teachers. It means challenging the assumptions that are firmly held, if infrequently questioned, about schools being places for workforce preparation. It also means linking the narrative with purposive arguments about why consumer materialism and schooling are ill matched in a democratic society. What follows, then, is an effort to confront and reduce consumer materialism in American schools. By illustrating the differences among "education," "schooling," and "training," and by providing evidence of hegemonically reinforced roles for teachers, an argument for critical transitivity emerges.[11] Other arguments reveal the widespread misuse of schools by corporate ideologues and their minions and include concerns regarding textbook adoption, curriculum standards, the proletarianization of teachers, and considerations such as the usefulness of technology for different populations. It should be clear from the start that this work is not arguing for an overthrow of capitalism. It is arguing, instead, that the worst vestiges of capitalism, including most prominently consumer materialism, are being foisted upon teachers and students, through their schools (via a kind of befuddled acquiescence), at the expense of critical transitivity.

THE PRIVILEGING OF TRAINING OVER EDUCATION

Schools are sites for consumer materialism, in part because of the nature of the organization and in part because the history of American schools includes the relatively recent bifurcation of the purpose of American schools: general education for citizenship versus specialized training for economic production.[12] McNeil suggests that the first purpose requires schools to offer information and processes of learning that result in knowledge. Theoretically, the information and processes are multi-faceted and broad. She notes that from an organizational standpoint, this purpose is problematic insofar as the outcomes of learning are unpredictable. Students learn at varying paces and while they share interests, there are important differences as well. The differences are not a problem for the first purpose because achieving knowledge is a messy and cumbersome affair that takes differences as necessary conditions for learning. It is almost as though "knowing" (via general education) is an inherently messy process, so that any organizing of information and learning will have to recognize—if not appreciate—those differences. But differences *are* a problem for the second purpose, because they get in the way of standardization and efficiency. To achieve specialized training, the function of the school is to fit learners into a preconceived economic scheme. It is similar to a "paint-by-numbers" metaphor where the lines, colors, and amounts of paint are given and the role of the painter (teacher?) is to fill in the lines of the predetermined picture (students?)—indeed, being sure not to paint outside them. For the second purpose, "schools process students through stratified steps leading to predictable, marketable credentials for the workplace. The steps, and some of the outcomes, can be managed, controlled. Thus the school is organized to be in conflict with itself."[13]

It was not always this way. Before widespread industrialism, schools were places where students would go, just long enough, to learn necessary information to further their purposes. Early American schooling expanded and reflected general education and literacy at a time when schooling was also seen as a means for social mobility, only not in terms of consumer materialism. Regarding the general-education purpose of schools, Cremin notes that "As almanacs, newspapers, pamphlets, and books dealt with matters of topical interest, especially after the Stamp Act crisis of the 1760s, a premium was placed on literacy in segments of the population where illiteracy had long been [stigmatized]."[14] Kantor further clarifies that "prior to 1880, schools were seldom seen as mechanisms to prepare youths for jobs. . . . Nor, by and large, did people expect that schooling beyond the elementary and grammar grades would influence one's chances for employment."[15] McNeil adds, "While having school-supplied skills (geography, accounting, literacy) might help a person find an apprenticeship, there was no notion of going to school in order to get a job or be trained for one, or to obtain a certificate of attendance."[16] Reading and ciphering learned, students would apply this knowledge as *they* intended it, or found utility for it. Literacy and economic achievement were linked, that is, those who were functionally illiterate had less earning potential on average than those who were literate, but the argument for schools as sites for specific forms of literacy (math and science achievement, industrial- and computer-oriented vocational training, etc.) is a mid- to late-nineteenth-century and twentieth- century development.[17] These arguments also lay the foundation for consumer materialism by recasting schools as reductionist institutions whose purpose it is to compartmentalize and transmit bits of information deemed "marketable."

Joel Spring suggests that an inherent tension here is one between cooperation of a particular kind and the agrarian individualism of the late nineteenth century.[18] The cooperation to which he refers was the result of immigration, urbanization, and the rise of industrialism. "Early American society was conceived of at a time when growth and progress resulted from everyone working for his own self-interest as an independent economic unit without the restraints of a tightly knit social organization. By the end of the century many Americans believed this conception of society was no longer relevant to the urban and industrial world of the post-Civil War period."[19]

Perhaps the roots of the push toward consumer materialism can be traced to arguments given in the nineteenth century by Horace Mann in favor of common schools. He advanced the "wealth position": individual wealth depends upon the general wealth of the community and schools are places where the traits that make productive workers can best be instilled.[20] Mann's position should not sound strange to contemporary ears, partly because the success of consumer materialism has dulled sensibilities about what is primarily pedagogic—not economic—about schools, and partly because the sensibilities that are dulled are easily dulled. That is, without a thoughtful position regarding the various purposes of schools (social, political, economic, pedagogic, etc.), Americans hear appeals to their materialist fears about jobs, productivity, and competition. By linking these concerns to schools, conversation about the purpose of schools is slanted. Mann understood the power of this link, but not quite for consumer materialist purposes. Mann's position was offered to sway voters in favor of common schools, but was also the way to have people swallow a bitter pill—funding in the form of taxes to support common schools. What he did was successfully argue that those who should pay for school are not only those who have children attending school. This way, more people pay because, according to the "wealth argument," it was in everyone's interest to see to it that schools succeeded in producing productive members for society.[21]

Part of the role of common schools, according to Mann and his supporters, was to instill good habits and quality traits like respect for authority, punctuality, and manners, via general and common curricula. As a foundation for good habits and quality traits, Mann and his supporters used a Protestant version of the Bible as a primary reader. Not surprisingly, opponents of the common-school movement included those of the Catholic and Jewish faiths, among others. But the point here is to clarify that Mann's position does not ultimately represent consumer materialism, even though it supports it, for while it narrows the focus of schooling and reinforces student roles as passive and teacher roles as transmission-oriented, it does not (perhaps because of its religious overtones) privilege the tangibility that characterizes consumer materialism. This bifurcation does not become apparent until the turn of the century, but schools today maintain purposes strikingly similar to those of Mann's time by asserting general-education purposes while practicing specialized training. McNeil's concern about conflicting ideas provides insight into how consumer materialism gains entry into schools at the same time that it mollifies the tension between the conflicting purposes. We can see how the ideas conflict by comparing business interests with those of labor and progressives around the turn of the century. Consumer materialism is one outcome of the debate and placates the tension by appearing to satisfy all parties, while primarily benefitting business in the long term.

At about the same time common schools were proliferating, industrial expansion increased dramatically. Arthur Wirth details many of the particulars of this period,[22] but our purposes only call for a brief history and general understanding of the players involved, their arguments, and the consequences for schools in the twentieth century. There were four major players: (1) business/industry; (2) managerial progressives; (3) labor; and (4) humanitarian progressives. Three out of the four groups ultimately opted for policies and practices that increased consumer materialism, even though the history of labor hints at different intentions.[23]

Businesses, well represented by the National Association of Manufacturers (NAM), wanted schools to be training sites in the manner of German technical institutes and argued that funds should be diverted from general education into "commercial and technical schools."[24] This position has changed little in over a century, with only the addition of advanced technology to serve its purposes. The NAM staunchly favored free enterprise and saw the increase in immigration at the turn of the century as an important source of cheap labor. They considered trade schools, continuation schools, and corporation schools to be models for reforming public education.[25] Continuation schools were too expensive, trade schools were too advanced, and corporation schools missed the point altogether: why have a corporate school paid for by the business when one could have a public system train students instead—at taxpayer expense?

Labor, represented by the American Federation of Labor (AFL), initially was skeptical about business calls for industrial training, but in the best Gompers tradition overcame any ideological problems and focused simply on the economic benefits for workers. It was, after all, the Political Workingmen's Party that fought class polarization and argued, via its various constituents, for a general education that did not educate the mind at the expense of the body *as well as* the reverse. There was, to be sure, an assumption that America could be egalitarian or a "band of republican brethren."[26] Other versions of this assumption were exemplified by Robert Owens and Francis Wright in their attempts to create communes as alternatives to classism. There were other labor groups that sought anarchist or socialist goals. Still others, in the Populist Movement, attacked the "vested interests." But the AFL and Samuel Gompers emerged as the major voice of labor, after a split with the Knights of Labor and after the defeat of the Populists, and they were committed to championing industrial education and consumer materialism. They were not eager to turn industrial training over to public schools, for, as Wirth points out, "[the AFL was] concerned that teachers were unduly influenced by the dominant business ethic and that children might be taught a distorted view of labor's role in society."[27] It was Gompers' accommodationalism, due to his strong faith that a profit system would improve workers' positions within industry that, ironically perhaps, rejected socialist ideas, but accommodated business interests.[28]

Managerial progressives counted among their numbers school administrators and educational theorists who opted for scientific efficiency arguments that favored a business approach to schooling. These were Taylorism advocates who thought science and method were the keys to routinization. Humanitarian progressives were also interested in scientific expertise, but they were interested most in how to avoid human suffering by efficient means. Wirth clarifies further:

> While business-oriented progressives were alarmed by waste, it was financial waste that bothered them most. When they discussed educational waste, they pointed to the "low yield of school products" measured on the yardsticks of cost accounting. Or, they deplored the impractical curriculum which failed to serve the requirements of business and industry. The humanitarian reformers, on the other hand, were appalled chiefly by the "human waste" as represented in the lives of slum dwellers eroded by poverty, vice, crime, and despair.[29]

Humanitarian progressives, such as Jane Addams, Ellen Gates Starr, and Robert Woods, found themselves arguing in favor of specialized training as a means for upward mobility *out of* debilitating poverty, not just increased wealth for status-quo comparison. They demonstrated their allegiance to the value preferences they thought were important, going so far as to advocate cooperatives and businesses that were run in democratic ways. Such democratic governance would develop "a new sense of reciprocity throughout, create a larger product, and share it on a better understanding and more equitable basis."[30]

The NAM considered such talk subversive and socialist and continued its efforts to have schools produce workers they desired. One interesting outcome of their effort was their call for federal regulation and support of education. This is interesting because the NAM, by so staunchly arguing for free enterprise, contradicted itself when it argued for government intervention. This point will return in chapter 4, but for now, what is important is understanding that the NAM was very influential in structuring schools in ways that benefitted business most.

In general terms, then, it is turn-of-the-century industrialism that provided the clearest illustration of the point. McNeil notes:

> This period of early industrialization is critical to any understanding of the situating of course content within the organization of the schools. It was during this time, when the school was being directly used as an agency of social control, that our present forms of high school organization were being established. These include administrators who function as business managers rather than as educators; curriculum differentiation by track and

time according to students' social class and expected job future; and emphasis on testable "outputs" of schooling rather than on longer-term learning.[31]

Take "education" to represent the first goal of schools (general education for citizenship) and "training" to represent the conflicting goal (specialized training for economic production). While schools purport to achieve "education," by touting the "coverage" of academic subjects such as English, mathematics, history, and science, they are primarily committed to "training" as the value of English, mathematics, history, and science, is widely taken to be in the utility of the subjects ("When will I ever *use* this?") or the competitive edge they represent in international comparisons. This, in part, is what makes the notions conflicting. To say on the one hand that the goal is "education," but then engage in "training" is to differ, fundamentally, over what schools should be doing. What makes this so interesting is the chicanery involved, that is, the purporting of "A" while doing "B," but saying "B" is "A" regardless.

Goodlad's study, for example, revealed that in the minds of elementary-, middle-, *and* high-school teachers, "training" was the least important goal for schools, after "education," personal goals, and social goals.[32] His study also revealed that "training" was the least important goal in the minds of parents whose children were in elementary or middle school. For parents of high-school students, "training" came in third behind "education" and personal goals. Ironically, the teachers' and parents' perspectives do not characterize society as policy mandates and educational planning continue to reflect "training." Spring notes that

nothing gives greater evidence of the potential conflict between public and private goals than the fact that the number-one goal of teachers and parents is intellectual ["education"]. Students maintain this is their number-one goal until high school, when it moves into second place after vocational ["training"]. This means that a majority of parents send their children to school primarily to learn academic skills and knowledge. Although on the surface this seems reasonable and a common sense conclusion, it is in conflict with the major public goals that have been used to justify the establishment and maintenance of public schools.[33]

Or is it? Consider the idea that what teachers and parents understand to be "education" is actually "training." This might mean that consumer materialism is evident in the assumptions made by both teachers and parents when they reveal their expectations for schooling. This might also mean that "education" and "training" are competing notions, rather than antithetical, but the current success of consumer materialism means that "education," as an idea, is understood inordinately in relation to "training." As the litmus-test notion for a "successful" school, "training" is the referee in a competitive game of test-score comparisons. Conceptually, however, there are important differences between "education," "schooling," and "training" that, when examined, offer hope for the project of distinguishing between American schools as democratic public spheres dedicated to the purposes of "education" and American schools as training sites for corporations.

CONCEPTUAL DIFFERENCES BETWEEN "EDUCATION," "SCHOOLING," AND "TRAINING"

"Education" is the broadest conceptual category and is neither limited to formal or institutional settings (as is "schooling"), nor does its value rely upon its utility or practicality (as does "training").[34] Said differently, "education" is not bounded by school walls and is not reliant upon professional teachers for its existence. "Education" does not depend upon externally imposed outcomes or goals. "Education," like learning, is also not reliant upon being applied in immediate practical situations. Instead, "education" exists, for example, when infants crawl, when children sing songs on the playground, or realize that the Tooth Fairy is a myth, when teenagers understand the meaning of peer pressure or demonstrate links and differences between certain books and Hollywood's reworking of them. "Education" exists when adults conceive of positions other than their own or when the elderly gain insight from a painting. It occurs, à la Robert Pirsig, by sneaking up behind you and tapping you on the shoulder. It occurs when we least expect it in "ah-ha!" moments alone or in the middle of a noisy crowd at a ball game or in thoughtful reflection on something said to us.[35] "Education" encompasses non-propositional knowledge ("I know 'how to' build the stool") as well as propositional knowledge ("I know that the sun is the center of our solar system."). "Education" may encompass memorizing Shakespeare or reciting Kwaanza precepts, but "education" goes beyond mnemonic devices and particulars. Education is not an end-point proposition. Phrases like "lifelong learning" could characterize the point, as long as the idea represents authentic inquiry, and is not a cliché for a series of programs. Authentic inquiry, in other words, may lead to sanctioned programs, but the programs are not necessary conditions for "education."

"Schooling," on the other hand, is precisely the formalization and institutionalization of content, mastery, experiment, etcetera. Originally understood in ancient Greece as leisurely study by elite groups, "schooling" is now represented by P-12 and college/university formal structures. It results in diplomas, degrees, and the like. "Schooling" can be part of "education," but to make "education" synonymous with "schooling" is to severely limit and reduce the concept of "education." "Schooling" exists when kindergartners practice their lines for the parent-day program, when high-school students complete lab assignments, when college students satisfy core course requirements, and when summer-program graduates of any age receive their certificates of attendance or merit. "Schooling," like "education," includes both non-propositional knowledge ("how-to" tie your shoe, "how-to" write an essay, "how-to" make clay pots, etc.) and propositional knowledge ("If a rock is dropped from the roof of a house, we know the rock will go downward."), but "schooling" is formal and intentional. It is structural insofar as it sets out the boundaries for inquiry and sets up the hurdles to overcome in order to get credit for work. "Schooling" establishes the criteria for achievement and procedures necessary for completion. Herein is one link between "schooling" and "training."

While "education" is not reliant upon institutional or formal structures for its existence, "training" is reliant on such structures. Where "education" can occur outside the realms of formal or institutional structures, "training" cannot. "Training" is specific, end- or goal-oriented, and reducible in its application to steps, specific procedures, and particular techniques. "Training" exists when flash cards are flashed at children (or adults), when high-school students follow procedures to complete a history project, when adults learn flower arranging, and when "skills" are the focus of whatever seminar or "in-service" program is going on at the time. Unlike both "education" and "schooling," which include non-propositional knowledge and propositional knowledge, "training" is only non-propositional knowledge-oriented. Willers distinguishes training from education by contrasting "know-*how*" with "know-*why*," such that knowing how to do *x* is good but knowing the hows, whats, and whys of *x*, discernibly, is better.[36]

Further, "training" is not limited to P-12 or college/university, but it requires the structuralism of "schooling" (e.g., on-the-job training, intern/apprenticeship training, etc.). Conceptually, then, "schooling" is the arbiter between "education" and "training." On one view ("education"), schooling is a formal process fostering both non-propositional and propositional knowledge. On the other view ("training"), schooling is a formal process fostering non-propositional knowledge. "Training" is restricted to "schooling" in a way that "education" is not. This sets up a tug-of-war over the purpose of "schooling," but only because consumer materialism exists to the degree that "education" does not. Said differently, the more American schools demonstrate consumer materialism (via the politics of textbooks and textbook adoption, curriculum expectations, the proletarianization of teaching, etc.), the less they demonstrate "education" and the more they demonstrate "training." The problem is only mildly intricate: because the constructed foundations for democracy in America are primarily Jeffersonian or Hamiltonian, and because both positions value "education" over "training" in terms of critical citizenship, the purpose or thrust of "schooling" is "education."[37] While "training" is valuable (necessary?), the problem is that consumer materialism successfully (purposefully?) confuses "education" and "training" in order to reduce, and thereby limit, both content and criticality. Limited content and reduced criticality mean stunted potential, increased gullibility and, as a result, an increase and perpetuation of consumer materialism. Because consumer materialism relies on imagery, impulse, marketing pretenses, and a "keeping up with the Jones" logic, it also relies on a carefully *trained* (student?) population for its existence and continuance. An educated population, on the other hand, questions images, holds impulse in abeyance, scrutinizes marketing claims, and does not rely on "the Joneses" for its identity.

Recall that consumer materialism elevates training as a way of furthering what Dewey called the "quest for certainty."[38] Consumer materialism posits predefined ends and objectives—as does training. Consumer materialism values the commodification of desire and plays upon it as though it were a game or an enticing concerto wooing listeners into states of "given-ness" or certitude where what is given is material achievement (as with a vender at a baseball game shouting "Peanuts!" at a child; the child's response is: a) they exist [given], therefore b) "Daddy, I want some."). Training is similar in that it promises jobs and economic competitiveness as endpoint purposes and lures adherents who are not only firm in their agreement with the perception of a predefined endpoint (à la Sally Struthers' assumptive television-commercial question, "Do you wanna make more money?"), but even more firm that schools are the venues for promoting such a vision. A capitalist reality, consumer materialism cannot be "kept out" of schools, after all schools are not divorced from the societies that they inhabit. At the same time, the balance in America is between the governing structure and the economic structure. Democratic pluralism is (in market terms) the consumer base to reach, but is also the harbinger of critical discernment to overcome.[39] Overcoming critical discernment means setting up at least the perception that an external reality is given, and that the reality is inordinately consumer materialist. For schools, as noted before, it means setting up vestiges of certainty and "givens" such as textbooks, curricula, and teacher roles.

"GIVENS," CONSUMER MATERIALISM, AND THE LINK TO TEXTBOOKS

Such considerations might allow us to better understand why textbooks represent "givens"for both students and teachers. While they are not the only representation of "givens," they are one of the best examples when talking about consumer materialism in schools. Textbooks, after all, are examples of the commodification of knowledge in an industry that has as its primary aim the selling of texts to state adoption agencies. The agencies represent policy makers, not parents or teachers. This is important because, as Goodlad's study indicates, parents and teachers perceive the role of schools as "education" or intellectual in their orientation whereas policymakers view the role of schools as sites for workforce preparation. Parents and teachers are understandably unclear about both the meaning of "education" and their use of the concept because policymaker initiatives (in the form of goals reports, standardized objectives, textbook requirements, etc.) consistently confuse "training" and "education." Textbooks become not only the symbolic representations of official knowledge, they also represent concrete ideological manifestations of exclusion.[40] Almost by default, what is *in*cluded is consistent with policymaker expectations for standardized curricula and state or national goals—all of which are undeniably conservative.

The texts, therefore, are both culture and commodity. On one hand, the narratives, content, and topics are cultural. They represent values, positions, and other cultural artifacts. The same narratives, content, and topics exist in packaged goods called "textbooks" which are bought and sold, making them, on the other hand, a commodity. So far, this is a simple distinction. But closer scrutiny reveals that what culture gets bought and sold is both contingent and political. It is not the case that culture is *a priori*. It is constructed, contested, reconstructed and recontested. What this means is that the double meaning of the word "value" lets us see the bridge between culture and commodity when talking about textbooks.

Consider that there are values such as competition, independence, rugged individualism, and playing by rules. Consider also that while each of those terms is *a* value, there is also value given to each of them. There is, for example (as we shall see in more detail shortly), such a high value placed upon free-market capitalism in textbooks that other economic systems are either downplayed in them or censored altogether from appearing in texts. Put the distinction in the form of a question: "How much value does your value have?" If your value is "multicultural understanding," you likely will find little in American textbooks, aside from tokenism or historical celebrity notation (Martin Luther King, Jr.; Jane Addams; Harriet Tubman, etc.). This means that textbook publishers are not getting the message from their "customers" that what is desired is a critical analysis of topics that are controversial or problematic or contestable. Publishers are therefore operating on their own meta-value. That is, the value ascribed to the project of publishing is bottom-line profit. This meta-value influences what ultimately is represented in texts because publishers publish what their "customers" want. Cameron McCarthy puts it this way:

> As publishers work to maximize their markets (and profits), textbook writing becomes more and more like an assembly line, with multiple authors producing submissions that are checked for quality control, readability, and overly conflictual issues by keen editorial staffs. When the textbook finally becomes a finished product, we have a tool for teaching that is often uninteresting and unchallenging to students and teachers alike. By bargaining away issues that might offend state adoption committees and conservative interest groups, publishers and textbook writers

contribute to the marginilization of cultural diversity and the suppression of minority history and identities in textbooks.[41]

Reducing the diversity of values in a pluralistic society to those values that sell best means that consumer materialism is at work in textbook adoption and use. Nearly half of the states in the United States have textbook adoption committees that decide which texts will be used and which texts will not. Michael Apple notes, "The economics of profit and loss of this situation makes it imperative that publishers devote nearly all of their efforts to guaranteeing a place on these lists of approved texts. Because of this, the texts made available to the entire nation, and the knowledge considered legitimate in them, are determined by what will sell in Texas, California, Florida, and so forth."[42] One illustration of the power that specific states have over what other states will adopt (because of publishing-industry profit concerns), is testimony given before the Texas Commissioner of Education and the State Textbook Committee by conservative textbook critic Mel Gabler. His concerns related to the Texas law requiring textbooks used for the seventh through twelfth grades to advocate and promote the free-enterprise system. Spring notes, "In Gabler's language, the law requires books to be 'unneutral.' In reference to this law, Gabler complained of a text that 'treats agricultural problems, on a number of pages, as something to be solved by government, rather than as problems that government helped to create by interfering with the free market.'"[43] In *Conflicts of Interest: The Politics of American Education*, Joel Spring writes:

> Obviously, students' ideas about economic and political problems can be shaped according to the way in which the sources of economic problems are identified and described. Certainly, the source of economic problems in agriculture is open to debate. It is also debatable whether or not America's prosperity has been solely the result of free enterprise. Since the early days of the nineteenth century, the federal government has been involved in financing roads, building railroads, managing the financial system, and helping business to accumulate capital. Whether or not government interference has been a key area of dispute is not recognized by the Texas textbook law. Essentially, Texas law defines what knowledge about economics should be standard.[44]

The history textbook story of the rise of industrialism is, according to Kincheloe, slanted toward a celebratory interpretation. His concern is that "[r]arely are questions of industrialization's social side effects raised: the despiritualization of labor, the ethic of deskilling, the irrationality of bureaucratization, the environmental destruction, and so on."[45] The debilitatingly mistaken adage about something being true because it is in a book takes on new meaning. Teachers are not prone to collectively or publicly question the texts because the authority of textbook adoption committees makes open questioning futile (and perpetuates the marginalization of teachers). This "*fait accompli*" ("given") syndrome is also shown by students who find it easier to soak up information without critique or challenge.[46] The result is consumer materialism because of consumer materialism. It secures its existence by perpetuating itself in classrooms. By commodifying information in order to sell it to textbook adoption committees, critical thought is taken out of the picture for the very people (teachers and students) most in need of it (and, importantly, most eager to demonstrate it). By the time state adoption lists are compiled, teachers have only a token role in the initial decision making, and this process is rife with marketing gimmicks and advertising pitches that play on the "givens" of textbook content.

As though being on a county, school, or department textbook-selection committee represents authentic power and choice, teachers see such roles in the ways that are laid out for them by a system of education that has not valued teachers in other than cursory or token ways during the entire process. Texas was used earlier to illustrate the political realities of textbook adoption at the end of the selection process. J. Dan Marshall's research, also based on the Texas system, illustrates the larger point about the specific process, who is involved, and what power actually resides where.[47] Marshall sought a "participant understanding" of the process and spent time in each of the three stages of the Texas textbook adoption process: (1) review and selection by the State Textbook Committee, (2) review by Texas Education Agency Personnel, and (3) review and adoption by the State Board of Education. Through interviews and observations he reveals the process, the perspectives of the participants, and how the system actually works.

At first glance, the process appears to offer teachers substantial power in deciding which textbooks will be adopted. The State Textbook Committee is, after all, comprised of fifteen educators who are appointed for one term.

At least eight of the members must be classroom teachers. During the summer of each year, the committee reviews all of the books submitted by publishers for the subject areas under consideration. Because of the amount of work, the committee uses "advisory groups" to help and meets with publishers over the summer to review and evaluate the texts. The committee chooses a maximum of five texts for each subject after holding an open hearing (for protesting and defending the texts), then recommends the final list to the Commissioner of Education.

For the second step, the list is screened by state-level curriculum specialists and the Commissioner of Education's office. The books that have been recommended by the State Textbook Committee may be required to have additions, corrections, and/or deletions made. Marshall notes, "The Commissioner may remove as many as three books from any list of five, but he [sic] cannot add books. When these reviews are completed and his decisions (if any) to delete books made, the Commissioner formally presents his lists of books to the State Board of Education for adoption at its November meeting."[48] The third and final step involves the State Board of Education, rounds of public hearings, and final decisions. The board can request changes in the textbooks and can remove texts from any list, as long as at least two books exist on the lists in each subject area. Importantly, the board cannot add books to the list. Again, Marshall: "Following their deliberations, members vote to adopt each book on each subject area list. From these final [State Board of Education] adoption lists, districts and schools throughout Texas select texts."[49]

Ostensibly, teachers are the initial and primary decision makers in the process. The State Textbook Committee begins the process and selects the initial texts. Recall that a majority of the members of the committee must be classroom teachers (at least eight). Recall, also, that the committee enlists the help of advisory groups, which can also be composed of classroom teachers. Yet two concerns remain and overlap: (1) inauthentic choice for most teachers, and (2) consumer- materialist influence in selecting the texts. For (1), the process results in a list *from which* districts and schools choose their books. Unless you are one of the eight or so teachers on the committee, you have pseudo-choice. Considering as few as eight teachers to be representative of teachers in a state as large as Texas works definitionally, but since the appointments are a one-time deal, it can only be definitional representationalism and not constituent representationalism. Said differently, teachers on the state selection committee find themselves representing teachers by *being* teachers, but because their appointments are so brief, they have very little time to hear the various (divergent?) perspectives of many teachers (until after selections have been made and in addition to the advisory groups noted above).

But here is the overlap with (2): even if you are on the committee, consumer materialism constricts authentic choice for *you*, much less your numerous constituents and colleagues. The textbooks are already "givens." The role of the committee is, in effect, to shop for goods already assembled. From the publisher's perspective, the role of the committee is *to be sold* on the merchandise. This is significant insofar as it represents the power that actually operates in the selection—publishers are active while committee members are faced with consumer-materialist choice.[50] Marshall notes, "The majority of textbook committee members who acknowledged having been influenced by publishers indicated that this influence usually occurred at the publishers' 'Round Robin' presentations. Whether made in school cafeterias or fine restaurants, these presentations were like polished theater. Not only did the committee members hear about textbook X, but they heard about it within a comparative context that highlighted the weaknesses of the competing texts."[51] One publisher explained it this way:

> The one thing you better do [in order to have a chance at making the list]: you better know your product [and] you better know your competitor's product. You better evaluate how you beat your competitor and then whenever you start to emphasize something say, "Well, I wish you would look at page so-and-so because this is the way we present The Articles of Confederation. . . . We've got three more pages of coverage of Teddy Roosevelt running up San Juan Hill than the competitors do." Those kinds of things. You pick out whatever you think is going to be a definitive plus and you *use* that![52]

The effects of the "pitches" are telling. They not only reveal the persuasiveness of advertising in a realm in which, according to Spring and Apple,[53] many people feel advertising has no place, the "pitches" indicate what happens to substantive academics and criticality: they are reduced to commodities. Once reduced, as in the "given" status of textbooks under consideration by state adoption committees, those making choices are really making a *kind* of choice. Call it *ex post facto* choice or Wal-mart browsing, the "choices" teachers are forced to consider "important" *are* important, but to publishers. The "important" decisions about content, usage, readability, etcetera, have already been made and standardized by a publishing empire interested in offending nobody by keeping noncontroversial content the same year after year. To make major alterations to textbooks, after all, costs publishers large sums of money. One result, then, is to "pitch" what has been modified (by close association with state departments of education[54]) to the members of the selection committee. Again, the unsuspecting, constantly changing group of teachers are subjected to sales schemes rife with consumer materialism.

Consider the following interview of State Textbook Committee (STC) members and publishers regarding the selection process:

STC Member 1: There were things that I might have missed if they [publishers] had not pointed them out. And this is generally true of all of them. I mean, I looked over the books, but perhaps not as carefully as I would have if no one had . . . [pause] You know, whenever they explained it . . . [pause] It did help to have them there. Of course they *all* had representatives.

STC Member 2: . . . Sometimes [publishers] were able to bring out some points about their programs that perhaps we hadn't caught.

Publisher: What I think [STC members] mean [when they recognize publisher influence] is that, by repeated presentation, either in conference or in general meetings, features of the books that they may not otherwise have seen were presented to them . . .

Interviewer: So it's really just a matter of receiving information . . .
Publisher: Well, I think that's what the committee members are talking about, yes. . . . It's information and it's a biased presentation, I suppose, of the information.[55]

One reading of this exchange suggests that committee members are interested in having publishers explain the details of their texts. A different reading, however, suggests committee members are like first-time car buyers. They are on a car-lot venue unfamiliar to them, but very familiar to car sales "associates." They are not intimately familiar with the car, whereas the "associates" not only know their product, they know their competitor's product as well. The committee members are subjected to the same kind of sales pitches for which people who sell cars are known: focus on the color, undercoating treatments, seat fabric, and any other "perk" that positions the *seller* in a position of power. What should be realized is that car sales "associates" and publishers make their living at such pitches, committee members do not. Committee members are one-time appointees to a commercial game played over and over by the publishers, by their rules of presentation, and usually on the designated "turf" of the publishers (whether it be a cafeteria or posh restaurant as noted before).

There are, therefore, some questions: To what degree is the arguably patronizing tone of the above exchange between committee members, publishing-house sales people, and the interviewer indicative of teacher power? To what degree are the choices made by the committee important or substantive choices? To what degree do publishers use consumer materialist devices like comparative shopping slogans and polished theatrical performances to make their text *appear* better, regardless of the truth? The marginalization of teachers, even in a structure that includes them, is one way consumer materialism influences the purpose of schools. This is not to say that there are not areas, pockets of resistance, that do not even use textbooks. This is also not to suggest that there are not those teachers who understand the game being played around them and limit the influence of textbooks by keeping them on their classroom shelves most of the time. Examples of dissidence can be found, but the energy used to be covert in this way is energy better used to interact with students; the negative influence of textbooks can be curbed by reducing the amount and power of consumer materialism in schools.

CURRICULUM AND CONSUMER MATERIALISM

Curriculum decisions are similar to the "given-ness" of textbooks. Georgia, for example, has a Quality Core Curriculum (QCC) that stipulates for teachers the content of their courses.[56] The QCC came about after the unanimous passage of educational reform legislation in 1985. The bill relating to the QCC was based on a recommendation from the governor of Georgia that happened to also be based on a report published by a commission he selected (aptly named, Governor's Education Review Commission).[57] Urban notes:

> That commission, in its first of two printed reports to the governor, stated that its recommendations represented "a consensus view of over 1,000 educators, business people, and parents."[58] This large, though selective, base (one wonders about labor, minorities, and other possibly unrepresented groups, perhaps even students) has been reinforced in its influence by the nonstop rhetoric from the Atlanta newspapers supporting passage of the bill. Their seeming decision simply to adopt the point of view of the governor and his commission and to make sure that the legislature did not trifle with the recommendations for reform indicates the existence of a powerful coalition of established individuals and groups seeking to force their will on our schools, their teachers, and students.[59]

The purpose behind the QCC is to better enable policymakers to hold teachers accountable for the instruction they "provide" their students. To see whether teachers are doing their jobs, the QCC has a test component that, ostensibly, indicates the degree to which teachers are successful in carrying out their roles as transmitters of information. Briefly, what occurs is this: the state Department of Education uses QCC components as the basis for tests administered at the end of the year for grades three, five, and eight. The tests are intended to represent measurements of what students *know*, given that what they should know is outlined and listed in the QCC itself. Once the tests are completed, the Department of Education looks at the percentage of students who responded to each question correctly as well as incorrectly. The department then makes claims about the success of schools based on the scores. Importantly, 90 percent of the variance (correct *and* incorrect responses) is accounted for in terms of school size and the percentage of students eligible for reduced-cost school-lunch programs. What results from this last factor is that there are lower expectations for smaller and poorer schools and greater expectations for larger and wealthier schools.

Another result of the general procedure is *ex post facto* reflection and subsequent generalization. Because the tests are administered at the *end* of each year for grades three, five, and eight (in order that nothing should be left out of the curriculum), scores come back to the schools at the beginning of the *next* academic year . . . by which time the third, fifth, and eighth graders are fourth, sixth, and ninth graders. Only after-the-fact speculation can be made concerning the population tested and the material on which they were tested. It might be argued that because the test is iterative, that is, because the test is repeatedly modified via "field-tested" questions year after year, it is better situated to be generalized for *incoming* third, fifth, and eighth graders. The truth or falsity of this assertion is not our concern here, but the sheer existence of the "iterativeness" of the QCC tests raises important questions about who defines the curriculum from which the test questions are constructed. It is also important to see what interests corporations might have in the overall process and end product. One larger point is to consider ramifications of QCC-like standardization and to question how consumer materialism relates to the issue.

We should recall the claim made at the very beginning of this text: consumer materialism is already ingrained in schools and is often represented in the language we use to talk about schooling. "Standards," "outcomes," "objectives," "goals," etcetera, bespeak consumer-materialist expectations for curriculum because they largely represent the intended "goods" to be produced. They also insinuate methods of instruction, for to begin with a standard means reducing or eliminating open-ended learning in favor of focusing on a preconceived end or "given." It is similar to teaching-to-the-test where content is restricted to "testable material" and where variations from the focus are eschewed. While the *theoretical* possibility for, say, open-ended dialectic is still one option within a standards-oriented curriculum, dialectic is, without apology, *in*efficient, thus not in keeping with standards-achievement. Because "standards" assume timely achievability, evidenced by the calls for accountability attached to "standards" policies and proposals, teaching and learning are reduced to procedural, methodical, and prescriptive means. Commodifying curriculum and instruction in this way reduces teaching and learning to prescriptive methods exemplified by "measurement-driven," "teacher-proof," or "cookbook" curriculum packages.[60] The "standards," "outcomes," "objectives," and "goals" that compel such processes are further representations of consumer materialism and illustrate the larger point: *the assumption that the purpose of school is to prepare students for future* *work.* In order to be "prepared," "prepared-ness" is defined, translated into "standards," "outcomes," "objectives," and "goals" and "taught" (transmitted?) in the way just depicted. What role do corporations play in this process?

From the Business Roundtable (a coalition made up of 200 companies) to The Conference Board (a 3,600-member business information service dedicated to creating networks of leaders discussing management practices, economics, and public policy) to Allstate Forums such as Labor 2000 (which convenes corporate leaders and government officials to talk about how business can improve education and training), corporate interests are numerous, prominent, and influential. Their intentions are not conspiratorial as conspiracies tend to be quiet affairs. Corporate interests and intentions are glimpsed from reading their open accounts of what schools should be doing to produce better products. For The Conference Board, Townley notes:

> The quality of our nation's education, linked directly to the quality of our workforce, has been pinpointed time and again as one of the keys to international competitiveness. Currently, the United States spends hundreds of billions of dollars on education. Yet, U.S. literacy ranks 48th out of 149 countries surveyed; and, unlike our competitors, we still don't have a national education agenda. Despite some isolated successes, many businesses are concerned about our poor return on investment.[61]

The Allstate Forum resulted in the following call:

> There needs to be a greater drive to make things happen on the education front. We, the business community, must become obsessed with improvement in education. CEOs and senior human resource people must be centrally involved. With their buy-in, potent business coalitions and meaningful business-education partnerships are possible. With such alliances, there is hope for a shared vision and a common solution. The alternative is the status quo: a continued decrease in America's competitive edge. . . . What can business offer? Clearly it can identify the changing requirements in the workplace as well as reasonable expectations. It can provide input on skill-building for educators and students alike, without attempting to impose a specific curriculum. It will not be a matter of simply submitting a list calling for computer literacy to this level or that. Rather it will be: "Here's what we need. What can you give these kids to suit our

requirements? And how can we help? What can we provide in the way of services and materials?"[62]

In addition to The Conference Board, the Allstate Forum, and the Business Roundtable, the CED (Committee for Economic Development) published a study that complained that students were not prepared to enter the workforce upon graduation.[63] The SCANS commission (Secretary's Commission on Achieving Necessary Skills) report, *What Work Requires of Schools*, called for, among other things, a standards-based approach to secondary schooling that would result in credentials employers would consider reliable.[64] Each of these reports share similar qualities: (1) they each emphasize competitiveness; (2) they each assume that the purpose of school is workforce preparation; and (3) they each intend to influence the curriculum.

Emphasizing competitiveness means spotlighting standardized tests for international comparisons. It also represents tacit support for tracking and the rugged-individualist ethos that continually elevates specific segments of the population at the expense of others. When competitiveness is pervasively seen as a necessary element of schooling, it is not a stretch to assume that competitiveness and workforce preparation are what schools should perpetuate. The assumptiveness of business attitudes, however, is interesting. Note that Townley's position is that "the quality of our nation's education, linked directly to the quality of our workforce, has been pinpointed time and again as one of the keys to international competitiveness." What is interesting about this is that (a) Townley mistakes "education" for "training"; (b) he equates dollar expenditures with literacy rankings; and (c) he assumes that those who have been doing the "pinpointing" (corporations and federal agencies) are in some way authoritative. Pinpointing a link between "education" and workforce preparation in this way achieves three goals: (1) it confuses "education" with "training" in order to (2) reduce effective teaching and learning to dollar-for-dollar ratios for ranking comparison as well as (3) reduce the critical transitivity of future workers.

Despite the Allstate Forum's claim that it is not "attempting to impose a specific curriculum," their report goes on to immediately outline what the process of their influence should be: "Here's what we need. What can you give kids to suit our requirements? And how can we help? What can we provide in the way of services and materials?" Such an outline reveals a few problems, not the least of which is consistency. The claim asserted is that businesses will keep their hands off specific curriculum development. At the same time, businesses wish to supply schools with a packing list of what they desire and expect teachers to "give kids" these particulars in order to "suit [businesses'] requirements." Aside from the obvious inconsistency, the call reveals just what businesses see schools doing: providing them with workers. It also reveals what businesses know about teaching and learning, for the call assumes that teaching and learning is merely a process of transmission from the teacher to the student and that student interest has little or nothing to do with successful learning. Like Townley, there is a mistaken authoritativeness in the Allstate Forum call. They know what they want in their workers, they see schools training ("educating") students to their specifications, and they understand that their interests will be attended to if only the curriculum would reflect what they want and teachers would pass on the necessary information.

The steady flow of reports such as those from Allstate and The Conference Board began first with *A Nation at Risk* and, later, *America 2000*, both of which made explicit connections between corporate interests and schools.[65] Clearly, then, business is not alone in seeing schools as sites for consumer materialism, since government reports are similar in their assumptions and their expectations. It is notable that the Secretary's Commission on Achieving Necessary Skills (SCANS) came out of the Department of Labor, not the Department of Education. While it might not have differed greatly otherwise, if at all, the Department of Labor's interest is symbolic of business influence. The follow-up to *What Work Requires of Schools* was *Learning a Living: A Blueprint for High Performance.*[66] Such government-sponsored initiatives demonstrate that corporations are not alone in arguing for the kind of initiatives that would even more tightly bind schools and businesses together.[67] In fact, the distinction between government and business is so blurred that democratic and capitalistic distinctions are subsumed under the oligopoly that characterizes America.[68] Perhaps an example of collusion, the consequences directly and seriously impact teachers and students.

For teachers, increasing business interests means increasing subordination and marginalization of their roles. Urban noted earlier the glaring absence of students, minorities, and labor in the development of the Quality Core Curriculum (QCC) program. While teachers were individually represented, power in the form of labor was not. What is important is that those who had the least involvement at the outset are now the most directly impacted. In the Atlanta Public Schools, for example, teachers must post the objectives for the day either on overheads or on chalkboards or on posters. Students in selected grades, as noted above, must sit for QCC examinations. Teachers not only administer the tests, they are, again ostensibly, held "accountable" for the progress (or lack of it) as indicated by the QCC scores. "Given," the QCC dictates the curriculum, periodic testing (of students *and* teachers), and even the means of instruction—akin to what corporations assume is necessary for global competition.

Some teachers follow the rules by placing the objective in clear view, then teach in unique ways to cover the material intended. Some teachers follow the rules by placing the objective in clear view and teach in traditional, didactic ways privileged by the QCC regulations. Some teachers realize the politics of disempowerment the QCC objectives represent and, while still posting the objectives on a daily basis, do their best to suspend the restrictive nature of the QCC initiative and teach in ways that connect the experiences and interests of their students with the knowledge that comes about from authentic interaction (rather than use the contrived speech patterns represented in teacher manuals). Regardless, the vast majority of teachers in the Atlanta Public School system post and teach as directed by the QCC objectives.

Georgia is not unique. Other states have similar programs. Virginia, for example, developed "Standards of Learning Objectives" that was so detailed that kindergarten music teachers were to be sure that students could "imitate (echo) simple two pitch patterns sung or played by the teacher."[69] Such specificity in standardized content clears the way for many teachers to go directly to the objectives and teach to them. Yet leaving students and teachers (due to sheer number or because of status?) out of the initial process of curriculum development or construction reinforces the very marginalization that Allstate Forums assume in the first place. It further means that the QCC and Standards of Learning Objectives exemplify consumer materialism in part because the objectives represent the interests of others—*for* teachers and students, not *with* them—and in part because the purpose of the objectives are for conforming and accepting and not for challenging. There is not, in other words, an objective that expects students to question objectives or the concept of objectives themselves.

PROLETARIANIZATION OF TEACHERS: ROLES, "GIVENS," AND CONSUMER MATERIALISM

Teachers acquiesce to such subordinate roles, in part, because the culture of teaching was fashioned early in their professional lives, usually as undergraduate or master's-degree students. For undergraduates, the "reality" of teaching was reinforced via apprenticeship programs where students, as student-teachers, either emulated their cooperating teachers (if they liked them or thought they were good teachers) or at least observed the "realities" of the classroom as disconnected from the cooperating teacher (if they did not like them or thought they were bad teachers). Student teachers in the Atlanta Public Schools who like their cooperating teacher, for example, observe how the cooperating teacher integrates the QCC objective listed on the board. Recall that regardless of the differences between teachers' attention to the QCC (uses it as a focus, puts it on the board but does creative activities to circumvent it, etc.), it nonetheless is posted in each room. Whether the student teachers emulate those cooperating teachers they consider good or disregard their cooperating teachers as useful-but-banal, they nonetheless are immersed into the cultural reality that QCC objectives are posted. They represent reality or "the real world."

What this represents is the "given-ness" of teaching.[70] Where textbook "choice" is really quasi- or pseudo-choice, it also is not questioned. It is usually accepted as the way the process works. This is the case, in part, because of the apprenticeship approach to teacher training. By initiating new teachers into the "givens" of teaching, any initial questioning of the "givens" results in noncritical acceptance. Couple this with the realization that teachers typically have a three-year probation period before they are granted tenure. During these formative three years, the system celebrates conformity. By the beginning of the fourth year of a teacher's career, it is the very rare person indeed who has been able to maintain a dual personality for those initial and ensuing years and who would come forward to argue policy and practice in their school. Joe Kincheloe puts it this way:

> As long as teacher educators believe that novice survival is a cardinal goal of professional education and that teachers learn to teach best by engaging in apprenticelike experiences, little substantive change will occur. Teacher education as apprenticeship induces neophytes to model the master teacher, rendering the study of teaching less essential than "correct"

performance based on the master teacher's opinion and local standards
within a particular school.[71]

Maxine Greene discusses the same theme in her book *The Dialectic of
Freedom*. She contrasts "wide-awakeness" and being the author of one's
own world with the "givens" also discussed here. She notes, "[Teachers]
may try to make use of [givens] or escape them or move around them or
make a mockery of them; but they feel themselves in some way doomed to
see them as objective 'realities,' impervious to transformation, hopelessly
there."[72] Recall the QCC. Recall, also, that consumer materialism
commodifies existence by reducing searching, thinking, and probing to
objectified and reductionistic particulars. Teachers are "doomed" in the way
Greene outlines and, as a result of seeing no way around the "realities,"
demonstrate consumer materialism in their daily practice and interactions
with students. She goes further in claiming that

> There is . . . an implicit encouragement of the tendency to accede to the
> given, to view what exists around us as an objective "reality," impervious
> to individual interpretation. Finding it difficult to stand forth from what is
> officially (or by means of media) defined as real, unable to perceive
> themselves in interpretive relation to it, the young (like their elders) are all
> too likely to remain immersed in the taken-for-granted and the everyday.
> For many this means an unreflective consumerism; for others, it means a
> preoccupation with *having* more rather than *being* more.[73]

One reason for consumer materialism in schools is what was known in the
1970s as the "proletarianization thesis." Proletarianization occurs when, for
example, curricula become "teacher-proof." The thesis suggests that teachers
are not only perpetuators of "givens" for their students, and thus considered
oppressors of working-class children, they are also exploited by consumer
materialism and persistently disempowered.[74]

Two aspects further clarify the importance of the proletarianization
thesis: de-skilling and cheapening. De-skilling, according to Carlson,
involves the fragmentation of complex interactions into "a series of relatively
routine and thus simple skills which can be taught to semi-skilled workers."[75]
Once this is done, control no longer resides with, say, teachers, but is vested
in a bureaucratic hierarchy. Accordingly, teachers perform routines with

central office administration overseeing the entire production process. The cheapening of labor of teachers results. Carlson notes:

> By lowering the skill requirements needed for a job, management is able to buy more low-priced labor on the job market. Experienced and well-paid union craftspersons in industry, for example, were replaced by semi-literate, non-union workers as "scientific management" replaced craft production techniques early in the century. So long as no special expertise was required to perform a job, the pool of potential workers was also dramatically increased; and this helped to keep wages low.[76]

By making teaching appear to be a series of step-by-step procedures, symbolized by QCC objectives and teacher manuals, teachers maintain a status similar to the semi-literate, non-union workers Carlson notes. It is not an attack on teachers, *per se*, but an attack on what many teachers hegemonically perpetuate: acquiescence, disempowerment, reliance on authority, and appeals to certainty. The perfect pawns to spread consumer materialism, teachers reinforce it for their students by holding consumer materialist expectations (via tracking) and by acting in consumer materialist ways (as technicians and clerks). One basis for this is teacher training programs that emphasize training over either schooling or education. The last chapter deals much more extensively with this issue, but teacher training is connected to proletarianization when colleges of education and their professors focus on practical outcomes and methods for achieving them. Such foci limit teachers or prospective teachers in developing broad, deep, connected grounds for revising what they *might* or what they *should* do. Instead of axiological investigation rife with questions, confrontation, and thoughtful scrutiny, teachers expect procedural certitude and easy grades from their program offerings and professors of education. A cycle is reinforced wherein teaching, teachers, and those charged with teaching teachers further consumer-materialist expectations. Henry Giroux is careful not to blame teachers for perpetuating consumer materialism when he explains what he faces as a professor in a college of education.

> Most of our students are very comfortable with defining themselves as technicians and clerks. For them to be all of a sudden exposed to a line of critical thinking that both calls their own experience into question and at the same time raises fundamental questions about what teaching should be

and what social purposes it might serve is very hard for them. They don't
have a frame of reference or a vocabulary with which to articulate the
centrality of what they do. They are caught up in market logic and
bureaucratic jargon. We can't defend what we do that way. We can't make
our best case. We always wind up on the defensive and appear to others as
second rate and marginal.[77]

While teachers are not solely responsible for the condition of their vocational
roles, teachers recognize (with frustration) the de-skilling they face in their
schools. But de-skilling coupled with cheapened value, as Carlson notes,
means that attracting critical visionaries to teaching is increasingly difficult.
There are, certainly, those teachers in schools today who consciously put
aside market logic and bureaucratic jargon in favor of critique and resistance
to subordination. Many schools have a few of these teachers. But they
demonstrate isolated power and are frequently ostracized by other teachers.
Interestingly, the limited power those few teachers demonstrate is a result of
achieving critical transitivity; this in the face of frequent intransitiveness on
the part of their peers and administrators.

Recall that critical transitivity is used by Freire to mean thoughtful
action and connected agency. He distinguishes between three degrees of
transitivity: intransitivity, semi-transitivity, and critical transitivity. Teachers
who are intransitive abjure the idea that they can alter their situations. These
are teachers who incessantly refer to "real-world" constrictions and offer "I
just can't do anything about it" rationales for the problems they face. Such
teachers see problems around them, that is, they are cognizant of their
situations but they see no way to overcome the problems. Teachers who are
semi-transitive embrace the idea that they can alter their situations.
Semi-transitive teachers, however, only see the world in unrelated segments
because semi-transitiveness is two dimensional and short term.
Semi-transitive teachers, for example, work hard to meet student needs in
each of the tracked classes they teach without confronting the issue of
tracking. Teachers who are critically transitive interpret problems as more
than black and white, two-dimensional phenomena. They connect, as Shor
notes, "personal and social meanings with a specific theme, text, or issue."[78]
Critically transitive teachers might begin by questioning Channel One
newscasts,[79] for example, and might turn the television off (even though the
rules require it to be on) given, say, a local event worthy of a "teachable
moment." So far, however, this is only semi-transitiveness. To achieve

critical transitivity means connecting concerns about power and money with the reality that students are a captive market for advertisers. The advertisers pay double the rate for prime-time television ads, resulting in gross annual revenues of over $100 million to the owners of Channel One (Whittle Communications). Questioning the amount of profit a private company makes from schools—which continually face budget constraints—begins to demonstrate critical transitivity. To demonstrate critical transitivity means overcoming the institutionalized deterrents to it. Institutional disempowerment resulting from proletarianization is one deterrent. Corporate culture application and manipulation is another.

NOTES

1. Hanna Arendt, *Totalitarianism* (New York: Harcourt Brace Jovanovich, 1968), 168.

2. Consumer materialism, recall, commodifies existence by reducing searching, being, thinking, etc., to objectified and reductionistic particulars. For schooling, it means, in part, that students see their roles as seeking "right" answers to questions instead of searching for meaning and understanding by contesting standardized curricula. Similarly, teachers see their roles as seeking preordained procedures that will allow the efficient transfer of information from them (or the adopted texts/curriculum) to their students. Peter McLaren uses a similar phrase (consumer capitalist culture) to make a connection between what he calls postmodern pathologies and the constitution of the body/subject. See Peter McLaren, *Critical Pedagogy and Predatory Culture: Oppositional Politics in a Postmodern Era* (New York: Routledge, 1995).

3. See Roger I. Simon, "Empowerment as a Pedagogy of Possibility," in *Education and the American Dream: Conservatives, Liberals and Radicals Debate the Future of Education*, Harvey Holtz, et al., eds., (Granby, MA: Bergin & Garvey Publishers, 1989), 134-146.

4. U.S. Department of Education, *America 2000: An Education Strategy* (Washington, DC: U.S. Government Printing Office, 1991).

5. Secretary's Commission on Achieving Necessary Skills, *What Work Requires of Schools: A SCANS Report for America 2000* (Washington, DC: U.S. Department of Labor, 1991).

6. Secretary's Commission on Achieving Necessary Skills Assessment Committee, *Learning a Living: A Blueprint for High Performance* (Washington, DC: U.S. Department of Labor, 1992).

7. National Alliance of Business, *The Fourth R: Workforce Readiness* (Washington, DC: National Alliance of Business, 1987).

8. Allstate Forum on Public Issues, *Labor Force 2000: Corporate America Responds* (New York: Allstate Forum, 1989).

9. Andrew Ashwell and Frank Caropreso, eds., *Business Leadership: The Third Wave of Education Reform* (New York: The Conference Board, 1989).

10. See, for one example, John I. Goodlad, "On Taking School Reform Seriously," *Phi Delta Kappan* 74 (November 1992): 236.

11. Critical transitivity is used by Paulo Freire to mean thoughtful *action*. He discerns between intransitiveness (which repudiates the power of individuals to change their existences, e.g., "I can't speak out about teaching-to-the-test because I might lose my job . . . that's the 'real world' and I can't do anything about it."), semitransitiveness, (individuals see the world as changeable, but see the world in unrelated segments such that semitransitiveness is two-dimensional and short term, e.g., groups feed the hungry without asking why hungry people exist in a society with yearly food surpluses), and critical transitiveness (demonstrated when individuals make, according to Shor, "broad connections between individual experience and social issues. . . . In education, critically [transitive] teachers and students synthesize personal and social meanings with a specific theme, text, or issue."). See Paulo Freire, *Education for Critical Consciousness* (New York: Seabury, 1973); and Ira Shor, *Empowering Education* (Chicago: University of Chicago Press, 1992), 127-128.

12. For an excellent and extensive treatment of this point, see Richard A. Brosio, *A Radical Critique of Capitalist Education* (New York: Peter Lang, 1994), 1-43*ff.*

13. Linda McNeil, *Contradictions of Control: School Structure and School Knowledge* (New York: Routledge, 1988), 3.

14. Lawrence A. Cremin, *American Education: The Colonial Experience 1607-1783* (New York: Harper & Row, 1970), 545. Cremin notes three main purposes: (1) personal advancement in an expanding economy; (2) religious denominational influence; and (3) growing participation in public affairs. (1) and (3) are more closely connected than are "general education" and "specialized training for economic production" noted in the chapter. Cremin underscores the meaning behind social mobility/personal advancement by recalling Thomas Smith's observation in 1583 that "whosoever studieth the laws of the realm, who studieth in the universities, who professeth liberal sciences, and to be short, who can live idly without manual labor, and will bear the port, charge and countenance of a gentleman, he shall be called master . . . and shall be taken for a gentleman." The connection, therefore, is made between social mobility and a deeper understanding of the world. This is in contrast to the similar-sounding argument for schools to provide the necessary skills for students to compete in an advanced world market. The former, while connected to social mobility and economic life, is not narrow or limiting in the same way as the latter.

15. Harvey Kantor, "Vocationalism in American Education: The Economic and Political Context, 1880-1930," in *Work, Youth, and Schooling*, Harvey Kantor and Davis B. Tyack, eds. (Stanford, CA: Stanford University Press, 1982), 15.

16. Ibid., 4. See also R. Collins, *The Credential Society: An Historical Sociology of Education and Stratification* (New York: Academic Press, 1979); Michael B. Katz, *The Irony of Early School Reform* (Boston: Beacon Press, 1968).

17. See Gordon Law, "Practical Schooling of the Nineteenth Century: Prelude to the American Vocational Movement," in *Preparation for Life? The Paradox of Education in the Late Twentieth Century*, Joan Burstyn, ed. (Philadelphia: The Falmer Press, 1986), 19-34.

18. See Joel Spring, *Education and the Rise of the Corporate State* (Boston: Beacon Press, 1972), 2-21.

19. Ibid., 2.

20. See, for example, Jonathan Messerli, *Horace Mann: A Biography* (New York: Alfred A. Knopf, 1972); and Joel Spring, *The American School: 1642-1985* (White Plains, NY: Longman, 1986).

21. Arguments similar to Mann's predated him, but Mann is responsible for the national push evidenced in the common school movement. For arguments prior to Mann, see Banjamin Rush, " A Plan for the Establishment of Public Schools and the Diffusion of Knowledge in Pennsylvania; to which Are Added, Thoughts upon the Mode of Education, Proper in a Republic" [1786], in *Essays on Education in the Early Republic*, Frederick Rudolph, ed.(Cambridge, MA: Harvard University Press, 1965), 3-23.

22. See Arthur Wirth, *Education in the Technological Society: The Vocational-Liberal Studies Controversy in the Early Twentieth Century* (Lanham, MD: University Press of American, 1980).

23. Ibid., especially pp. 43-55 and 66-92.

24. See Search, "Presidential Address," *Proceedings*, National Association of Manufacturers, 1898.

25. See Ellwood P. Cubberly, *Public Education in the United States: A Study and Interpretation of American Educational History* (New York: Houghton Mifflin, 1947), 573-576, 645-646.

26. See John R. Commons et al., *History of Labour in the United States*, Volume I (New York: Macmillian, 1961).

27. Wirth, *Education in the Technological Society*, 54.

28. Gerald N. Grob, *Workers and Utopia* (Evanston, IL: Northwestern University Press, 1961).

29. Wirth, *Education in the Technological Society*, 67-68.

30. Robert A. Woods and Albert J. Kennedy, *The Settlement Horizon: A National Estimate* (New York: Russell Sate Foundation, 1922), 220.

31. McNeil, *Contradictions of Control*, 6.

32. John I. Goodlad, *A Place Called School* (New York: McGraw-Hill, 1984). Goodlad actually uses "vocational" to mean training for economic production or preparation for getting a job, "intellectual" to mean education for general citizenship using academic knowledge, "social" to mean preparation for social life in a complex society, and "personal" to mean the development of expression and individual responsibility. For the purpose of consistency, this text uses "education" for Goodlad's "intellectual," and "training" for Goodlad's "vocational."

33. Joel Spring, *American Education: An Introduction to Social and Political Aspects* [fifth edition] (New York: Longman, 1991), 6.

34. See for example, J. Glenn Gray, *The Promise of Wisdom* (New York: Harper & Row, 1968).

35. See Robert Pirsig, *Zen and the Art of Motorcycle Maintenance: An Inquiry into Values* (New York: Bantam, 1974).

36. Jack Conrad Willers, " The Conflict of Substance and Process in Philosophy of Education," *Philosophy of Education Society Proceedings* (1966): 87-97.

37. Jefferson clearly outlined his ideas regarding "schooling" in his work on "The General Diffusion of Knowledge." Elitist, his idea was to ultimately separate students into two tiers, with the "best" students going on to university. The thrust of his plan, regardless of elitism and the early forms of tracking, was for "educated citizens." "Training," in the form of apprenticeships, was outside the role of the school. See Thomas Jefferson, "Bill for the More General Diffusion of Knowledge [1779]," in *The Educational Works of Thomas Jefferson*, Roy J. Honeywell, ed.(New York: Russell & Russell, 1964), 199-205; Garrett Ward Sheldon, *The Political Philosophy of Thomas Jefferson* (Baltimore: Johns Hopkins University Press, 1991); and Richard Matthews, *The Radical Politics of Thomas Jefferson* (Lawrence, KS: University Press of Kansas, 1984).

38. John Dewey, *The Quest for Certainty* (New York: Minton, Balch and Co., 1929).

39. See Brosio, op. cit., and Charles E. Lindblom, *Politics and Markets: The World's Political- Economic Systems* (New York: Basic Books, 1977), 161-222.

40. For and extensive treatment of this subtheme, see Michael W. Apple, *Official Knowledge: Democratic Education in a Conservative Age* (New York: Routledge, 1993).

41. Cameron McCarthy, " Multicultural Education: Minority Identities, Textbooks, and the Challenge of Curricular Reform," in *What Schools Can Do: Critical Pedagogy and Practice*, Kathleen Weiler and Candace Mitchell, eds. (Albany, NY: SUNY Press, 1992), 124.

42. Ibid., 51.

43. Joel Spring, *Conflicts of Interest: The Politics of American Education* (New York: Longman, 1988), 128-129. Gabler's testimony is from *Transcript of*

Proceedings before the Commissioner of Education and the State Textbook Committee, July 14-16, 1986 (Austin, TX: Kennedy Reporting Service, 1986), 2.

44. Spring, *Conflicts of Interest*, 129.

45. Joe L. Kincheloe, *Toward a Critical Politics of Teacher Thinking: Mapping the Postmodern* (Westport, CT: Bergin & Garvey, 1993), 206.

46. What is at issue here is the *collective* and *public* and *open* critiques from teachers which are conspicuously absent from the general discourse on schooling. Teachers question and critique, but they do so in very small groups or in isolation behind their closed classroom doors.

47. J. Dan Marshall, "With a Little Help from Some Friends: Publishers, Protesters, and Texas Textbook Decisions," in *The Politics of the Textbook*, Michael W. Apple and Linda K. Christian- Smith, eds. (New York : Routledge, 1991), 56-77.

48. Ibid., 58.

49. Ibid., 59. See also, J.D. Marshall, *The Politics of Curriculum Decisions Manifested through the Selection and Adoption of Textbooks for Texas* (doctoral dissertation, University of Texas at Austin, 1985). ED 270 900.

50. See Richard P. Feynman, *"Surely You're Joking, Mr. Feynman!" Adventures of a Curious Character* (New York: Basic Books, 1989), 264-276. Feynman recounts his role as a physicist on a California textbook-adoption committee. He catalogues attempted bribes from textbook publishers, inaccurate scientific information in textbooks, and how the "bidding wars" between publishers took precedence over scholarship.

51. Marshall, "With a Little Help from Some Friends," 60-61.

52. Ibid., 61. Italics in original.

53. See Michael W. Apple, *Official Knowledge: Democratic Education in a Conservative Age* (New York: Routledge, 1993); and Spring, *Conflicts of Interest*.

54. See, for example, M.A. Tulley, "A Descriptive Study of the Intents of State-Level Textbook Adoption Processes," *Educational Evaluation and Policy Analysis* 7 (Fall 1985): 289-308; R.B., Edgerton, "Odyssey of a Book: How a Social Studies Textbook Comes into Being," *Social Education* 33 (1969): 279-286; and Marshall, "With a Little Help from Some Friends," 63. Marshall notes, "Most major publishing houses maintain a close relationship with the Texas Education Agency—one that serves the dual purpose of keeping the publishers attuned to the directions in which Proclamation guides are likely to change while maintaining a professional and personal bond between themselves and Agency staff' (64).

55. Ibid.

56. Georgia Department of Education, *Georgia's Quality Core Curriculum for Grades K-12* (Atlanta, GA: Georgia Department of Education, 1994).

57. Governor's Education Review Commission, *Priority for a Quality Basic Education*, 12 November 1984.

58. Ibid., 2.

59. Wayne J. Urban, "The Illusion of Educational Reform in Georgia," in *School Reform in the Deep South: A Critical Appraisal*, David J. Vold and Joseph L. DeVitis, eds. (Tuscaloosa, AL: The University of Alabama Press, 1991), 131.

60. Joseph W. Newman, *America's Teachers: An Introduction to Education* (New York: Longman, 1994), 45, 81, 106.

61. Preston Townley, *Business Leadership: The Third Wave of Reform* (New York: The Conference Board, 1989), v.

62. Allstate Forum on Public Issues, *Labor Force 2000: Corporate America Responds* (New York: Allstate Forum on Public Issues, 1989).

63. Robert C. Holland, Introduction to *CED and Education: National Impact and Next Steps* (New York: Committee for Economic Development, 1989), 2. The CED also put out *Investing in Our Children: Business and the Public Schools* in 1985 among other reports.

64. See Secretary's Commission on Achieving Necessary Skills, *What Work Requires of Schools: A Scans Report of America 2000* (Washington, DC: U.S. Department of Labor, 1991).

65. National Commission on Excellence in Education, *A Nation at Risk: The Imperative for Educational Reform* (Washington, DC: U.S. Department of Education, 1983); and U.S. Department of Education, *America 2000: An Education Strategy* (Washington, DC: U.S. Government Printing Office, 1991).

66. Secretary's Commission on Achieving Necessary Skills Assessment Committee, *Learning a Living: A Blueprint for High Performance* (Washington, DC: U.S. Department of Labor, 1992).

67. Other federal publications include U.S. Department of Labor and U.S. Department of Education, *The Bottom Line: Basic Skills in the Workplace* (Washington, DC: U.S. Department of Labor and U.S. Department of Education, 1988); Report of the Panel on Secondary School Education for the Changing Workplace, *High Schools and the Changing Workplace: The Employer's View* (Washington, DC: National Academy Press, 1988); and U.S. Departments of Labor, Education, and Commerce, *Building a Quality Workforce* (Washington, DC: U.S. Departments of Labor, Education, and Commerce, 1988).

68. See Charles Lindblom, *Politics and Markets: The World's Political-Economic Systems* (New York: Basic Books, 1977).

69. Commonwealth of Virginia, *Standards of Learning Objectives for Virginia Public Schools* (Richmond, VA: Commonwealth of Virginia Department of Education, 1983), 2.

70. For a similar point regarding the way educational research perpetuates "what is," see R. Floden and H. Klinzig, "What Can Research on Teacher Thinking Contribute to Teacher Preparation? A Second Opinion," *Educational Researcher* 19, no. 5 (1990):15-20.

71. Kincheloe, *Toward a Critical Politics of Teacher Thinking*, 14.

72. Maxine Greene, *The Dialectic of Freedom* (New York: Teachers College Press, 1988), 22.

73. Ibid.

74. See, for example, Harry Braverman, *Labor and Monopoly Capital* (London: Monthly Review Press, 1974); Guglielmo Carchedi, *On the Economic Identification of Social Classes* (New York: Routledge & Kegan Paul, 1977); Barbara Ehrenreich, " The Professional-Managerial Class," in Paul Walker, ed., *Between Labor and Capital* (Montreal: Black Rose, 1978), 5-48; and Nico Poulantzas, *Classes in Contemporary Capitalism* (London: New Left Books, 1975).

75. Dennis Carlson, *Teachers and Crisis: Urban School Reform and Teachers' Work Culture* (New York: Routledge, 1992), 72.

76. Ibid.

77. Henry Giroux, *Border Crossings: Cultural Workers and the Politics of Education* (New York: Routledge, 1992), 16.

78. Shor, *Empowering Education*, 127-128.

79. Channel One is the program fed to schools via television monitors, cable, and satellite dishes supplied free of charge to schools provided they watch a ten-minute "newscast" with commercials. Whittle Communications was the provider (before T-III Communications bought them out) and will be discussed in greater detail in chapter 3.

CHAPTER 2

Corporate Culture and Schools: Consultants in Search of New Markets

"We are also planning new 'Education Connection' workshops to show metro area teachers the endless amount of quality educational programming and curricula available from MediaOne and Cable in the Classroom."[1]

The manifestation of consumer materialism is seen in the increasing application of organizational management programs on and in schools. Sometimes under the guise of "professional development schools," sometimes coming in the form of "in-service training," teachers are faced with the encroachment of corporate culture. The Allstate Forum illustrates the effort when it assumes business practices and tactics can commodify teacher roles and the role of schools for achieving a "successful" corporate culture.

These business practices, and the tactics developed to implement them, can perhaps be shared with educators: focusing on society as a customer and recognizing the importance an educated [trained] citizenry plays in a competitive economy. A company faced with a dramatically changed market must differentiate itself from its competitors. Schools, now faced

with a dramatically changed world, are also revising their view of what can
be done to enhance the quality of their products.[2]

Ways to "enhance the quality of their products" include developing a keen
awareness of corporate culture requirements and emphasizing technicist
ways to manipulate that culture for centralized goals. Deal and Kennedy,
Peters and Waterman, and Dyer all argue that "corporate culture" consists
of patterns of behaviors, beliefs, rituals, symbols, and myths that help
stimulate members of an organization toward success.[3] Success, in turn, is
defined by those individuals who shape the culture of the organization. Deal
and Kennedy contend that companies generate their identities by "shaping
values, making heroes, spelling out rites and rituals, and acknowledging the
cultural network have an edge."[4] Part of this edge, they contend, is in having
heroes whom workers can imitate. Significant to understanding "corporate
culture" ideology is explicating the functionalist and behaviorist foundations
held by proponents of "corporate culture." These foundations best serve
business interests for two major reasons: proclivity for control and
generalizability of standards for accountability.

Behaviorists consider the human being an entity to be externally
molded. If the person controlling a given human being wishes to stimulate
a desired response, tactics like reinforcement, modeling, and conditioning
follow.[5] Kilmann, Saxton, and Serpa exemplify the behaviorist position in
corporations when they distinguish between the positive and negative
impacts a culture has on an organization.

> A culture has *positive* impact on an organization when it points behavior
> in the right direction, is widely shared among the members of work groups,
> and puts strong pressure on group members to follow the established
> cultural guidelines. Alternatively, a culture has *negative* impact on an
> organization when it points behavior in the wrong direction, is widely
> shared among group members, and exerts strong pressure on group
> members.[6]

The only (rather obvious) difference between what is considered positive and
negative in this case relates directly to whether employee behavior is being
pointed in the "right" or "wrong" direction. What are the implications of this
seeming truism?

Promoters of "corporate culture" orchestration readily point to the leadership role of executives and managers (by the very definition of their title, controlling and manipulative), who are seen as setting the tone and serving as models for their subordinates.[7] Deal and Kennedy concede this point and argue that the practice of cultural management by "symbolic managers" is becoming not just an added management technique, but the only effective solution to the danger of loss of control in an organization.[8]

For corporate executives and managers to point behavior in the "right" direction, schemes of standardization are formulated for the purpose of accountability and profit; these schemes have as their origin scientific management. Recall the use of scientific management to bifurcate the purpose of schools around the turn of the century. Also recall how Carlson illustrated the role of scientific management in proletarianizing teachers. Frederick Taylor is the "father" of the movement and advocated the use of time-and-motion study as a means of analyzing and standardizing work activities. His research called for detailed observation and measurement to find the optimum mode of performance.[9] Gareth Morgan outlines five principles that Taylor advocated as follows:

1. *Shift all responsibility for the organization of work from the worker to the manager*; managers should do all the thinking relating to the planning and design of work, leaving the workers with the task of implementation.
2. *Use scientific methods to determine the most efficient way of doing work*; design the worker's task accordingly, specifying the *precise* way in which the work is to be done.
3. *Select* the best person to perform the job thus designed.
4. *Train* the worker to do the work efficiently.
5. *Monitor* worker performance to ensure that appropriate work procedures are followed and that appropriate results are achieved.[10]

Accountability and standards thus become the focus of a well-run organization. Businesses that incorporate the appropriate symbols, myths, and beliefs with Taylor's characteristics of production and accountability become the apex of success for "corporate-culture" advocates.

Consider fast-food chains. The respective symbols, a smiling clown or a fatherly pitchman, are coupled with the belief that a delicious meal can be purchased for a nominal fee and received in a very short amount of time. Workers are expected to follow the designated speech for each customer ("Would you like fries with that?") and should embody the prescribed, happy demeanor. Managers direct workers to complete their tasks in the most efficient manner possible, noting duties and procedures specific to the "drive-thru," "register," and "grill."

Deal and Kennedy applaud fast-food-chain approaches to "corporate culture." They even detail the process of an exemplary model to follow.

> The first model is to be found in the recognized king of the franchisees, McDonald's. McDonald's dominates fast-food franchising because of a very strong culture—almost a mystique—that bonds its far-flung franchisees together. The core beliefs of this culture revolve around Quality, Service, Convenience, and Value (QSCV)—a slogan repeatedly drummed into the heads of management and the work force. Franchisees are educated into this culture at Hamburger University, where, in a program more extensive than any other in the franchising industry, newcomers are indoctrinated into the culture that is McDonald's. . . . Once the franchisees are in the field, the McDonald's culture is continually reinforced by inspectors and by contests to determine who best reaches the standards McDonald's sets for all its franchises. Ceremonies honor the most successful franchisees, and regional associations among the franchisees keep awareness of the parent company's values up to snuff. . . . Atop this culture sits a highly visible hero—Ray Kroc. But there are many other heroes as well: waitress of the month, franchisee of the year; the originator of Egg McMuffin—a franchisee. An assembly of heroes keeps the culture alive and strong.[11]

For "corporate culture" advocates, Hamburger University is exemplary: a place where slogans are "repeatedly drummed into the heads of management and the work force "; a place for "indoctrination" such that no matter how far apart graduates might go, they can rely on a strong "culture" to "bond" them together; a place where, like the originator of the Egg McMuffin, one becomes a "hero" by reproducing the material goods of the company that, cyclically, advance the company and its profits. Like a surreal Orwellian dreamscape, Hamburger University is the place, literally, where indoctrination is applauded and where a controlling behaviorism thrives.

Educational institutions risk becoming similar institutions of consumer and worker acquiescence. As with corporate managers directing their workers to be "on" the "drive-thru," "register," or "grill," educational administrators also direct teachers to perform similar "tasks." In addition to their classroom responsibilities, teachers patrol the cafeteria and hallways and monitor the bathrooms. Scripted speech may not be as noticeable as in a fast-food establishment, but careful review may yield phrases that intimate the impact of behaviorist speech patterns or Madeline Hunter vocabulary ("My, isn't Susy sitting nicely today?"). State-mandated learning objectives, like the QCC and Standards of Learning Objectives, are slogan-like and constitute the menu teachers serve their students, with one major difference. Students have little or no choice in selecting what they want, nor do teachers have any major input.

Yet here is where some opportunists within the "corporate culture" world find a new niche, an eternal business opportunity. They seize the notion of worker "choice" or worker "participation" and wrap companies in the "gussied-up" paper of "cooperative, democratic" ventures. Attempting to distance themselves from the rewards-based behaviorism and contrived-but-controlling systems supported at Hamburger University, the "new wave" corporatists argue for advanced business models for schools.[12] Kearns makes the case that "the modern school should look less like a factory and more like our best high-tech companies, with lean structures, flat organizations, and decision making pushed to the lowest possible level . . . with fewer middle managers, and those that remain act[ing] less like controllers and more like colleagues and collaborators."[13]

Part of the charade here is that the argument, while calling for "flat organizations," actually reinforces the hierarchy it purports to reject by offering that decision making be pushed to the *lowest possible level*. The structure may change, but increasing the girth of the lowest possible level is akin to Reaganomics: shrinking the middle class by forcing the middle class into the expanding lower class (with the hegemonic support of the very people who are pushed "lower"). Another part of the charade is the insinuation that oligopolies are seriously interested in authentic collegiality and collaboration. Perhaps what is sought is Egg McMuffin collaboration, where the appearance of mutuality means celebrating only that innovation and creativity that results in increased profit and market share for executives and stockholders.

Edward Deming provides another example of "new wave" corporatism. On the positive side, Deming generally supports the idea that people have a fundamental desire to learn and he operates from an optimistic view of human nature. The particulars of his proposals, however, are oriented toward corporate consulting. He offers fourteen points, in the tradition of consultants, that promise systemic change. The list is important to note, not so much for what it says, but for what it implies.

1. Create constancy of purpose for improvement of product and service.
2. Adopt the new [Deming] philosophy.
3. Cease dependence on inspection to achieve quality. Build in quality in the first place.
4. End the practice of awarding business on the basis of price alone.
5. Improve constantly and forever every process.
6. Institute training on the job.
7. Adopt and institute leadership.
8. Drive out fear.
9. Break down barriers between staff areas.
10. Eliminate slogans, exhortations, and targets for staff.
11. Eliminate numerical quotas for the staff and goals for management.
12. Remove barriers that rob people of pride of workmanship.
13. Institute a vigorous program of education and self-improvement for everyone.
14. Put everybody in the organization to work to accomplish the transformation.[14]

Aside from the apparent redundancy and self-serving nature of #2, if we took Deming's #10 seriously, we might dispense with his entire list. Nonetheless, the widespread attention, if not acceptance, given to Deming indicates an infatuation with "kinder and gentler reform." Deming's success, after all, has been primarily in Japan where hierarchy is deeply ingrained and where appearances of "cooperative teams" belie structural subordination of women.[15] Training on the job is a reality (#4), regardless of preparation, and driving out fear (#8) is beneficial to workers. In the "new world," however, where "outsourcing" means lost jobs for workers, driving out fear is not a corporate interest.

As with the implications of Hamburger University, "new" consultants also have an eye on schools. Recall the comparison made earlier regarding the roles of business personnel (incessantly reduced to "human resources") and school personnel. Alan Blankenstein translates Deming's terminology into school language:

> In order to see how Deming's principles, which were originally developed for business, might apply to schools, we need to translate a few of his terms. Principals and superintendents can be considered "management" or "leadership." Teachers are "employees," "leaders," and "managers" of students. Students are "employees," and the knowledge they gain and later contribute to society is the "product." Parents and society are the "customers." Legislators are the "board of directors."[16]

Such a crass comparison reinforces business interests and consumer materialism by equating and thus reducing, among other things, knowledge as a "product."[17] Once knowledge is commodified, standardized test scores can be said to represent what students "know." Scores from tests (CAT, IOWAs, etc.) can then be used to place students in "appropriate" tracks ("ability grouping"), stratifying students to become future leaders, managers, and employees.

A step below intransitiveness, such a perspective elevates business hierarchies of control at the same time as it calls for collaboration. To play the game, momentarily, one might ask why teachers are not listed as "managers" or "leaders" (in the first sense[18]). If the structure of schools were reformed, (that is, formed again, in the purported visionary and collegial sense noted earlier) might teachers lead their own schools and have principals manage the school's business affairs? Even the "new" consultants refrain from such an arrangement, fearing, perhaps, a rise to power of the small but growing population of teachers who demonstrate critical transitivity.

Blankenstein's anachronisms also reveal the kind of reductionism and utilitarianism against which this text argues. By linking parents and society to "customers," he insinuates a "customer is always right" position. If parents desire, for example, a particular curriculum, teachers should or must adhere to their wishes, regardless of pedagogy. The point might be a question of terminology, but not *only* terminology. There is more to it than *simply* wording. Kohn adds:

That it is so difficult to agree on the educational correlative to a company's customer—one who *purchases* a product—should alert us to the possibility that the question is misconceived. Attempting to answer it is about as sensible as trying to figure out which member of a family is most like a colonel and which is most like a lieutenant. . . . To talk about learning in terms of buying and selling not only reflects a warped view of the activity but contributes to the warping.[19]

Parents and policymakers already demonstrate a corporate, bottom-line mentality regarding test scores and appeals to accountancy, both of which warp learning. As a result, teachers are consistently subjected to the kind of "corporate-culture" mentality outlined above.[20] Calls for accountability, testing, and standardized curricula all point to business schemes and "corporate culture" production. Recall the transfer: schools assume the role of a business, administrators assume the role of managers, teachers assume the role of workers, students are relegated to the "getting" of necessary products (knowledge), and all are encouraged to consider the climate "positive" because there are predetermined symbols, behaviors, beliefs, and rituals to support the claims and people "feel" a part of the team.

Referring again to Morgan's outline of the five characteristics advocated by Taylor, consider the similarities between businesses and schools outlined in Table 1. What easier way is there to ensure the success of major corporations in the United States? The beliefs from Horace Mann's common schools regarding "hard work" and "obedience to authority" could be induced from kindergarten through high school, but now with business approval and corporate support, the consequences of the beliefs benefit individuals and groups of individuals less and corporations more. The result is hegemony; the school itself becomes a factory (or high-tech firm) poised to produce workers for growing companies and competitive enterprises. The rituals of tracking and stratification become paths along which travel future managers and future workers as determined by the performance of "appropriate" or "inappropriate" behaviors. It seems ironic, however, that "corporate-culture" advocates readily overlook the possibility that in their system—which so much depends on the inculcation of the proper "myths"—the overriding myth might actually be applying "corporate-culture" manipulation strategies to schools.

Table 1

KEY

Administrators = Managers
Teachers = Workers
Students = Products

CORPORATIONS	SCHOOLS
Shift all responsibility for organization of work from the worker to the manager.	Base the teacher's role on a prescribed agenda set by supervisors, principals, superintendents, and central office (state department) policymakers.
Use scientific methods to determine the most efficient way of doing work.	Develop more standardized tests for easier evaluation. Teachers follow teacher guides and prepackaged worksheets that reinforce testing and accountability.
Select the best person to perform the job thus designed.	Expand tracking to further stratify students. Teachers should be tested to be sure they qualify to be an educator by taking the NTE or other national standardized examination.
Train the worker to do the work efficiently.	Provide teachers with in-service training on "effective teaching" methodologies and on staff development.
Monitor worker performance to ensure that appropriate work procedures are followed and that appropriate results are achieved.[21]	Evaluate teachers on student performance, on outcomes of the SAT, and on classroom behavioral observations.

Teachers are nonetheless faced with corporate-culture expectations in their daily school lives. Represented in those schools by "visioneering" charts, slogan buttons, and in-service day programs filled with overhead presentations, teachers are subjected to corporatist "team-building" games and performances. The effort is technorationalist in that it offers "tried and true" methods, from businesses and human-resource consultants, on how to influence the culture of the school. As though schools are not already demonstrating a "corporate culture," or varying versions of it, "facilitators" are brought in to reinforce forms of "cooperation," "communication," and "commitment" that obstruct critical intellectualism.

Teachers resist the patronizing nature of such efforts, sometimes consciously but more often out of the malaise that comes with repetitiveness. Teachers have heard it all before, in other words. To face another in-service means more butcher paper taped around the room for fake "brainstorming" sessions that will only reflect what central-office administrators want anyway. It's the same old procedure.

The problem remains that there are conflicting messages. Mass-media accounts of schooling so intimately connect corporate interests with the interests of schools that teachers' identities are confounded. Peter McLaren puts it this way:

> Manufactured consumer needs have taken precedence over labor power while the commodity form has subsumed subjectivity and identity under the laws of capital accumulation and the regime of productivity. Subjectivities and identities of citizens [*qua* teachers] have been virtually reterritorialized by new postmodern electronic mediating devices of television, radio, film, and computers such that the stress on interpretation that was formerly linked to bourgeois individualism has given way to a simulated self that has become socially integrated through the politics of consumption with its surfeit of conservative ideologies. Identity in postmodern times mirrors opinion polls, and forms of organized resistance collapse into public apathy and mass inertia.[22]

For those teachers able to see the impact of corporate-culture meta-narratives, they find themselves even more troubled due to their isolation and (resulting?) disempowerment. By proletarianizing teaching and reinforcing consumer-materialist expectations, schools (legislators?) fortify corporate-culture dispositions at the expense of teacher and student interests and identities. One way this is done is by promoting technology as the panacea for employment and global competitiveness. If technological literacy is the focus of schools, so corporatists assume, manipulating teaching and learning (as well as teachers and students) in that direction assures consumer-materialist success.

By raising concerns about cultural capital exchange rates relating to technology, its funding, and certain outcomes, we can see continuing efforts at maintaining a proletarianized teaching force. We can also see how corporate interests affect schooling in not-so-obvious ways—a kind of Sartrean conspiracy in broad daylight. We can conceive of technology in terms of business interests, marketing, and product familiarity. This is significant as we turn our attention in chapter 3 to school-business partnerships. Before considering that topic, our task is to reveal links between cultural capital, technology, and consumer materialism.

CULTURAL CAPITAL AND TECHNOLOGY'S LINK TO CONSUMER MATERIALISM

The term "cultural capital" comes from Bourdieu and represents, in basic terms, ways of dressing, talking, acting, and socializing in addition to ways of speaking, communicating, and behaving.[23] McLaren notes that "cultural capital can exist in the embodied state, as long-lasting dispositions of the mind and body; in the objectified state, as cultural artifacts such as pictures, books, diplomas, and other material objects; and in the institutionalized state, which confers original properties on the cultural capital which guarantees it."[24] Add computers/technology to McLaren's list of cultural artifacts and the link to the institutionalized state to which he refers is striking. Computers, in other words, are the artifacts for economic production that are institutionalized in schools (surrogate training sites for corporations).

Unless one wishes to argue, Platonically, that computers are an imperfect representation of computer-ness, computers/technology are constructed; that is, they developed (and continue to develop) at the hands of the men and women who crafted (and craft) them. Regardless of their human/subjective origin, however, computers now appear immutable and ever present. This is particularly true to students in American schools who are on the receiving end of vast expenditures of (a) money for technology, and (b) time given over to talk of a future century and the pervasiveness, nay, requirement, that "technology-skills" will play in their employment in that future. Couple this process of institutionalization with the material manifestation of computers in classrooms, and the picture becomes more complete. The ontology of schooling intends consumer materialism via technologization. In other words, the computer, as cultural artifact, is a highly valued and valuable cultural-capital commodity.

Neil Postman outlines technological innovation and change in both historical and cultural terms. Specifically, he divides history into three major eras with very different implications regarding life and culture. His third era, technopoly, is the current era and submits culture to the "sovereignty of technique and technology."[25] One result of such "sovereignty" is the reification of fast-paced efficiency and the anticipation and expectation that change (such as software upgrades and hardware alterations [mega-bytes, giga-bytes, etc.]) begets change. Consequently, the very time touted as "being saved" because of technological change, is actually used to "keep up" with the change that was supposed to "save time" in the first place. Taylorism's zeal for efficiency recurs. What this ultimately means for schools is an expensive game of tail-chasing, as schools are faced with technological expectations (satellites, computers in every classroom, etc.) that, when funded, are either funded from specially legislated state and local budgets (as short-term expenditures or perhaps taken from other areas of the overall budget with no increase in that overall budget); funded by lotteries, which operate on the very backs of those who can least afford to gamble; or funded by business partnerships that profit on a captive market.[26] Perhaps worse is the technological chase set up by the previously mentioned paradoxical regression out of which neither technologists nor the rest of society can easily escape. Consider two points: (1) technology is embraced by schools far more than it is scrutinized for possible long-term ethical, economic, and pedagogical deficits; and (2) the rapid pace of technological change just noted is conspiratorial insofar as the change/growth/competition argument ultimately favors a particular section of society at the expense of the poor and disenfranchised.

For those students whose homes already house computers, reality fits nicely into the system of cultural exchange outlined above. They own the goods or the means of production that situates them amicably in a world that values the commodity they have. Those students, however, who are from homes which do not (or do not yet) have computers struggle to engage a world alien to what they know. These students are trying to trade commodities perceived as less valuable than the commodity of technological literacy. As with the dilemma of bilingualism, students are faced with the huge challenge of finding their roles in a society that is portraying successful existence in terms of specialized competence. Students from poor homes develop a kind of "boomerang perception": they come to schools that do not value their cultural capital and hear about what cultural capital *is* valuable, but return to their homes after school unable to trade the very capital they were just told was advantageous.[27] Like legislating English as "the" official language and requiring of all students a particular and provincial manner of speech, differing worth is mutually applied to distinct knowledges (school and home). It takes care of one problem by ignoring other (larger) ones. Sanctioning technological literacy as "the" means of success in the next millennium, for example, and dotting classrooms and schools with computers and computer labs misses an important cultural reality (or larger problem): those who have, will have more—while those who do not have, will continue not to have.

While there is nothing novel about this situation, when seen in light of technological expectations and the stratified valuation of cultural capital, it reveals a pretension of technology and its paradoxical ramification. On one hand, technology is the reality (*fait accompli?*) with which everyone must live. On the other hand, those who cannot afford technology have the burden of living with technology, but without personal and translatable access to it. Similarly, technology's claim of equity ("user friendliness," and increasing numbers of computers in classrooms to reach more and more students) is like an invitation from the neighborhood bully to play ball. Deny the opportunity and be beaten up. Accept the challenge and still be pummeled, as bullies are bigger than those they bully anyway. Poor and disenfranchised students pay the price of technological illiteracy and the nontransfer of their cultural capital, not because of any lack of aptitude, but because capitalistic restraints define *for* them that they will be perpetually behind. Joe Kincheloe puts it this way, "Schools will privilege those students who exhibit the dominant cultural capital while punishing those students who possess very different forms of cultural capital. Thus epistemologies that do not examine contextual factors focus only on hard statistical correlations that dismiss social factors such as cultural capital and its effect on academic performance."[28]

Put in pecuniary terms, even if used computers were, for example, available at affordable prices, the second- or third-hand user is restrained in what they can do, at the same time those able to afford the latest models with largest capacities continue to advance far ahead of those with older models. The scenario may define a realistic version of what people will *have* to do to become members of the dominant society, but the scenario leaves out the vital component of cultural capital. It presupposes that all *will* value what has been institutionally sanctioned as valuable because membership in the dominant society is a laudable given.

That technology has become a necessary and pervasive part of existence is not in dispute. Access to information, speed of that access, and almost any word-processing and presentation preparation feature possible, are all praiseworthy additions technology brings to the world. Faxing papers and letters, E-mailing colleagues around the world, surfing the Net hour after hour, these activities generally exemplify expedience and/or entertainment and have the potential to broaden views and expand thoughts.

John Dewey would concede the advantages of technology and would probably be in the forefront of those advocating technological innovation. He notes that "[a] vision of a day in which the natural sciences and the technologies which flow from them are used as servants of a humane life, constitutes the imagination that is relevant to our own time. A humanism that flees from science as an enemy denies the means by which a liberal humanism might become a reality."[29] Dewey would also likely position himself in favor of increased spending on technology, perhaps even from school-business partnerships. Computers in every classroom would be a fine means/ends—but only if the enterprise of technology went toward "liberal humanism." Herein is a concern for Dewey. The concern is threefold: (1) that advances in technology are firstly and primarily realized by the upper classes of American society, (2) that the pace of change far exceeds critical scrutiny of the change, and (3) that, for all of the rhetoric arguing for fast change and technology's ability to foster it, most Americans neither need nor want the speeds possible and would not be able to make meaning of the vast amounts of information able to be garnered by technology even if they wanted to.

Regarding the first concern, Ratan shows that while Americans spent $8 billion on computers in 1994, "wealthy and upper-middle-class families form the bulk of the 30% of American households that own computers."[30] Mark Shields adds that

> technological advances are reinforcing national socioeconomic inequalities. In three huge national surveys conducted in 1984, 1989, and 1993, the U.S. Census Bureau found big gaps in access to computers by income, race, and education. But the most disturbing finding was that those gaps hadn't diminished over the decade covered by the surveys. As a 1990 report by the Congressional Office of Technology Assessment concluded, 'changes in the U.S. communication infrastructure are likely to broaden the gap between those who can access communication services and use information strategically and those who cannot.'[31]

Regarding the second and third concerns, Postman argues the following:

> Attend any conference on telecommunications or computer technology, and you will be attending a celebration of innovative machinery that generates, stores, and distributes more information, more conveniently, at greater speeds, than ever before. To the question "What problem does the information solve?" the answer is usually "How to generate, store, and distribute more information, more conveniently, at greater speeds than ever before." This is the elevation of information to a metaphysical status: information as both the means and end of human creativity. . . . For what purpose or with what limitations, it is not for us to ask; and we are not accustomed to asking, since the problem is unprecedented.[32]

Because he was intimately concerned with purpose, Dewey's expectations of technology went beyond information. He substituted "objects" for "information," but Dewey's point was to contrast the certainty connected to "objects" with useful "data": "By data is signified subject matter for *further* interpretation; something to be thought about. *Objects* are finalities; they are complete, finished; they call for thought only in the way of definition, classification, logical arrangement, subsumption in syllogisms, etc. But data signify 'material to serve'; they are indications, evidence, signs, clues to and of something still to be reached; they are intermediate, not ultimate; means, not finalities."[33] Postman's point about elevating information to a metaphysical status means, in Dewey's terms, raising *objects* to exalted status. Consumer materialism does the same. It also establishes the standards for acceptance of the status-quo (via comparisons).

This calls to mind Antonio Gramsci's concern about science and technology. He argued that given the pervasiveness and continual rise of technology, social control was no longer left primarily to the police and to armies but instead was accomplished through the distribution of a technology-oriented system of norms and imperatives. "The latter were used to lend institutional authority a degree of unity and certainty and provide it with apparent universality and legitimation."[34] Gramsci calls this "ideological hegemony," which is a type of domination that not only exploits who we are within the larger questions of reality, it also composes day-to-day experiences that shape behavior.[35] The degree to which computers control behavior (e.g., specific commands at certain times, permission grants to perform inevitable functions) is the same degree to which Gramsci's concerns are valid. Teachers might teach differently and students might learn differently (possibly a great idea), but the question is "*Which* teachers and students would teach and learn differently?"

Recall Dewey. The particulars of his technology stance (objects, data, etc.) are subsumed under his larger argument about the principle of interaction.[36] For Dewey, external conditions *and* internal conditions are unified by experience.[37] Experiences are "educative" when they result in more unification and when continued inquiry occurs (and recurs). The role of the teacher, accordingly, is as a kind of regulator. Teachers have as their "immediate and direct concern . . . the situations in which interaction takes place. The individual, who enters as a factor into it, is what he is at a given time. It is the other factor, that of objective [external] conditions, which lies to some extent with the possibility of regulation by the educator."[38] The lessons, games, techniques, materials, and equipment teachers use, the way they talk and what they say, for instance, all comprise the objective/external "situations" to which Dewey refers. These make up, in Dewey's words, "that environment which will interact with the existing capacities and needs of those taught to create worth-while experience[s]."[39] Yet as Seals notes,

> Computers, quite obviously and understandably, stand Dewey's argument on its head. When incorporated into the external environment of the students' educational situation, computers present a feature of that environment crucially outside the power of the educator to control, manipulate, or regulate. The inflexibility associated with computer "conversational" interaction forces the educator to practice manipulation of the other side of the educational situation. In short, the internal state of the student must be brought to the point of matching the latest member of the classroom's external environment. Since computers can't be moved from their preferences concerning styles of interaction, students must be moved from theirs.[40]

At this point, we might suggest that there is no problem here after all. The purpose of schooling, so this argument goes, is to change the internal conditions of students. Dewey even admits to this when he suggests his companion principle to the principle of interaction. The companion is the principle of continuity and it holds that, like "educative experiences," changes for the better and growth as a result of interaction must obtain for "education" to be said to occur. On this point, computers can only be said to give teachers a new job to do: they must train students to use computers and to develop "computer skills." As a result, students are enabled to learn on their own by using computers. Dewey is satisfied and computers no longer represent a problem. Unfortunately, as Seals points out,

> [t]his objection . . . misses the point of the problem of the inversion of the principle of interaction. The problem occurs, not after students adapt to computer use, but before and during their adaptation to it. That is, the problem of the inversion of the principle of interaction cannot be used to argue about any alleged interruption or enhancement of a student's continual growth qua student. It may be true that computers, inflexible and strict as they are in their interactions with humans, indoctrinate students into passivity, docility and compliance. It may also be true that computers, entertaining and fascinating as they can be, unlock untold treasures of educational interest for some students. But those problems, whatever merit they may have, have no bearing on the current issue. Instead, the problem of the inversion of the principle of interaction concerns an anthropological point and arises at the place where students are being trained to computer use. The upshot of identifying computers as a conversational subculture, and an inflexible, strict, and narrow one at that, is that cultural differences

among users will determine differential responses to interaction with computers. Therein lies the rub. As a conversational subculture in their own right, computers are guaranteed to interact more or less well with members of other, more or less well-adapted and adaptable subcultures.[41]

Seals goes on to illustrate the point using McLaren's *Life in Schools*.[42] In *Life in Schools*, McLaren compares his nine-year-old stepdaughter's traditional suburban school with Driftwood, the school at which he is a teacher located in the "troubled" "inner-city" Jane Finch Corridor of Toronto. McLaren comes home one afternoon and is greeted by his daughter. She is cheerful this particular afternoon and is wearing a pair of cardboard glasses she made in school that day. McLaren recounts:

> "How was school today?" I asked.
> "Just great, dad!" she exclaimed. "Everybody got to make a pair of these glasses in art. The teacher bought all the material."
> I nodded, then asked her, "How do the kids in your class behave?"
> "Everybody does what the teacher tells them to, pretty well. Nobody even talks in class without the teacher's permission."
> "Nobody even talks," I echoed blankly.[43]

In contrast, McLaren reveals that in his school, just the hint of commands stirs instantaneous confrontation. His students resist traditional authority and become violent if pushed to conform to archetypal expectations.

> Now imagine, further, introduction of computers into these dissimilar cultures. A reasonable expectation will be that students already acculturated to obeisance to teacher's commands will easily adapt to those of the computer. On the other hand, students in whom inflexibility of interaction evokes frustration, anger and physical attack can not be counted on to take kindly to computer command. Problems will arise just at the point where their internal conditions (i.e. their culturally accepted and habitual responses to forms of interaction) must be manipulated, regulated, or changed to make them into computer compliant learners. That, of course, is exactly the problem of the inversion of the principle of interaction.[44]

In part, this means that the socioeconomic background of students provides an important context for understanding teaching and computers. Whatever realizations come about from this, one point is clear: those who "have" tend toward conservatism, as they have much to conserve. Consequently, as conservatism advocates respect for authority, obedience, docility, etcetera, those who "have" already possess a cultural predilection to computer use.

Those who do not have, since they have little or nothing to lose anyway, tend to reject authority and its cultural consequences.

Because computers, their use, the teaching of them, and their inclusion in classrooms are increasingly pervasive issues facing American schools, questions about cultural capital, interactions, etcetera, reveal concerns inherent to technology. Given consumer materialism, however, those kinds of issues are rarely the focus of the public's attention. The more pertinent question, so the consumerist logic goes, is when computers will be in every classroom and who will pay for them. Corporations are eager to exploit the topic of technology by arguing that unless "we" are "technologically literate," the United States will be unable to compete in the next century. To assure the acceptance of this mantra, corporate interests, via school-partnerships and donations, increasingly control what kind of technology teachers and students face in their classrooms. Chapter 3 explores school-business partnerships and it is to that investigation that we now turn.

NOTES

1. From the August 1997 brochure titled "The Big Picture" (Atlanta, GA: MediaOne, 1997), 1.

2. *Labor Force 2000*, 60.

3. See Terrence Deal and Allan A. Kennedy, *Corporate Cultures: The Rights and Rituals of Corporate Life* (Reading, MA: Addison-Wesley, 1982); Thomas J. Peters and Robert H. Waterman, *In Search of Excellence: Lessons from America's Best Run Companies* (New York: Harper & Row, 1982); and W. Gibb Dyer, Jr., *Culture and Organizations: A Case Study and Analysis* (Cambridge, MA: MIT, Sloan School of Management, 1982).

4. Deal and Kennedy, *Corporate Cultures*, 15.

5. See B.F. Skinner, *Walden Two* (New York: MacMillian, 1948); *The Shaping of a Behaviorist* (New York: Knopf, 1979).

6. Ralph H. Kilmann, Mary Saxton, Roy Serpa, et al., *Gaining Control of the Corporate Culture* (San Francisco: Jossey-Bass, 1985), 4. (Italics added.)

7. See Lee G. Bolman and Terrence E. Deal, *Reframing Organizations: Artistry, Choice, and Leadership* (San Francisco: Jossey-Bass, 1991), and Terrence E. Deal and William A. Jenkins, *Managing the Hidden Organization* (New York: Warner Books, 1994).

8. Deal and Kennedy, *Corporate Cultures*, 193.

9. See Frederick W. Taylor, *Principles of Scientific Management* (New York: Harper & Row, 1911).

10. Gareth Morgan, *Images of Organization* (Beverly Hills, CA: Sage, 1986), 30.

11. Deal and Kennedy, *Corporate Cultures*, 193-194.

12. See, for example, James E. Liebig, *Merchants of Vision: People Bringing New Purposes and Values to Business* (San Francisco: Berrett-Koehler, 1994); William Lundin and Kathleen Lundin, *The Healing Manager: How to Build Quality Relationships and Productive Cultures at Work* (San Francisco: Berrett-Koehler, 1993); and Herman Bryant Maynard, Jr. and Susan E. Mehrtens, *The Fourth Wave: Business in the 21st Century* (San Francisco: Berrett-Koehler, 1993). Maynard and Mehrtens go so far as to suggest shifts in business outlooks: "from exploitation to caring, from materialism to spirituality, and from consumerism to a concern for social and economic justice. Greed has become less acceptable; there is a movement away from materialism toward intangibles such as honesty, truth, courage, self-worth, the quality of relationships, and personal fulfillment" (4).

13. David Kearns and Denis Doyle, *Winning the Brain Race* (San Francisco: ICS Press, 1988), 38. Kearns was CEO of Xerox before becoming Deputy Secretary of Education under George Bush.

14. W. Edward Deming, *Out of the Crisis* (Cambridge: MIT Press, 1988).

15. See, for example, James E. Rosenbaum and Takehiko Kariya, "From High School to Work: Market and Institutional Mechanisms in Japan," *American Journal of Sociology* 94, no. 6 (May 1989): 1334-1365.

16. Alan M. Blankenstein, "Lessons from Enlightened Corporations," *Educational Leadership* (March 1992): 72.

17. For a detailed analysis of closely related issues, see Dennis Carlson, "'Updating' Individualism and the Work Ethic: Corporate Logic in the Classroom," *Curriculum Inquiry* 12, no. 2 (1982): 125-160.

18. Blankenstein connotes two versions of leadership: principals, for example, are leaders in a general and overarching sense while teachers are leaders in a narrow and specific sense.

19. Alfie Kohn, "Turning Learning into a Business: Concerns about Total Quality," *Educational Leadership* (September 1993): 59. (Italics in original.)

20. Stanley Aronowitz and Henry Giroux, *Education under Siege: The Conservative, Liberal and Radical Debate over Schooling* (South Hadley, MA: Bergin & Garvey, 1985), 9.

21. Morgan, *Images of Organization*; See also Samuel Bowles and Herbert Gintis, *Schooling in Capitalist America: Educational Reform and the Contradictions of Economic Life* (New York: Basic Books, 1976), 55-102.

22. Peter McLaren, *Critical Pedagogy and Predatory Culture: Oppositional Politics in a Postmodern Era* (New York: Routledge, 1995), 102.

23. See, for example, Pierre Bourdieu, "The School as a Conservation Force: Scholastic and Cultural Inequalities," in *Contemporary Research in the Sociology of Education*, J. Eggleston, ed. (London: Methuen, 1974); and Pierre Bourdieu and J.C. Passeron, *Reproduction in Education, Society, and Culture* (Beverly Hills, CA: Sage, 1977).

24. Peter McLaren, *Life in Schools: An Introduction to Critical Pedagogy in the Foundations of Education* (New York: Longman, 1994), 198.

25. Neil Postman, *Technopoly: The Surrender of Culture to Technology* (New York: Alfred A. Knopf, 1992), 52.

26. See Southern Regional Education Board, "Educational Technology: K-12 Planning and Investments in SREB States." (Atlanta: Southern Regional Education Board, 1995); Richard Barnet and John Cavenagh, *Global Dreams: Imperial Corporations and the New World Order* (New York: Simon and Schuster, 1994); and Edward S. Herman, *Triumph of the Market: Essays on Economics, Politics, and the Media* (Boston: South End Press, 1995), 6-11.

27. See Elizabeth V. Spelman, *Inessential Woman: Problems of Exclusion in Feminist Thought* (Boston: Beacon, 1988). Spelman illustrates the point in terms of race (and gender) when she notes that "White children in the U.S. got early training in boomerang perception when they were told by well-meaning white adults that Black people were just like us—never, however, that we were just like Blacks." See also, María C. Lugones, "On the Logic of Pluralist Feminism," in *Feminist Ethics*, Claudia Card, ed. (Lawrence, KS: University Press of Kansas, 1991), 41.

28. Joe Kincheloe, *Toward a Critical Politics of Teacher Thinking: Mapping the Postmodern* (Westport, CT: Bergin & Garvey, 1993), 46.

29. John Dewey, *Individualism Old and New* (New York: Capricorn, 1962 [1929]), 155-156.

30. Suneel Ratan, "A New Divide between Haves and Have-Nots?" *Time* Spring 1995 (Special Issue), 25.

31. Mark A. Shields, "Academe Enters the Age of Anticippointment," *TECHNOS* 4, no.1 (Fall 1995): 31. See also, David McGrath, "Computerize or BUST!" *Contemporary Education* 66 (Fall 1994): 58-60.

32. Postman, 61.

33. John Dewey, *The Quest for Certainty* in Jo Ann Boydston, ed., *The Later Works of John Dewey, 1925-1953*, Vol. 4. (Carbondale, IL: Southern Illinois University Press, 1988), 80. (Italics in the original.)

34. Henry Giroux, *Ideology, Culture, and the Process of Schooling* (Philadelphia: Temple University Press, 1981), 39.

35. Antonio Gramsci, *Selections from Prison Notebooks* trans. Hoare and Smith (New York: International Publishers, 1971).

36. See John Dewey, *Experience and Education*, in Jo Ann Boydston, ed., *John Dewey, The Later Works, 1925-1939*, Vol, 13. (Carbondale, IL: Southern Illinois University Press, 1988), 3- 62.

37. Ibid., 24.

38. Ibid., 26.

39. Ibid.

40. Greg Seals, "Ritual: The Hidden Curriculum of Education in Cyberspace," *Insights* 32, no. 1 (June, 1996): 7.

41. Ibid., 7-8.

42. McLaren, *Life in Schools,* op.cit.

43. Ibid., 49.

44. Seals, op. cit.

CHAPTER 3

The Kroger Connection

"Just as the sources blamed for the American economic woes had less to do with education than with misguided federal policies and corporate investment strategies the current focus of educational policy has less to do with education than with creating new corporate profit centers. Children as children just don't enter into the calculations."[1]

An interesting lineage of "2000" plans began with America 2000, which begat Goals 2000, which begat county and district attempts at "2000-ness," in the form of Cherokee County 2000, Hanover High 2000, and others. A fascinating incarnation of "2000-ness," however, began in the summer of 1993 with Kroger 2000. Kroger is a major supermarket chain in the Midwest, Southeast, and Mid-Atlantic regions of the U.S. Under the heading of "Partners in Education," Fulton County, Georgia, teamed with Kroger to promote a program titled "The Kroger Connection." The footer for the flyer is "Kroger 2000: For Goodness Sake." This chapter explores the meaning behind school-business partnerships and raises questions about funding conflicts and the degree to which business agendas influence schooling. As though aware of the concerns this chapter raises, Kroger 2000 offers the following reassurance about their program: "This is real life, hands on partnering as Kroger connects education and business in a win-win situation." Who really wins, and why, is the major focus of this chapter.

The task, then, is to provide examples and illustrations of actual partnerships and adopt-a-school partnering programs.[2] In so doing, the intention is to show that there *are* benefits of partnering schools with businesses but that the benefits are essentially for businesses and only residually for schools, teachers, and students. When the benefits for corporations are scrutinized, they reveal an emphasis on training-oriented schooling, marketing, and consumer materialism over possibilities for education-oriented schooling, authenticity, and critical transitivity. Such an emphasis, if it remains unchecked, risks undermining the potential for democratic citizenship and is sure to further reinforce the oligopoly currently enjoying power. The point here is to understand the subtheme assumptions, such as the purpose of schooling as job preparation, in order to question who benefits most from such a purpose. By bridging illustrations and examples of corporate involvement together with schools, corporate assumptions about the purposes of schooling are further revealed.

Assumptions are pervasive, for example, about what it means to be a teacher, what qualifies as "student success," and what funding sources schools should have and should use. Corporations view teaching much as one would view traditional methods courses in colleges of education: perfunctory, procedural, generalizable, and non-propositional. Teaching is not left to teacher interpretation, because teaching, on the traditional and corporate view, is fundamentally a series of steps and strategies to be carried out in linear, sequential fashion. Corporations also use national goals, particularly those that celebrate the need for international comparisons and increased competitiveness, to qualify what teaching entails and what success connotes. Goal #3, Goal #4, and Goal #5 from *Goals 2000* are highly touted by businesses and corporations. Goal #3 states, "By the year 2000, American students will leave grades four, eight and twelve having demonstrated competency in challenging subject matter including English, mathematics, science, history and geography, and every school in America will ensure that all students learn to use their minds well, so they may be prepared for responsible citizenship, further learning, and productive employment in our modern economy." Goal #4 is, "By the year 2000, U.S. students will be first in the world in mathematics and science achievement." Goal #5 is, "By the year 2000, every adult in America will be literate and will possess the knowledge and skill necessary to compete in a global economy and exercise the rights and responsibilities of citizenship."

Success is thus made contingent upon quantified measures and conformity to capitalist competition expectations. Science and mathematics, as a result, are useful instruments for consumer-materialist presumptions about what counts as valid curriculum reform. Such reform also allows corporations to maximize the larger exploitative circle: business interests shape national goals in the first place, national goals are used as the rationale by businesses to "reform" schooling and teaching, and the consequences for curriculum (also noted in the national goals) include the kind of reductionism upon which consumer materialism and corporate profit rely.[3]

This is perhaps not surprising. It is also not merely an exercise in revelatory narration. Revealing flaws in programs and narrating what those flaws are to people does not require reflection, thoughtfulness, or action on their part. Reflection, thoughtfulness and action, however, *are* part of what is necessary to elevate schools from being training-oriented sites for consumer materialism to being education-oriented sites for critical transitivity—the goal of this text. To achieve critical transitivity means interrogating the veracity of national goals assumptions and businesses' use of those goals. It also means overcoming "infomercial" affectations and consumerist lethargy. It means dispensing with reductionism, passive acceptance, and reliance on imagery. Instead, critical transitivity requires authenticity and not contrivance such that connections are made between disparities of power and privilege, their causes, and potential solutions.

"Infomercials" are useful examples of the problem of technorationality and consumer materialism because they represent the kind of approach to existence consumer materialists embrace and are loathe to *consequentially* critique (i.e., act against in critically transitive ways). Said differently, infomercials are the embodiment of contrivedness and capitalistic pretense, but are successful because large enough numbers of people watch them and believe what they are told, and thus the format proliferates. Similarly, the acceptance of business-aligned national goals elevates capitalistic pretense by further narrowing the role of schools to competitive sites producing techno-workers for a new century. Recall Goal #5. Knowledge is reduced and linked with particularistic "skills" for global economic competition. Exercising rights and responsibilities of citizenship is an afterthought. First is a competitive literacy; second a non-propositional epistemology. Once these two objectives are met, rights and responsibilities of citizenship are ex-post-facto actions deeply tainted and restricted by consumer materialism.

When "ab-cruncher" infomercials, for example, were revealed to have used larger models in the beginning of their sales pitch and smaller and thinner "doubles" at the end of their pitch, consumers still watched and still consumed. A competitive literacy existed: what beautiful people looked like, what means/product existed to achieve status-quo notions of beauty, what the cost of the product was, etcetera. The nonpropositional epistemology was how to put the "ab-cruncher" together, how to use the gadget, how many repetitions were recommended, etcetera. Two sets of rights/responsibilities result: (1) the consumer's right for total satisfaction with the product, "or your money back," and the responsibility to use the "ab-cruncher" to achieve "beauty"; and (2) the right of the business to sell the product and the responsibility to honor the obligation of the money-back guarantee. Missing, however, are *consequential* critiques. Because the promotions continue(d), well after it was widely revealed that "doubles" replaced the "heavier" models initially pictured, there was no consequence to the misrepresentation. Since the point is to make money in a capitalist society, rights and responsibilities are tainted and/or subsumed under materialist logic. Consumers are the focus, rather than citizens. It is similar to "Hooked on Phonics," where literacy is reduced to credit-card purchasing such that *being* literate is contingent only on *getting* cassette tapes and workbooks.

The malady shared by both examples is convenience-consciousness: reduce the amounts of time people are required to spend attaining status-quo images or giving to contemplative scholarship and more money will be made. Convenience and ease are selling points to people who see reality inordinately in terms of time, expense, and energy. The imagery is too appealing and simply narrating the deceit will not lead to critical transitivity. Indeed, by literally "buying into" the programmed commodification that "Hooked on Phonics," "ab-crunchers," and the like represent, consumer materialism is reinforced. Arguments against this reductionism and commercialization face "free- market defenses" such as "consumer responsibility."

"Free market defenses" are used by business advocates to make the duplicity of "ab-cruncher" infomercials palatable when, for example, business advocates remind us that even in the illustration of "ab-cruncher" scams, consumers are responsible for their own actions. This "responsible-consumer thesis" suggests that individuals are in charge of their faculties and make responsible purchasing decisions.[4] Culpability for purchases, accordingly, is assigned to the consumer. If one spends $49.95 on phonics cassette tapes, responsibility is for the holder of the credit card. Note the one-sidedness of the responsibility. A kind of after-the-fact blame game, responsibility for human fallibility is not for businesses that knowingly (aggressively?) exploit those frailties (such as vanity, schooling status, social comparisons, image consciousness), only those that flagrantly defy loosely interpreted consumer laws.

But the casualties of the marketing schemes are already tainted by fault if they "decide" or "choose" to purchase *x*, *y*, or *z* in the first place. Having the right to choose *not* to buy *x*, *y*, or *z* is the only criterion necessary for "no holds barred" advertising campaigns.[5] The existence of the right *not* to choose, in other words, means businesses push the limits of honest representation and minimize, literally, exceptions and concerns. One need only look at the small print that follows car- lease advertisements or cigarette warnings. The small print discloses limitations of availability or the existence of exceptions to the original claims or possible side-effects of use. Symbolically, truth is minimized or shrunk or subsumed under wanton imagery. Screaming pitchpeople first get consumers' attention; truth is an afterthought sublimated in tiny print alongside registered trademark information.

Obviously, techniques of marketing are linked to these concerns and are important to understand because they allow us to see how those techniques are used in promoting school-business partnerships. Less crass than "ab-cruncher" infomercials, school-business partnerships nonetheless share many of the same assumptions regarding method, marketing, and consumer materialism. Each is concerned with packaging its program, pricing it accordingly, considering demand factors, perceived values, and competition.[6] For businesses involved with schools, packaging their programs ranges from closely connecting their programs with national goals to reinforcing the assumption that schools should be sites for workforce preparation for a global economy. Like "ab-crunchers" appealing to the $19.95-persuaded market, businesses bring the appeal of funding *with* them *to* schools. Free goods are difficult to decline. Demand for svelte figures is a status-quo concoction, much like business assumptions for the purpose of public schools. Fueling that demand means businesses lament openly the presence of ill-prepared workers, regardless of mitigating circumstances,[7] then offer salvation by satisfying much of the demand they fueled in the first place. They do so, in part, by reinforcing the status-quo perception that one kind of competitiveness is both necessary and sufficient to achieve an "educated" (i.e., "trained") population of workers. For "ab-crunchers" one must compete with the most physically fit images (genetically predisposed?); for school-business partnerships, schools compete with other schools and other nations to achieve *Vogue-* like perfection and *Forbes*-like success rankings. Competition also means that if x company is involved with schools, y company should also "partner" with a school because the logic of competition does not allow one company a monopoly on a "sure thing." Businesses do not escape the status quo they perpetuate, in other words. We will remind ourselves of these points as we work through the illustrations and case studies that follow, but we will also look for the larger themes mentioned earlier: assumptions about teachers, student success, and the funding that corporations bring to school-business partnerships. We will also consider what returns on their "investments" companies expect from schools.

Volunteerism and community involvement are positive themes that can also be seen in the following illustrations. Yet the fleeting examples of altruism are clouded by the profiteering that haunt these same examples. We will consider contrived philanthropy, targeted advertising, and market campaigns that feature agendas of greed as the "flip side" of corporate influence, no matter how positively ingrained the popular-cultural icons might be, nor how much corporations insist that schools are the primary beneficiaries of corporate involvement.

THE KROGER CONNECTION

Kroger, recall, is the large and successful supermarket chain in the Midwest, Southeast, and Mid-Atlantic regions of the U.S. In 1993 Kroger distributed copies of their "partnering" program with Fulton County, Georgia schools (See Figure 1). "The Kroger Connection" is, upon careful scrutiny, a summer employment program for teachers. The flyer characterizes the job opportunity in terms of teacher roles: "Enrich teaching experience by gaining a better understanding of today's workforce and beyond"; and "Become liaison between business and the classroom by helping students obtain a winning career match.

Little is left to interpretation. Kroger wants teachers to work for them and when they return to their classrooms in the fall, wants teachers (as unpaid "liaisons") to promote Kroger as a place where students can find a job. Kroger, in this way, furthers the assumption that the primary purpose of schools is to prepare future workers. Kroger also stands to benefit from those teachers who *do* encourage their students to seek employment with the company.

Look again at the flyer. It has at the top a "Partners in Education" logo including the image of a mortar board. Mortar boards symbolize scholarship insofar as they are traditionally worn at graduation ceremonies.[8] By connecting a summer employment program with symbols of scholarship, Kroger furthers the imagery that their interest is educational. The flyer reinforces this by using the term "education" four times and "classroom" once. "This is real life, hands on partnering as Kroger connects education and business in a win-win situation." Kroger is actually attempting to connect employees (those teachers who fill one of the Kroger slots) with potential employees (students contacted by teacher/Kroger workers). The "connection" to schools is in recruiting teachers from them to work behind bakery, seafood, and deli counters.

Figure 1: The Kroger Connection
(Reprinted by permission of The Kroger Company, Atlanta, Georgia)

Kroger and Fulton County Partners In Education

proudly present

The Kroger Connection

Teacher Summer Employment Opportunity

Summer employment.

Opportunity to learn the multi-facets of rapidly growing food retailing.

Enrich teaching experience by gaining a better understanding of today's workforce and beyond.

Become liaison between business and the classroom by helping students obtain a winning career match.

Come be a part of the future and take the Kroger challenge!

This is real life, hands on partnering as Kroger connects education and business in a win-win situation.

Contact Partners In Education at 763-6772 if you are interested.

Deadline: Friday, June 11, 1993

To be clear, Kroger enjoys a good reputation and is successful enough as a business to continue expanding and adding stores. Double-coupon savings, 24-hour operations, and extra 5-percent discounts for seniors add to Kroger's positive image. Jobs at Kroger are worthwhile positions and those who fill those positions are as hardworking and upstanding as most citizens in the U.S. In terms of business, the company offers extensive benefits to some of its workers, but many positions are part-time and allow Kroger (as with many businesses) not to extend full health benefits or savings and retirement plans. Most of the employees in area stores are also not typically college-educated. This point is only important when we consider which people the Kroger flyer targeted and which people it did not. The flyer was not distributed to engineers or accountants or any other groups that have college degrees as a common basic requirement. Teachers are different, however. Like nurses, they have a hard time defining themselves as professionals, even with certification requirements and college degree standards.[9] The Kroger flyer only reinforces the nonprofessional regard attributed to, in this case, teachers. "Opportunity to learn the multi-facets of rapidly growing food retailing." Teachers, who already face inordinate procedural duties in their schools, *would be* successful in such a position, but this is beside the point: retailing and teaching are not the same, current expectations for teacher practice notwithstanding.

The bottom of the flyer includes another logo; this one has Kroger's name in corporate symbol form and font, but it is connected to "2000" reminding readers of the plethora of "2000" reports that began with *America 2000*, followed by *Goals 2000*, etcetera. The corporate slogan, "For Goodness Sake" is underneath "Kroger 2000." The enticements for summer work are in keeping with the spirit of national education goals, they are not out of sync with them. On first glance, the flyer may appear anachronistic, that is, not fitting the thrust of the national goals movement, but it actually exemplifies subthemes in the goals reports: schools exist to supply workers for companies and teachers are the hirelings to advance the cause of international economic competition. Seeing teachers as deli-clerks is not insulting, so the flier assumes, because teachers are also "liaisons" who will return to their classrooms and recruit "new hires" for their corporation. Like corporate-culture consultants who rename clerks "associates" and hairdressers "cosmetologists," Kroger assigns teachers the moniker "liaison." By so doing, Kroger blurs the distinctions between the roles of teachers and the roles of other workers by reducing the complexities of teaching to the simplified and simplifiable—though no less important—roles of producers.

STOP & SHOP, SHOP, SHOP

Kroger is not the only grocery chain to connect itself with schools. Stop & Shop, Safeway, Shop Rite, Von's, Bruno's, and Publix Supermarkets all have programs targeting schools. The programs advertise that a portion of all sales will go toward purchasing school equipment, typically computers and printers. This kind of corporate involvement exists because schools lack adequate funding to buy enough equipment. As a result, schools are forced to accept grocery receipt "charity." Consider the issue of school funding.

Schools are largely funded by property taxes, with nearly 47 percent of financial support coming from local communities. The federal government contributes only 6 percent or so to school coffers.[10] What this means is that school districts with large amounts of taxable wealth will have more money to spend on the schools in those districts. Areas with fewer amounts of taxable wealth will have less money to spend. Spring comments that "there is a major difference between the $17,435 per student spent in the Long Island community of Shoreham-Wading River and the $7,299 spent per student in New York City."[11] Since property taxes are the major source of local revenue, they advantage the wealthier communities because of the interplay between property *value* and property tax *rates*. Newman illustrates this by considering two school districts of about the same size that are located in the same state. One district is an upper-middle-class suburb where homes have an average market value of $200,000. The other district is much less affluent and where homes have an average market value of $50,000. For sake of the illustration, Newman assumes that the properties in question are taxed at full market value.[12]

> The residents of the upper-middle-class suburb have set their school tax rate at $1 per $100 of property value. The average home in this suburb, therefore, brings in $2,000 for the local schools. With the average family paying school taxes of $2,000 each year, these citizens can truthfully say they are trying hard to support public education. . . . The residents of the less affluent community have set their tax rate twice as high—at $2 per $100 of assessed value—yet the average home in their community generates only $1,000 for the schools. These residents can say they are trying twice as hard, but their *effort*—a technical term in school finance that means exactly what it says—yields only half as much.[13]

Such funding disparity provides the opening for businesses to "aid" schools. Stop & Shop helps by contributing a small portion of its sales toward the purchase of computers. The portion contributed is so small, in fact, that "register tapes documenting $250,000 of grocery purchases from Stop &

Shop, for example, nets a school an Apple Macintosh Classic 2/40; and $125,000 in tapes an Apple IIE color computer."[14]

This is not a donation from Stop & Shop as much as it is Stop & Shop's acting as the conduit for customers who spend money at participating stores. That is. Stop & Shop puts itself in the position of "aiding" schools *when* customers shop at their stores. The fewer customers, the longer it takes to raise the $250,000 to purchase *one* computer. The more customers, the faster the donation will take place. Schools get "needed" equipment and Stop & Shop gets a gold star for philanthropy. Stop & Shop also gets repeat customers, increased volume, and increased sales.

Stop & Shop's motive is profit; the same as in any business. This point is the focus of critique. The issue in question is that Stop & Shop, like other food stores, utilizes disparities in school funding as an opportunity to increase volume and revenue. Underlying this concern, furthermore, is the basic question regarding why schools are faced with shortages in funds for the very computers grocery chains are supplying in the first place. Kozol explores one response to this question in his book *Savage Inequalities*, noting first that corporations oppose paying school taxes. "City and state business associations, in Chicago as in many other cities, have lobbied for years against tax increments to finance education of low-income children. 'You don't dump a lot of money into guys who haven't done well with the money they've got in the past,' says the chief executive officer of Citicorps Savings of Illinois. 'You don't rearrange deck chairs on the *Titanic*.'"[15]

Kozol continues,

> In recent years, however, some of the corporate leaders in Chicago who opposed additional school funding and historically resisted efforts at desegregation have nonetheless attempted to portray themselves as allies to poor children—or, as they sometimes call themselves, "school partners"—and they even offer certain kinds of help. Some of the help they give is certainly of use, although it is effectively the substitution of a form of charity, which can be withheld at any time, for the more permanent assurances of justice; but much of what the corporations do is simply superficial and its worth absurdly overstated by the press.[16]

Corporations would rather "donate" computers than pay taxes because "donations" can be curtailed. Corporations benefit doubly. They enjoy tax breaks for locating in their respective municipalities *and*, with only some of the money they would pay in taxes, cast themselves as beneficent charities and responsible members of the community. In so doing, corporate interests are able to leverage the curriculum as well as the general purposes of schooling by reinforcing the community belief that schools exist to prepare future workers.

PIZZA HUT: BOOKIN' IT!

PepsiCo Inc.'s Pizza Hut has a national BOOK IT! campaign. If students meet the reading goals set by their teachers each month, they receive a free individual pan pizza. In this example, the corporation is not influencing the curriculum because the goals are set by teachers. Viewed positively, what Pizza Hut influences is student reading. Viewed negatively, Pizza Hut is bribing students and taking the intrinsic worth out of reading. Viewed more broadly, however, we should consider what benefits the company reaps from such a program. When first graders win a free individual pan pizza, they do not make their way to the local Pizza Hut and eat by themselves. Their families take them. Their families also eat with them. For the "free" individual pan pizza, Pizza Hut makes money on the meals the family eats.

> That was apparent one recent evening when five-year-old William Griggs went to a Pizza Hut in a Virginia suburb of Washington, D.C., to claim the free pan pizza he earned for reading aloud with his parents. Of course, the kindergartner didn't make the trip to the restaurant by himself. While William got a $1.99 tomato-and-cheese pan pizza for free . . . his mother, sister, and another adult spent $15.81 for a sausage-and-green-pepper pizza, two light beers, an orange soda and a Pepsi. Multiply that by the 16 million children going to Pizza Hut to claim their Book It pizza each month.[17]

This represents a variation on the "bait and switch" ruse: lure customers with free gifts, then steer them to purchase other, more expensive goods. In the case of Pizza Hut, they lure students with a free personal pizza, then capitalize on the meals those who must join the students consume. There really is nothing new here. Stores offer similar promotions on regular bases, but there is one major difference: the school-business campaign exploits student achievement for profit. Unwitting children are pitted against their parents in a sort of consumer-materialist love test. Students work hard to achieve the goals outlined for them and are awarded a free pizza. Parents who refuse to take their children to redeem the free pizza coupon risk undermining the work the child has done and are saddled with the "you don't love me" test that children (unfairly, if understandably) raise in such situations. While similar exchanges are not rare to families, programs that knowingly foster agendas that precipitate such a test force families into consumerist battlegrounds already charted by corporate marketing researchers to the advantage of business interests. Molnar puts it this way:

> . . . BOOK IT! unethically uses schools to get Pizza Hut inside students' homes. Since the BOOK IT! program can create a classroom atmosphere in which a child who doesn't join in feels odd, it is very hard for a parent to demand that a son or daughter not participate. Parents who may want nothing to do with Pizza Hut are forced to either go along with the program or face struggles with their children. Moreover, children who do participate and meet their reading goals feel cheated if they are not then taken to Pizza Hut for the promised reward.[18]

Pizza Hut nonetheless benefits from promoting itself as interested in learning, interested in children, and interested in supporting schools and the community. While PepsiCo and Pizza Hut do not put their corporate logo on the BOOK IT! buttons students wear or on the posters used to promote BOOK IT! in classrooms, they *do* put their logo on General Mills cereal boxes when they promote their BOOK IT! program. On a recent Golden Grahams cereal box, Pizza Hut provides a free coupon to any student in grades K–6, ostensibly to get the word out that Pizza Hut has the BOOK IT! program. Note that PepsiCo and Pizza Hut are the primary benefactors of such promotion and sponsorship. Perhaps a double-edged sword or a catch-22, one wonders whether subversive, non-logo advertising is worse than advertising *with* the logo, but the overarching point is that students who get rewarded with a small, personal pizza for reading achievement are pawns in a game of corporate profiteering.

SIX FLAGS OVER LITERACY

Six Flags Theme Parks, Inc. also has a reading program. Their program is called "Read to Succeed" and rewards those in the "600-Minute Reading Club." Students who complete the form receive a complimentary ticket into the theme park. Like the Pizza Hut program, the curriculum is not controlled by the business. A close look at the "winner's card," however, reveals the same machination used by Pizza Hut: provide one free good in order to capitalize on those who must accompany the winner/awardee. The "winner's card" asks the student (or whomever is filling out the card) to "list the number of people in your party, not including the winner(s)." For both Pizza Hut and Six Flags, families are beguiled into buying meals and tickets they might not otherwise buy. Once the students are in the theme park, the "extras" that admission tickets do not cover are objects for further spending.

Food, trinkets, and souvenirs are business profits-in-waiting and, given that the students who "win" admission are in grades K–6, their appeals for buying "everything in sight" are only matched by their appeals for going in all directions of the park at once.

The scenario is not predicated by critical reflection on capitalist marketing techniques. The targeted consumers here are K–6 graders. Their eyes are caught, like adults, by shiny objects and flashy baubles. Want overtakes need and this is another point at which the "responsible-consumer thesis" fails. It fails because the structure of consumer materialism puts K–6 graders *and* their adult guides in the contrived position of *reactive* agents *to* concocted external objects.

The double contrivance is significant because if businesses are successful at defining the sphere in which reactions are to *their* contrivances, the businesses win the game. That is, there is no way the "responsible-consumer thesis" can hold once consumers are reacting to the second tier of contrivance. Once students are *in* the park, in other words, the business *will* profit. There is no choice. The necessary condition (choice) of the "responsible-consumer thesis" simply does not follow. Not only must those accompanying the "winners" pay entrance fees to the theme park, all must now react to the contrived surroundings. Toys are eye-high to children. Food is perfectly represented in large and alluring pictures near rides. Walking clowns and movable carts even bring balloons and sweets *to* potential customers, so that going into side attractions is not necessary.

This, again, is nothing new to a society like the one in the United States. Decisions like those faced by K–6 graders and their adult guides are ones Americans face daily. The problem, however, is that the enticement is directly related to reading success. Marketed as a reward for meeting reading goals, the point is not whether similar consumer-choice scenarios face students daily, but whether corporations take advantage of student learning by offering token awards that result in sales increases commensurate with the number of family members of reading club "winners."

COLGATE TOOTHPASTE

The Colgate-Palmolive Company operates what it calls a "Dental Health Classroom Project" in which the company apparently attempts to promote good dental hygiene. As with any successful school-business marketing campaign, the company "helps schools out" by distributing tubes of its toothpaste, high-gloss promotional pamphlets outlining for parents "five easy steps" for teaching their child proper dental care, and a plastic ring that has "Colgate Superstar Magic Club" emblazoned on it. Unlike Pizza Hut,

Colgate prominently displays its corporate logo on the materials it provides—including the promotional pamphlet bulleting the five easy steps. In addition to the five easy steps the pamphlet outlines, it also comes with suggestions like brushing with fluoride toothpaste. Not any fluoride toothpaste will do, however—the pamphlet encourages the use of "Colgate Junior" toothpaste. The pamphlet also suggests using a particular kind of bristle; a soft toothbrush. It recommends, not surprisingly, the "Colgate Junior" toothbrush to match the paste.

Another example of contrived philanthropy, Colgate is unwilling to promote good dental hygiene for the sake of good dental hygiene. It must promote good dental hygiene for the sake of "Colgate Junior" sales. Underfunded teachers find themselves in positions of near-gratitude: forced to be thankful to a corporate giant and coerced into being a second-hand peddler of Colgate goods. Meanwhile, Colgate gets credit for "helping" teachers and schools. Whither credit to schools as commercial sites for toothpaste advertising? Recall Kozol:

> But that is the bitter part of it. The same political figures who extol the role of business have made certain that these poor black children would have no real choice. Cutting back the role of government and then suggesting that the poor can turn to businessmen who lobbied for such cuts is cynical indeed. But many black principals in urban schools know very well that they have no alternative; so they learn to swallow their pride, subdue their recognitions and their dignity, and frame their language carefully to win the backing of potential "business partners." At length they are even willing to adjust their schools and their curricula to serve the corporate will: as the woman in Chicago said, to train the ghetto children to be good employees.[19]

Kozol is specifically referring to a context in which poor black children in urban schools are the focus of contrived philanthropy. The point is not limited to this context, though. Like the administrator in Kozol's study, teachers everywhere are also caught. As with computer donations, when a school does not have materials or equipment, it matters less from where they come as long as schools have them. Beggars are not choosers, so the platitude goes. Teachers find themselves being grateful to companies that, again, benefit doubly. Not only does Colgate have its product advertised on school materials, the company gets a tax deduction for supplying schools with the sample products.

Evidently, there has never been an issue as to whether or not efforts like Colgate's merit a tax deduction. The only issue has been what type of deduction such programs allow. Do they, for purposes of taxation, count as charitable contributions or as ordinary and necessary expenses of manufacture, promotion, and delivery of a product? The former sort of deduction is greater because tax codes allow corporations to exempt charitable gifts, up to a certain amount, from taxation. The latter type of deduction is taken as part of and against gross taxable income. This issue, however, was settled some twenty-five years ago in *The Singer Company v. The United States*.[20]

In that case, U.S. Court of Claims Judge Laramore held, for a unanimous court in substantial accordance with pre-trial findings of fact by Trial Commissioner George Willi, that Singer's sales of sewing machines to schools at a 45 percent discount of retail price in 1954 did not constitute a charitable contribution. They did not because Singer had a reasonable expectation of a *quid pro quo* from these discounted sales. Students trained on Singer sewing machines were likely to purchase Singer machines later for personal use. In light of the predictable profitableness of the donations, Singer was required to forgo its attempt to recover back taxes in terms of codes covering charitable donations. Nonetheless, the company was allowed to pursue recovery in terms of business expense. So, too, do Colgate and other major corporations who supply schools with "learning aids."[21]

CHANNEL ONE

One of the most-discussed school-business partnerships came about from the 1991 Whittle Communications initiative called "Channel One." Under the auspice of "The Edison Project," the Channel One promotion was to supply schools with television monitors and satellite dishes. In exchange for the free hardware and the appropriate wiring, approximately 8 million students in 10,000 schools are required to watch a "news" program that has commercial interruption. The earliest version of the Channel One "newscast" was a student version of national evening-news broadcasts: topical coverage of politics, the environment, and world affairs. Students were less than attentive until Channel One was revamped to be more like an "MTV" or "Entertainment Tonight" broadcast, such that the already shallow degree of "in-depth" coverage gave way to even more shallow treatments of topics.[22] All along, the broadcast included commercials for candy bars, jeans wear, and tennis/sport shoes with more than a third of all teenagers in America's schools required to watch at least 90 percent of the time. This literally represents a captive student market: a student market that accounts for $80 billion worth of annual product revenue. "At $157,000 for a thirty-second ad—double the advertising rate of prime time network news—Whittle grosses $630,000 from the four ads run each day, bringing him gross annual revenues of more that $100 million." [23]

Similar to other funding issues discussed so far, Channel One is a private-enterprise answer to public-policy problems. Unable or unwilling to alter local property-tax revenue structures, many school districts are expected to meet competition goals that champion the use of technology, but without enough funds to make sufficient purchases of technology. This raises other concerns, such as whether technology is a panacea or an over-hyped infinite regress with classist consequences, a concern that was explored in chapter 2. The general concern is linked, nonetheless, to what might be called bribery-induced extortion.

Using the hype over technology as a platform for selling candy bars, Channel One offers money-strapped schools technological hardware. Schools receive television monitors, satellite dishes, wiring, videocassette players/recorders, etcetera. *In return*, schools provide K-III (the communications company that bought out Whittle Communications) with a captive market. Where technology is the bribe, the extortion is the requirement that 90 percent of all students within a given participating school watch Channel One 90 percent of the time. By using the contractual authority that comes with the "free" technology, students (as a captive market) have their time (and money?) taken from them. This is very different from the "real-world" argument that supports Channel One. On this view, advertising is merely a way of life in a society that can not divorce itself from schooling and vice versa. There is, however, no procedural or technical alternative.

While teachers have been reminded by their principals that they are to have the television monitors turned on to achieve the 90-percent/90-percent figures, intransitive teachers follow such rules and regulations because "that's the way the world is" or "that's what the contract requires." Semitransitive teachers, differently, turn the television on to meet the minimum requirements but have no problem with a noisy classroom during the time in which the program is running. To achieve critical transitivity, though, teachers (with students) must investigate the use of Channel One itself: that is, use Channel One as an object lesson at the same time that it is required viewing. A Harold Rugg-esque move,[24] it means contesting and challenging the advertising, the power of Chris Whittle, the content selected for presentation on Channel One, the way it is presented, and what possible consequences might obtain.

METROPOLITAN LIFE INSURANCE

An active school-business partnership advocate, Metropolitan Life Insurance is proud of its involvement with schools. It boasts of four major initiatives and three subinitiatives: Education Forums, Future Teacher Scholarship Programs, Regional Forums on Teacher Education Reform, and Grants for Research and Policy Development. Under the Grants for Research and Policy Development, Metropolitan has three subinitiatives: Partnership with the Committee for Economic Development (CED), Study of the Teaching Profession, and Study of the Teacher as an Ally in Reform. For its Education Forum, Metropolitan held a symposium in New York City in 1985 that included "1,000 business, education, labor, and government leaders to explore ways to pursue educational excellence."[25] Similarly, the subinitiative Partnership with the Committee for Economic Development cosponsored meetings to ensure "that the dialogue among classroom teachers, school administrators, and business leaders would continue."[26] Connecting business interests and schools is something that the president and chief executive officer, John Creedon, understood when he wrote:

> Part of the effort on the part of business has to be a recognition that our schools are important to business as such, not only as a matter of corporate responsibility, but also as a matter of economics, because the people who will be our employees in the future are the people who will be coming out of the public schools. That's our market, and if they are not given the skills, training and ability to learn in those schools, they won't have it. So it's a matter of self-preservation, in a way.[27]

Creedon demonstrates a fundamental misunderstanding of schooling. Abilities are not *given*. They are fostered or squelched, perhaps, but neither teachers nor Metropolitan Life Insurance have the power to *give* an ability. Akin to the Aristotelian premise that individuals are, by their nature, inquisitive, abilities are inherent. The mistaken assumption goes hand in hand with the larger supposition, however: that schools exist to inculcate students with the skills businesses want them to have when they leave school to become corporate employees. By sponsoring round-table discussions, teacher scholarship programs, and summer employment initiatives, Metropolitan is sure to be included in policy formulation. Influencing the roles of teachers, the roles of schools, and even specific curriculum, Metropolitan seeks more return on each of the dollars it "invests" in education.

Creedon also uses "corporate responsibility" to characterize his company's interest in schools. "Corporate responsibility" will be discussed more at length in the Burger King illustration that follows, but Creedon's claim of "corporate responsibility" is distinctive because it is set *against* economics. He noted the importance of schools "not only as a matter of corporate responsibility, but also as a matter of economics." The notion of corporate responsibility *is* economics. There is no "but also" about it. When corporations proclaim their own civic duties they are advertising and selling themselves. The question is whether companies would perform civic duties if there were no economic benefits to reap.

One of the difficulties of arguing against business involvement is that not only are businesses *already* deeply involved, it is antithetical to a critically transitive position to exclude business perspectives. Schools are not divorced from the societies they inhabit: yet the *degree* of corporate involvement, evidenced by Metropolitan, is as striking as it is convoluting. When businesses are involved in questions of schooling, the conceptual distinctions among education, schooling, and training should be augmented to include an investigation of teacher and student roles. For Creedon, he not only misunderstands abilities, he misunderstands the role of teachers. He sees them as *givers*; providers of the "skills" he wants his future employees to *have*. It is a classic top-down approach to management (recall Taylorism), which is as problematic as it is ingrained in both corporations and schools—regardless of "cooperative" "coprofessional" "team" monikers affixed by corporate consultants.

BURGER KING

It was noted before that business attempts to influence or control school policy are not a conspiracy, as conspiracies tend to be quiet affairs. Barbara Gothard, of Burger King Corporation, illustrates the open, perhaps cavalier, way in which businesses look at schools. She provides a background history of the efforts of Burger King to influence schools. Part of the rationale for Burger King involvement is the company's need for 200,000 workers each year. Because 70 percent of Burger King's workforce is under age twenty-one, having and retaining young workers is vital.[28] One way of reaching such a workforce is by associating with schools and marketing that association as part of the overall strategy.

> Kyle Craig [Executive Vice President for Marketing] was influenced by his wife, a teacher. With his marketing background, he recognized the wisdom of focusing the company's contributions strategy. At a meeting of the National Association of Secondary School Principals in Orlando in late 1983, Craig became convinced that support of education made sense for

Burger King. The idea had the virtue of being utterly consistent with the corporate vision. It was keyed directly to the need to motivate and upgrade the quality of present and future employees. It offered the potential for meaningful involvement at the national, state, and community levels. It also offered an opportunity for Burger King to assume a leadership role in an area that we felt desperately needed corporate involvement. So it was that Jeff Campbell [President and CEO] announced, late in 1983: "To demonstrate the company's social responsibility to the communities we serve, Burger King has dedicated its corporate contributions to the support of education."[29]

We should carefully consider the point asserted here because it illustrates the kind of argument corporations (including Metropolitan Life noted earlier) give to perfume (contrive?) their philanthropy agenda. Campbell claims that "social responsibility to the community" is the central purpose behind corporate (in this case Burger King's) contributions. Conceptually, however, social responsibility does not carry a "return" requirement. That is, getting a return on your investment is not a necessary condition for "social responsibility." One can be "socially responsible" and not gain any material profit from it. What this suggests is that "social responsibility" is the concept touted to mean "social policy benefitting corporations." It is beside the point but relevant in a larger sense, that members of the community earn only minimum wage with limited benefits.

Furthermore, fast-food chains exemplify the same Taylorism that routinizes existence. To be good at one's job means following the procedures and the scripted speech outlined for workers. Fast-food chains are also venues, as Gothard admits, for workers under the age of twenty-one. This is the group in society most vulnerable to consumer materialism because such workers are not only at an age when cars and clothes are considered vital, they are at an age when they can work to buy those things.[30] In order to achieve material goods, though, students face Taylorism and the routinization that follows. Importantly, students find Taylorism in their schools as well as in their work at Burger King. The difference is that students get material reward for their efforts at Burger King. Homework or scholarship or thoughtful reflection on course content are made ancillary to spending money or car insurance premiums or differently—in the most gripping cases—by students working to support their families.

Two points here: One is that when businesses use student-success measures as indicators of school failure and as an impetus for corporate involvement, they do not consider whether students' extracurricular work negatively effects their achievement, thus perpetuating the problem. The second point is the assumptiveness or presumptuousness of business when it comes to schooling. Like Townley from chapter 1, Burger King (via Craig and Campbell) sees schools as sites for "motivating and upgrading the quality of present and future employees." For Burger King to assert a "leadership role" in schooling means reinforcing the essentialism that is already much of the problem. Accordingly, students face one of the "givens" so rarely challenged: that schools exist to "prepare" future employees. To take a leadership role on this assumption means reinforcing the position that privileges Burger King: use public schools (supported not by Burger King taxes, but by property taxes) to train Burger King employees. Teachers and students who have conflicting notions of the purpose of public schools (that is, those who see schools more in terms of democracy than in terms of capitalism), are faced with questioning the very terrain that has been given over to consumer materialism.[31] Brosio alludes to this when he notes that "the subaltern groups are in almost every case struggling defensively. Furthermore, they fight with fewer resources at their disposal and the contestation occurs on sites/terrains which are far from being level playing fields."[32]

HONEYWELL

Honeywell is a Minneapolis-based high-technology corporation employing over 94,000 people worldwide. The company was strongly influenced by a corporate responsibility plan initiated by George Dayton, the president of a Minneapolis department-store chain. Along with his family, Dayton set out a corporate philanthropy plan to which Honeywell ascribes. As a result, Honeywell gives "approximately 2 percent of its U.S. pretax profit (about $7 million in 1986) to the Honeywell Foundation. . . . The Foundation's Board of Directors earmarks 45 percent of its annual contributions for education programs."[33]

It is important to note, again, that Honeywell is a high-technology corporation. High-technology firms typically require specialized employees. Increased salaries accompany these higher-status positions and the level of schooling of employees in high-technology firms is also usually above that of other major businesses. Honeywell's school partnerships reflect this situation.

It somehow seemed logical that as a high tech company with a highly educated work force, we should recognize and support education programs. It was a comfortable area of involvement for our executives and employees. As we worked at it, the pattern of our involvement shifted from a reactive to an active stance. In 1980, a group of employees responsible for managing our local contributions process in the Twin Cities decided to initiate a project with the Minneapolis schools rather than wait for a request. The group contacted school administrators and offered to augment district resources for an important project that school resources were unable to cover. *Because district resources were focused on the average student, we developed a program for high-potential students. In this way, we could help round out the district's focus.*[34]

Two points: (1) school funding and (2) target groups. For (1), schools suffer from a mistaken public perception that too much money is spent on education. Returns on investment, per-pupil expenditures, and simmering arguments about people having to pay school taxes even when they have no children or when their children have already graduated from district schools, all point to a kind of dissatisfaction with school revenues. Such dissatisfaction encourages outside sources of funding, so that while the perception exists that schools spend too much *public* money on schools, taxpayers typically welcome private funding. Corporations such as Honeywell take advantage of this problem by "coming to the rescue" of schools that have funding restrictions.

There is an important subpoint here, however, that allows businesses to "rescue" schools and target populations that will benefit their companies: reduced corporate taxes. Corporations often receive tax credits merely for existing. Used primarily to attract businesses, county and state government lure businesses by eliminating or severely reducing the amount of taxes (including taxes that support schools) businesses pay. As this argument goes, businesses deserve the tax credits because they will be employing increased numbers of workers and the workers will be paying taxes. On this view, schools *benefit* from corporate welfare handouts.

For (2), Honeywell supplied monies to the Minneapolis schools in order to target "high-potential students." As with any marketing strategy, Honeywell used its "high-technology" status as a justification for funding programs for upper tracks. Potential workers in computers would come from the upper-echelon of students, so this market is the one to support. If successful, high-school students interested in technology would look favorably upon working at Honeywell. Regarding different populations of students and divergent socioeconomic backgrounds, Honeywell boasts of its "affirmative action and equal opportunity strategies."[35] The Defense Systems

Division at Honeywell

> provides scholarships to senior students from the communities in which it
> is located. The Division looks for students who have demonstrated high
> potential for scientific, engineering, or technical careers in industry or the
> public sector. The Division scholarship program for minority and
> handicapped students takes a three-pronged approach: full four-year
> scholarship, summer employment with specialized tutorials, and
> employment after graduation. We know that when more
> people—particularly minorities, women, and the handicapped—are
> encouraged to pursue the disciplines in demand at Honeywell, our work
> force can better reflect the ethnic and cultural diversity of the population.[36]

Even with claims of equal opportunities, Honeywell effectively limits
minority participation by focusing on "upper-track" students in high school.
That is, while their scholarship program appears to indicate equal
opportunity, they look for "senior students" who have "high potential" for
work in "scientific, engineering, or technical careers." But by funding
"upper-track" initiatives, Honeywell effectively limits diversity because
"upper-track" classes are disproportionately upper-middle-class or
upper-class and white.[37]

Honeywell also finds itself in comfortable territory arguing a business
position for the advanced echelon of students. Sapon-Shevin notes that
"gifted education material abounds with the language of economics."[38]
Fetterman, like Honeywell, sees opportunities for corporate competitiveness
and global economic possibilities. "This educational arena [upper tracks]
must become a national priority if we are to survive and prosper in the
international marketplace," he notes.[39] Honeywell puts it like this: "Many of
Honeywell's education programs support company [profit] strategies.
Programs that help students make successful transitions from school to the
workplace support our employment strategies."[40]

Even Honeywell's initiative for at-risk students is linked to training.
With the Loring-Bethlehem Community Center, the Center for Community
Action, and other businesses, Honeywell helped to create the Minneapolis
Education and Recycling Center (MERC). Confusing, again, education with
training, Honeywell targets "at-risk" students. Students in the program are
working toward a high school diploma "while gaining work experience and
earning wages in the center's business."[41] In short, students follow
employees to learn about the jobs performed in the Building Services
Division at Honeywell. Building Services in the recycling arm of Honeywell
and students at-risk find "on-the-job, real-world" connections between what

it means to work and what it means to work at Honeywell. On-the-job programs of this kind are very different, make no mistake, from the upper-track initiatives attracting future scientists and engineers. There is no talk of college scholarships for this population. At-risk students, after all, are the ones relegated to the lowest rungs of the corporate ladder.

AMOCO: SCIENCE ENRICHMENT AND TEACHER QUALIFICATIONS

Amoco Corporation developed an enrichment program in 1985 that was funded by the Amoco Foundation and staffed by Amoco Production Research Center scientists. The effort was directed at increasing "hands-on" science learning in Tulsa, Oklahoma–area schools after two Amoco research scientists, Eric Bandurski and Marwin Kemp, taught science classes to young people on Saturdays. With the Tulsa Junior League and Tulsa schools, Amoco made its way into teaching.

> Bandurski and Kemp designed the curriculum and obtained the equipment for the physical science experiments; Dr. Paul Welch, a local veterinarian, wrote the life science unit. Bandurski, Kemp, and other Amoco scientists then trained 16 Junior League volunteers who worked in two of the first four participating schools. The Tulsa section of the American Chemical Society furnished the volunteers and funding for a third school, and parents staffed the fourth program. As the number of participating schools increased, the Junior League trained a corps of parent volunteers for each school. These volunteers enable schools to enliven science curricula with small group experiments that stimulate curiosity and participation.[42]

John Laubenstein, the director of the Amoco Foundation, applauds the effort by suggesting the more volunteers know about Amoco, the better able they are to explain Amoco's position on the environment. "People in Yorktown, Virginia, are concerned about the environmental impact of the Amoco refinery. Science Enrichment has given Amoco scientists an opportunity to discuss these issues with the students."[43]

Two larger agendas are present: (1) take teaching out of the hands of certified teachers and reduce the requirements of teaching to such a degree that corporate scientists can train volunteers to be teachers; and (2) in part as a result of (1), via the Science Enrichment program, scientists paid by Amoco would explain Amoco's environmental policies to students.

For (1) the Amoco program makes the following point: teaching requires only step-by-step proceduralism or a cookbook approach that, consequently, can be done by anyone. They achieved such reductionism by using a group experiment sheet that listed the following instructions:

> Weigh the bottom of a clean, dry petri dish on the two-pan balance.
> Place the top of the petri dish on the table top.
> Place a 10 oz. plastic cup in the petri dish top.
> Fill the cup with water until water runs out the holes drilled in the side.
> Place the aluminum "boat" on top of the water in the cup.
> Touch the hole in the side of the cup with a wooden stick . . . . [44]

The perspective represented by the "experiment" is traditional and many teachers in public schools use tools of this kind in their lessons. Perhaps useful in terms of order, organization, and control, the experiment's success is actually the problem. Akin to Willers' lamentation that the problem with behaviorism is not that it does not work but that it does, the problem with outlines of this kind (standardized, generalized, procedural, prescriptive, nonpropositional) is that they offer certainty in support of consumer materialism but at the expense of critical transitivity. The form represents *a priori* thinking such that teachers need only superficially consider content and method.[45] By successfully recasting the role of teacher in this way, Amoco sets itself up not only to "teach," but to teach about its environmental friendliness.

For (2), the conflicts of interest represented in the congratulatory claim are too large to ignore. Amoco scientists will teach students about the environmental effects of the Amoco refinery. It appears akin to asking RJ Reynolds whether or not cigarettes cause cancer. Critical transitivity is not the point of this form of perfidious teaching. This is not to suggest, however, that teachers in American schools are scholastically qualified as scientists or poets or geographers. Teachers, flatly, are not as qualified as they could or should be. Consider, however, reasons why this situation exists. If schools do function on the assumption that (1) details, what purpose is there in being scholastically adept? Said differently, if teaching is reduced to goal-oriented, lesson-plan-focused, behavior-demonstrable criteria, there is no need to bother with propositional knowledge claims. One has only to look at the pre-answered nonpropositional knowledge assertions (how-to). Where propositional knowledge claims and nonreduced approaches to teaching require justification (and scholarship), nonpropositional knowledge claims need no justification other than the performance of the object of (nonpropositional) knowledge. Teachers are caught. On one hand, they are expected to challenge students, foster inquiry, and do all the interesting projects that make learning authentically interesting. On the other hand, they are expected to cover specific material in a given amount of time, increase test scores so their school will look good when the scores are published in the local paper, and be baby-sitting disciplinarians *in loco parentis*. On one hand, teachers have students in their care whose potential is limitless. On the other hand, teachers have raw material to prepare for future employment. The competing notions are not antithetical, but the degree to which the second outline *constructs* teacher roles is the degree to which the first outline *constricts* them so effectively.

When Amoco reduces the art and science of teaching to particularistic functions any volunteer can do, the notion of teaching as a profession becomes increasingly remote. A profession, after all, has a defined body of knowledge, performs a unique societal role, and demonstrates autonomy. If Amoco diminishes the intricacies involved in teaching on the first hand to minimalist tactics and strategies on the second hand, it effectively wrests power away from teachers and takes it for itself.

CHOICES

Perhaps the best illustration of many of the problems explored thus far is the CHOICES initiative. CHOICES is U S WEST's program to get average students to make "better choices" in school. By "better choices" U S WEST means those choices that will lead to more "good" decisions and "positive" consequences.[46]

> The CHOICES program seeks to improve student motivation by helping participants determine those factors that affect who and what they are (attitudes, goals, appearance, self-discipline, neighborhood, gender, and interests). Each child is given a fortune cookie and is asked to determine those elements in the fortune cookie that cannot be changed from those that are under their personal control and can be modified by individual choices.... CHOICES' final objective is to persuade the participants that school and career are "connected." Success in school directly translates into positive results in the working world because high school does more than teach minimal basic skills that are needed in the workplace. It also equips graduates with a mindset for confronting career challenges. The decision-making process used in school when selecting classes and earning grades provides the model for making career decisions and achieving high levels of vocational performance. Cultivating school habits of consistent

attendance and good relationships with peers and teachers make it easier
to meet similar demands in the workplace.[47]

The program uses volunteers from local businesses to "lead" a two-class
seminar for ninth graders. The volunteers are "trained," and the intention is
to have students realize "that from the moment that each participant wakes
up he or she is confronted with alternatives."[48] Figure 2 is part of the initial
"lesson." Importantly, the trained volunteers only have two class periods to
instill CHOICES values, so "teachers are encouraged to expand and
reinforce its message with additional instruction provided in a
CHOICERCISES workbook. These individual lesson plans enable students
to understand principles of self-evaluation, decision-making, time and money
management, and academic "lesson" planning."[49] Witness a narrative
illustration of a CHOICERCISE. The program began with a grant from U S
WEST, Inc., but supports itself financially through the sale of programs like
"Parenting for Education" and "CHOICES." It also advertises itself in terms
of reducing drop-out rates. The success of the program is illustrated as
follows.

> One-third of the U.S. population now has access to a CHOICES seminar.
> Radio, television and print advertisements by sponsoring companies inform
> potential participants of CHOICES' purposes and availability. To date,
> more than 2,250,000 students in 46 states and 2 foreign countries have
> been enrolled in the program. . . . Surveys and comments of volunteers,
> students, and teachers attest to high levels of satisfaction. A composite of
> eight student polls conducted in all regions of the country showed
> near-unanimous agreement that CHOICES made the survey respondent
> more aware of the value of education and better able to make decisions.[50]

On the view of U S WEST, student drop-out rates are reduced, better
choices are made by students, and career orientations are reinforced. Four
issues need consideration: (1) the assumptiveness about the training-oriented
role of school; (2) using (1) as a foundational "model" for career
decision-making; (3) the recurring problem of what it means to teach; and
(4) advertisements that highlight drop-out rates and "corporate
responsibility" themes, but do not reveal the ulterior motive behind the
initiative (i.e. using schools as corporate training sites without corporate
funding).

Figure 2: CHOICES: Decisions and Consequences
(From The Conference Board, *Corporate Support of Dropout Prevention and Work Readiness*, 1993, p. 24. Reprinted by permission of the publisher.)

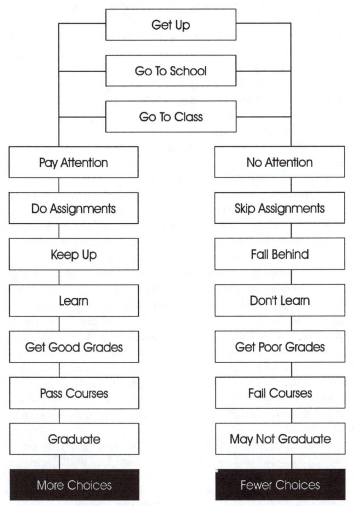

For (1) we should recall Berenbeim's supportive explanation of the US WEST initiative. He noted that "success in school directly translates into positive results in the working world because high school does more than teach minimal basic skills that are needed in the workplace. It also equips graduates with a mindset for confronting career challenges."[51] The first sentence is the deeply-held consumer-materialist assumption that schools exist to prepare future workers. The second idea indicates much of the problem with accepting the assumption of the first sentence. The second idea holds that schools "equip" students "with a mindset" regarding future career decisions. Teaching and learning are thus reduced, again, to transmission processes for "equipping" students with a corporate "mindset." Because the first assumption is so widely and deeply held, to the delight of corporations, the second part—the next step in narrowing learning to careerism—is an easy and immediate next step.

Both parts of (1) are also assumed to be used in "deciding on" which classes to take in school. Such a process "provides the model for making career decisions and achieving high levels of vocational performance."[52] Unfortunately, the "model," as it is presented, does not indicate the degree to which tracking effectively eliminates choices or "decisions on" which classes to take. "Models" will be considered in more detail in chapter 5, but it should be made clear that a model, in the sense it is used in the quote, is a contrivance. It is a shell or an overarching mechanism that abates decision making by supplanting a series of pre-formed and prescribed procedures *for* students. Akin to recipe-following, more conformity is required than interpretation or individual transposition. In terms of power, those who determine the "minimal basic skills" and those who decide the "mindsets" with which students will be "equipped" are integral players in the game of "providing models." To control the process, in other words, is to control the outcome. Gratefully, students and teachers are too diverse for the reductionist model to achieve total success. Nonetheless, the expectations represented in the widely-held corporate assumptions about schooling, teaching, and learning indicate the degree to which consumer materialism is established and reinforced.

Teaching is one way to illustrate this point and it is our third consideration in this section. Like Amoco before, U S WEST reveals what it thinks teaching entails (and, with sad irony, what teaching often does entail). Similar to traditional lesson plans, U S WEST supplies teachers with specified outlines of exercises, called "CHOICERCISES" regarding what they should do. The "CHOICERCISE" used for this analysis is subtitled "A Day in My Life" and offers the kind of details that diminish teacher roles.

Furthermore, recall that the corporation-trained volunteers have two class sessions with students. The link to the role of teachers is at this point because teachers (not corporate volunteers) are "encouraged" to continue what the corporate volunteers began. The "CHOICERCISE," then, is what the corporation sees teachers as being able to do and, more to the point, *not* able to do. The CHOICERCISE lists objectives for the students and also lists the materials needed (overhead projector, CHOICES Overhead #2, worksheet, etc.). The CHOICERCISE also lists directions for the teacher. This is not for the corporate volunteer. Instead, it is, in effect, the corporation telling the teacher what to do and how to do it. The very first direction, for example, is as follows: "Tell students that today's activity is part of CHOICERCISES, classroom exercises to help each of them 'build academic muscle.' Explain that the concepts presented in the CHOICES program can be further developed into personal skills and knowledge to help each of them maximize his/her high-school education." Part not-so-subtle advertising, part "human-resource pep talk," the directions conjure up images of teachers actually using the phrase "build academic muscle."

Direction #3 tells teachers to "Ask students for their definitions of the word Consequences. With your help, come up with a class definition and write this on top of the chalkboard. Generally, the translation should be: The results/what happens because of a previous decision/action." The contrivance is blatant: teachers are to pretend they are interested in what students are saying. Write the definition on the *top* of the chalkboard—not in the middle, for some reason. What you write on the *top* of the chalkboard should be what U S WEST thinks the definition should be. Direction #6 tells the teacher to "Pass out the worksheet called: A Day In My Life. (Teacher note: If your class completed Exercise #1, you may choose to direct students to Hello, It's Me Worksheets as a personal information source for this activity.) Explain to students that completing this worksheet will require them to work privately and seriously. Answers are not right or wrong, but what seems most true for each of them." Direction #7: "Give students the rest of the class period to work on this worksheet. The actual amount of time needed will vary with each class. You may also find that in some classes you will want to stop students after each section of the worksheet to discuss questions and issues that came up. Use your own judgement in this regard." Given all of the directions, the ending to #7 is intriguing. "Use your own judgement." If teachers actually followed such a plan, any judgement they would be using would not be their own. Using one's own judgement is against the thrust of such particularism. Interested in controlling teachers and regulating students (to work privately and seriously), the outline is as indicative of corporate understanding of pedagogy as it is insulting to teachers.

This is not to say that lesson plans like the CHOICERCISE are not daily expectations teachers are required to meet (that is, make up and submit to department heads, assistant principals, curriculum specialists, etc.), for lesson plans and objectives are central to the *current* role of teachers.[53] The point, however, is that the reason teachers are required to have such devices is because corporate reductionism demands it. Controlling teacher actions and the ideas they present, under the guise of "basic skills requirements" is the first step, as noted above, in a process of control that reinforces teacher roles as subordinate and proletarianized, as indicated by CHOICERCISES.

For (4) above, U S WEST uses advertisements to highlight drop-out rates. They note that "15,000 Washington kids dropped out of school before graduation. . . . So the people of U S WEST® volunteered to teach a high school course called CHOICE. . . . Not surprisingly, more Washington kids have decided to stay in school this year." How many more students stayed in school is not revealed. It is also not revealed whether the students who stayed in school did so as a result of taking a CHOICES course. Nonetheless, U S WEST takes credit for "working with educators," being a responsible part of the community for providing corporate "volunteers," and coming to the aid of "dropout kids." The advantage of the advertisement is two-fold: it positions corporations as munificent and it furthers the perception that businesses *can* and *should* be intimately involved in making the curriculum, controlling the role of teachers, and deciding the purposes for public schools.

CHEVRON AND FORD

Also missing from the U S WEST advertisement is the kind of tracking their program reinforces. The CHOICES program, remember, is targeted at "mid-range" ninth-grade students. These are students who are neither in the top 10 percent nor bottom 10 percent of their class.

A similar approach to reaching "average" or "less than average" students is illustrated by Project 2000. Project 2000 is another in the seemingly endless series of "2000" reports that Chevron Corporation and Ford Motor Company offer as a way to enrich an "inter-disciplinary curriculum for 'average' students (entering high school freshmen who have scored between the 25th and 65th percentile on standardized achievement tests)."[54] Operating on the characteristically "human resource" mentality discussed in chapter 2, Project 2000 begins with the following chart (See Figure 3). Not only does the chart indicate the overtly corporate orientation of school-business partnership initiatives, it brushes over with broad strokes the intricacies involved in schooling. It also appeals to reductionism and scientism by culling "needed resources" and selecting only those sites that "match project goals." Sorting in this way means that partnerships will "work" if those who "partner" fit the working requirements corporations set up. In a larger sense, what is *not* on the chart is perhaps most revealing. When the chart begins with "Form Coalitions among Public and Private Sectors" it is not forthcoming about whose desire it is to form the coalitions or in whose interest it is to form the coalitions.

When students are identified by ability, higher expectations for "high-ability" groups and lower expectations for "low-ability" groups are the risk. Chevron and Ford, through Project 2000 (another example of the plethora of "2000" programs), took great pains to mix the 80 percent of the middle in terms of standardized test scores and socioeconomic backgrounds. According to their data, drop-out rates fell significantly. The question remains whether what students came to school *for* was a classist curriculum for vocational orientation or an egalitarian curriculum for critical transitivity. Brosio recalls Greer's suggestion, for example, that "schools have always failed the children of the non-powerful, except that, unlike the late twentieth century, when certificates granted by formal schooling are the sine qua non for employment, the earlier flunk-outs and drop-outs could make it in America by doing the difficult dirty jobs."[55]

The point here is the inherent conflict of interest that schools perpetuate by engaging in school-business partnerships. By arguing for "the middle" students to have "equal opportunity" as a result of Project 2000, Chevron and Ford are perpetuating the conservative myth that schools are institutions devoted to equality and democratic possibility. Instead, Chevron, Ford, and other corporations influence public schools to *conserve* consumer materialism. By controlling the means of production and the distribution of wealth, corporate platitudes about the United States being the "land of opportunity" are only true if corporate values are accepted. Targeting "middle" students and influencing their acceptance of "hard work" ethics *for* corporations *for* money means that a false realism defines for tracked students the "givens" of "the real world." Colin Greer writes that the United States

has a public school system designed to preserve that contradiction—by institutionalizing the rhetoric of change [represented in microcosm by Figure 3] to preserve social status. The educational theory of its schools is a theory of a society based on scarcity; limited success and much failure is the educational equivalent of definitions of full employment that accept high levels of unemployment as tolerable. In fact the public school stands

Figure 3: A Model for School Partnerships
(From The Conference Board, *Corporate Support of Dropout Prevention and Work Readiness*, 1993, p. 16. Reprinted by permission of the publisher)

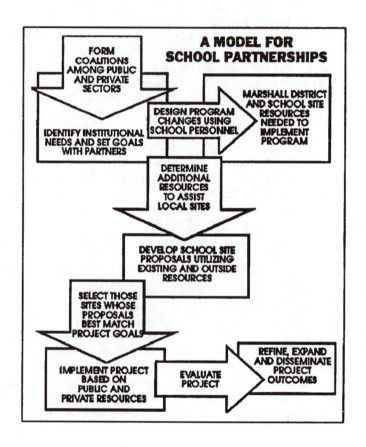

as an instrument of the conservative strategy for defusing movements for social change which seriously challenge the established order . . . [56]

One way to defuse movements for social change is to construct and reinforce Goals 2000-like plans. Another way is to have students face occupational and career decisions earlier and earlier in their schooling. Thus far, the illustrations have been of school-business partnerships as they typically operate. What follows, however, are illustrations of business influence in schools that are slightly different from many of the formal school-business partnerships just outlined. Some, like Junior Achievement, are long-standing programs. Others, like the Capital Area Training Foundation, are relatively recent. They share, however, the fundamental desire to inextricably link schooling to vocationalism. In so doing, they lay the groundwork early for future expectations from both parents and students as well as teachers and administrators.

JUNIOR ACHIEVEMENT

Junior Achievement (JA) began in Massachusetts over seventy years ago and was organized by businessman Horace Moses as a companion club to 4-H. Primarily an eastern-seaboard initiative until after World War II, JA expanded nationwide and is now franchised in all fifty states and eighteen foreign countries.[57] JA is distinct from other examples in this chapter in that it is a nonprofit corporation (as of 1957).

In Hawaii, JA promotes student-run "companies" in a program that has ninth through twelfth graders working with business community volunteers to establish and run a business from start-up to liquidation. "Businesses pay a $600 underwriting fee for each student-run company, which is made up of about 20 students and three advisers meeting one night a week for 20 weeks. In the 1985-86 school year, 47 JA companies with 886 students were operated on Oahu, while 13 companies were set up on the Neighbor Islands involving 389 students."[58] The perceived success of the student-run company program led to the formation of Project Business, an in-school program designed to supplement eighth- and ninth- grade social-studies classes. Additionally, JA developed a curriculum for an economics class that could be taken by eleventh and twelfth graders as an elective. This course is paid for by a program fee of $800 provided by sponsoring businesses—businesses that also provide a consultant to "assist" the economics teacher in charge of the course.

JA is renowned for bringing corporate and civic leaders, professionals, and workers of all types into schools. Instructional time is given over to "visitors" who donate their time and energy to talk to fifth and sixth graders about future career options. The idea is to get students thinking about what it is they might want to do when they leave school.

On the surface, as with many adopt-a-school and school-business partnerships, the program seems worthy. Indeed, the program *has* worth. Those who become involved in JA programs are concerned about the future of the students to whom they speak and interact. These are people who devote their time and effort to working with children. The merit of JA resides with the individuals who attempt to carry out the general goals of JA. Careful review, however, raises a question about those general goals and the larger purposes that inform the actions of volunteers: why are students encouraged at such a young age to consider occupations? As though pushing consumer materialism on younger and younger students, JA, like other business interests, sees itself focusing on young minds. The focus, however, is directed toward utilitarianism; narrower and narrower specialization valued overwhelmingly for its hyper-usefulness. Hence, the consumer-materialist question, "But when will I ever *use* this?" To conclude, however temporarily, that *x* or *y* is *what* one will do when one "grows up" not only risks dispensing with broad or liberal study, it furthers the mindset that a meticulously honed focus is the purpose of public schooling.

It is one step away from commodification such that schooling is seen in sophistic particulars: "I don't need to study algebra, I'm going to be a musician." "I don't need Shakespeare or Hentoff, I'm going to be an engineer." Schooling becomes a shopping list and students go to the school market to purchase what they need to make the recipe they understand they are supposed to follow. This is what school is about, after all. At least this is what businesses, and JA, represent by their presence—unintended or intended, it makes no difference. They are furthering an agenda of contrived particularism by forcing students into "real-world" decisions about jobs. Such efforts are highlighted and supported by the Carl D. Perkins Act and the School to Work Opportunities Act of 1994. The "school to work" legislation provides grants to states and communities that develop systems and partnerships that are "designed to prepare young people for additional [training] and careers."[59]

An oppositional, critically transitive position means investigating the disparities of power and privilege represented by those pushing specific careers on middle schoolers. What advantages do they reap? Who are they encouraging and who are they discouraging? Why? Are there gender disparities? Are there classist assumptions about who *can* achieve *x*, *y*, or *z* occupation? Why?

KAPOW

In Dade County, Florida, a similar approach to JA is taken with even younger students. "Kids and the Power of Work" (KAPOW) is a Miami initiative partnering businesses with elementary schools "to prepare kids for the working world."[60]

> "We teach them about what kinds of careers are available," said Lynn Heyman, director of community and volunteer resources at the [Miami Children's] hospital. . . . While some experts doubt the lasting impact of these kinds of programs, others say the programs are critical in preparing children to enter the workforce and give businesses a say in the education of their future employees.[61]

Phillips quotes John Casbarro, the regional program consultant for KAPOW: "The goal is to prepare students for the workplace in a way that has not been done in the past. Kids always say, 'Why am I studying this and what good is this going to do me?'"[62] Examples of preparing students for future careers in ways that have "not been done in the past" include having students interact with lawyers from Burger King (where students negotiate for milk and cookies) and having students "operate" on mannequins in a mock operating room. Funding for the program comes from school-to-work grants and in 1994 totaled $1.3 million. Companies, including American Airlines, AT&T, Coulter Corp., and the Metro Dade Aviation Department, pay "some" of the costs of the program, but the substantial amount of funding is from governmental agencies.

Three contrasting points arise regarding whether there is anything "wrong" with such a program: one position says "no," there is nothing wrong; one position says "yes," there is something "wrong"; the third position suggests that being "wrong" is at least partially beside the point. The first position holds that businesses not only have the right to influence future workers, they have an obligation. The second position, however, sees something overly intrusive and controlling about a program that encourages fourth graders to consider careers by constructing a "given reality" about existence that *requires* career exploration (at earlier and earlier ages). Because children are naturally inquisitive, formulaic and calculated boundaries for their inquiry are anathema. This means, perhaps ironically, that if a child inquires into a series of careers, so be it. The problem is the contrivance of the *program* to *get* children to narrow their focus in occupational and vocational ways. Children negotiating for milk and cookies are negotiating for milk and cookies, period. A game, an interesting exercise at negotiation, a complex set of social interactions, the negotiation is not the problem. Children *can* learn from such experiences. To *intend* fourth-grade students to narrow the value of their learning to adult visions of pecuniary, vocational ends, however, is to corrupt the general inquisitiveness of childhood.

Lindblom offers insight into the third perspective. He sees businesses holding "privileged positions," but *de facto*, when they are beneficiaries of government grants like the ones KAPOW enjoys.[63] This is, he maintains, the nature of politics in a capitalist society:

> Any government official who understands the requirements of his position and the responsibilities that market-oriented systems throw on businessmen will therefore grant them a privileged position. He does not have to be bribed, duped, or pressured to do so. Nor does he have to be an uncritical admirer of businessmen to do so. He simply understands, as is plain to see, that public affairs in market-oriented systems are in the hand of two groups of leaders, government and business, who must collaborate and that to make the system work government leadership must often defer to business leadership. Collaboration and deference between the two are at the heart of politics in such systems. Businessmen cannot be left knocking at the doors of the political systems, they must be invited in.[64]

"Real-world" positions of this kind, accurate though they might be in their narration, risk sidestepping the problem. Such positions are in jeopardy of being "accomplices" in the constructed "givens" that make KAPOW programs not only acceptable, but perceived as *necessary*. There is nothing *necessary*, however, about externally-induced career orientation for fourth graders. Children expressing interest in *x*, *y*, or *z* occupation, positively fleeting though the interest might be, is primarily chosen by viewing or interacting with authentic representations of career paths and is natural. Contriving external stimuli to *get* children to consider adult-chosen *a*, *b*, or *c* career, a la KAPOW, is, again, a corruption of natural growth and the innocence of youth.

CAPITAL AREA TRAINING FOUNDATION: CONSTRUCTION ACADEMY IN THE HIGH SCHOOL

In Austin, Texas, Lanier High School has a new program, thanks to construction industry representatives. The program is called the Construction Academy and has as its objective "to give students an opportunity to explore the construction industry as a career choice."[65] Like many of the other school-business relationships noted in this chapter, the Construction Academy advances what Shor calls "careerism."[66]

Groups of fifteen students are chosen to participate. They enter into "cooperative" ventures with construction companies, earn high-school credits for their work, and are "paid for work-based learning experiences."[67] The reason for the program is that construction workers are retiring in Austin at a faster rate than workers are entering construction jobs. The Central Texas chapter of the Associated Builders and Contractors, Inc. (ABC), and the Austin chapter of the Associated General Contractors of America (AGC) negotiated with the school district to form the Academy. Students get credit, and pay, for the apprenticing they do with area contractors.

Advocates of such a program see businesses helping out those students who are not typically academically advanced. But they confuse the plan by inferring that the program is vital to further study. Students, for example, can "escrow" credits toward a two-year degree at Austin Community College. One industry representative offers, "We don't want to discourage them from college....We want strong students. . . . They have to be intelligent, with their heads screwed on right."[68] With overt recognition of child-labor laws, the program also asserts its concern for safety.

These particulars are beside the point. Industry is effectively not only giving up on certain students' potential for liberal study, they are making education appear the opposite. That students in the program are not being "discouraged" from college study (1) does not mean they are being *en*couraged; and (2) the "advanced study" that *is* open to them (via "escrowed" credits) is a two-year training degree. The program fosters reductionism, careerism, and in part as a result, intransitivity. To suggest that students "choose" to be in such programs obscures the problem. While some students see clear advantages to not learning broad, deep, and differentiated curricula (i.e., not restricted to a western-civilization canon), the advantages of such "choices" primarily benefit industry. When those "choices" are directly influenced by industry, arguments for libertarian individualist choice become corporate-induced conflicts of interest.

Critical transitivity, note, is not beyond those students who are chosen for the construction training program, unless the program institutionally precludes it by subordinating questions to carrying out orders. Said differently, there are attempts within vocational circles to use occupational realities as means for critical investigation.[69] These efforts differentiate between functional empowerment and critical empowerment and while they fall short of probing why functional empowerment might defeat critical empowerment in the first place, the number of students and the level of participation they demonstrate nonetheless highlights both interest and ability.

"The world will always need plumbers." Knee-jerk logic is thus confronted and its unilateral two-dimensionality is refuted. Instead of accepting "real-world" arguments that silence dissent, students and teachers are finding dimensions beyond those illustrated by the Lanier Academy. Where the Lanier Academy represents the outcome of tracking (and corporate profits made as a result), Lakes' notion of emancipatory work education raises questions of race, class, gender, sexual orientation, etcetera, as lenses through which work assumptions are scrutinized. Businesses are not interested in this kind of scrutiny, however. As with Silberman's concern in 1970, the more vocationally-oriented the student, the more likely the student is to conform.[70] Since conformity is the cousin of the status quo, businesses rely upon it to perpetuate consumer materialism. Enter McLearning.

McLUNCH, McLEARNING, AND McSCHOOLING

In Boulder, Colorado, some students are facing a similar fate to those who are selected for the Lanier Academy. Businesses use students to use business as the curriculum. Where "credits" were earned for construction work in Austin, McDonald's inventory, payroll, and ordering procedures are used for mathematics instruction in Boulder. The McDonald's menu is used for meal planning in home economics and McDonald's marketing plans are the basis for business classes.

Two high schools in the Boulder Valley School District replaced their own school-lunch programs with ones run by McDonald's. According to school officials, the intent was to have students eat a hot meal on campus rather than driving off campus to local restaurants.[71]

> Until McDonald's came along, the Boulder Valley School District offered lunches at its two high schools based on a health reform plan established by a parent task force eleven years ago. Lunches included 50 percent whole wheat flour in all bread products, as well as fresh fruits and vegetables every day, and low levels of refined sugar. Nancy Paluh, manager of the district's food service, points out that one of the first steps McDonald's took upon arriving at Fairview High School was to exhume a deep-fryer "that hadn't been in use in twenty years."[72]

The problem this raises is not only nutrition, but federally subsidized school-lunch programs for the poor. McDonald's does not qualify for the National School Lunch Program because the food it serves does not meet the nutritional criteria. Fifteen percent of the students in Boulder were affected by the change, but McDonald's, like the Construction Academy in Austin, offered a business solution. Rodd puts it this way, "McDonald's came up with the kind of response Oliver Twist might have appreciated: Target those students—along with teen parents and the disabled—to staff the McCafeteria. (You want lunch? Work for it!)."[73]

The corporate takeover does not end with this narrative, however. Kaplan puts it this way

> Two sets of materials distributed by McDonald's—one on helping children "develop healthy practices and attitudes that will stay with them for a lifetime" and the other designed to help them to "learn how to practice good eating and fitness habits"—were judged by the Consumers Union to be "objective and not commercial." One was even endorsed by the President's Council on Physical Fitness and Sports. But like a kit offered for middle-schoolers by Anheuser-Busch on the dangers of drinking and another by Kellogg's urging fitness and sound nutrition for children in grades 3 and 4, these offerings cannot be considered entirely benign. Unless these firms have totally changed their product profiles, their presence in classrooms in any guise implies at least that school leaders are not averse to sharing class time with purveyors of alcoholic beverages and sugar-packed nutritional nightmares.[74]

The example of McDonald's is an initial look into the issue of privatization. Schools are already privatized to the degree that food, transportation, textbooks, and other "hard" services are provided by private firms. The concern is that McDonald's can not only be the lowest bidder for food service provision, but that they directly influence the curriculum and infuse consumer materialism into earlier and earlier grades. McDonald's has help. The NEA and the AFT are odd allies in the push to connect businesses and schools even more tightly together. Both organizations support school-business partnerships and the increasing role corporations play in deciding the purposes and meaning of school.

NEA: PROMOTING CONSUMER MATERIALISM

The nation's two largest teacher unions, the National Education Association (NEA) and the American Federation of Teachers (AFT), are two strong proponents of school-business partnerships, reductionism, and consumer materialism. Both organizations argue for a closer link between businesses and schools and both organizations provide guidance to teachers on how to make those connections. Why? What is it that makes *these* organizations, particularly, so prone to reduce teaching into commodified steps and procedures that favor business influence?

Consider, for example, the "NEA Policy on Business Education Partnerships." The preamble asserts that school-business partnerships are beneficial to both groups. Its characterization of corporations and schools, however, clarifies the power structure between the two entities: corporations *over* schools. "American business has expertise in research and development, problem- solving, and on-the-job training experience that can help the schools improve education techniques, strategies, and methodologies."[75] Corporations do the difficult work (researching and developing and representing "real-world" venues) in order that schools can reduce *their* findings to "techniques," "strategies," and "methodologies." Preparing students for jobs is the reinforced role schools assume.

The preamble goes on, "Business leaders are in a position to articulate current and projected employment needs, to suggest ways to make curriculum content more relevant to the needs of the business world, and to ensure a well-educated citizenry from which to draw a skilled workforce."[76] To assert, as the NEA policy goes on to do, that "public education employees must be involved as equal partners with business" belies the point. Once corporations are reified as the group calling the shots for schools, attempts to assert equal-partnership status are hollow. Hollowness turns to hypocrisy when the policy statement warns that "Partnership arrangements must not result in programs that stress the marketing and/or the promotion of products with students. *The public schools must not be used for commercial purposes.*"[77]

Using public schools for commercial purposes is *exactly* what is promoted when the NEA welcomes business leader influence on the curriculum. If public schools must not be used for commercial purposes, why the proclivity toward job preparation? Why the focus on future employment needs? Why emphasize corporation-expected skills? Perhaps the reason is because the political reality demands it—parents demand it, students demand it, and teachers perpetuate it. The NEA is, after all, one of the most powerful political lobbies in Washington. As such the NEA not only influences policy, they negotiate issues that keep them in power. By embracing corporate values and promoting business interests, evidenced in its policy on partnerships and in its publication *Bring Business and Community Resources into Your Classroom: A Handbook for Educators from the National Education Association*, the NEA maintains its influence. It also, unfortunately, reduces the role of teachers.

The *Handbook* provides teachers with detailed instructions on topics like "Building Awareness Regarding the Need for Business and Community Resources," "How To Write Objectives," "How to Assess Resources Needed to Support the Achievement of Objectives," and "How to Determine Specific Sources of Resources to Assess." The *Handbook*, as result (and like Amoco's and U S WEST's reduction of teaching), achieves two goals, both of which are necessary for training-oriented schools but neither of which is in the best interest of education-oriented schools: (1) it sanctions and encourages business involvement and (2) it patronizes teachers by reducing their roles to "cookbook" followers. These goals are not accidentally together, either; they go hand in hand. Teachers who do not consider the technorational listing of procedures problematic are either critically aware of the "reduction game" and play around it (without overt challenge) or are so used to following prescriptions that they are too tired to object or are the very teachers businesses use (with increasing success) to further the consumer-materialist agenda represented by the NEA *Handbook*.

Again, this is not to say that jobs do not exist or that people interested in job preparation are not entitled to training. It is not a denial of reality, in other words. It is, instead, an argument against using public schools as corporate sites that value commodity logics over critical transitivity. Further, this is not to say that simply because the NEA published a preamble and document that it is pervasively accepted and made operative by teachers. It is to say that when the nation's largest teacher "union" so warmly embraces business interests, it at least technically represents the sell-out of what was a potentially powerful oppositional voice. If the largest union invites wolves to dinner, it at least appears that teachers endorse the consumer-materialist logic evidenced in the documents. With businesses, politicians, and the NEA willing to promote school-business partnerships, the metaconversation about the purpose of school is "given."

AFT ADVERTISING: MARKETING MARKETABILITY

The conversation is furthered when, for example, the American Federation of Teachers (AFT) takes out a full-page advertisement—made to look like an article—to make the case for overt business involvement and influence (See Figure 4).[78] Albert Shanker, then president of the AFT, was arguing for increased attention to school performance. He wanted arduous national standards so businesses would pay attention to teacher evaluations and recommendations. Until employers have a way of figuring out what an "A" in algebra actually means (and whether algebra is a fancy name for "consumer math"), what schools do will have no value.

Figure 4: Linking School to Work

(From Albert Shanker, *Where We Stand: Linking School and Work*, an advertisement in *The New Republic*, 15 May 1995. Reprinted by permission of the American Federation of Teachers.)

Where We Stand

By Albert Shanker, President
American Federation of Teachers

Linking School and Work

A recent *New York Times* story found that employers don't believe schools are preparing young people for their workplaces. But this may be the result of a phenomenon known as the "self-fulfilling prophecy." Self-fulfilling prophecy is a sociological term used to describe events that occur because people believe they will. The classic example is large numbers of people making a run on a bank because they believe it is failing. Their run makes the bank fail.

The *Times* story ("Employers Wary of School System: Survey Finds Broad Distrust of Younger Job Applicants," February 20, 1995) was based on a national survey done by the Census Bureau for the U. S. Department of Education. The Census Bureau surveyed 3,000 employers across the nation last August and September. Employers were asked, "When you consider hiring a new nonsupervisory or production worker, how important are the following in your decision to hire?" The Census Bureau used a scale of 1 through 5. A score of 1 indicates that the quality is not important or not even considered while a score of 5 indicates that the quality is considered to be extremely important. (See table below.)

Clearly, most employers give little weight to the last three items, which deal with the perfor-

Prospective employers are more interested in how many years students spent in school than in what the kids did while they were here.

mance of students in school. In fact, they are more interested in how many years students spent in school than in what they did while they were there. (See the fifth item from the bottom.) This probably means that employers seldom bother to ask for teacher recommendations or transcripts of grades, and they probably don't pay any attention to where a student went to school. Is there any doubt that the word gets back to students who are still in school that these things don't count? And if they don't count, why should students work hard to get good grades or attend schools with reputations for high standards rather than easy ones?

It's obvious that the less attention employers pay to school performance, the less incentive kids have to achieve and the more poorly prepared they will be. One way out of this problem would be for employers to ask for information about student achievement and take it seriously. But it's not that simple.

In Japan and Germany, where there are close links between what students do in school and the jobs they get when they graduate, employers know what a grade means. Like most other industrialized democracies, these countries have school systems with external standards and examinations. If students take certain courses and pass certain exams, there is no question about the material they have studied and their level of achievement. This is true for students going on to university, but it is also true for young people who are entering the job market right from school.

In the U.S., every school district is free to set its own curriculum and standards, and employers have no way of figuring out what an A in algebra means—or even whether "algebra" is just consumer math that has been given a fancy name.

Until businesses can have confidence in student transcripts and recommendations, they will go on disregarding them—and students will continue to conclude that what they do in school does not count. States that are now working on Goals 2000 should keep this in mind. The external standards they create for their students can help re-establish the essential link between school achievement and the job market.

Qualities That Count With Employers	
Quality	Score
Attitude	4.6
Communication skills	4.2
Previous work experience	4.0
Recommendations from current employees	3.4
Recommendations from previous employers	3.4
Industry-based credentials certifying skills	3.2
Years of schooling completed	2.9
Score on tests administered as part of interview	2.5
Academic performance (grades)	2.5
Experience or reputation of applicant's school	2.4
Teacher recommendations	2.1

At first glance, the ideas appear to be bending over backwards to appeal to businesses. Closer scrutiny only makes matters worse. Not only did Shanker use Census Bureau data derived from 3,000 businesses to represent discourse on schooling needs, he went on to make academic quality contingent on corporate desires. This is another way of stating *Goals 2000*. Shanker made the seemingly obligatory comparison to Germany and Japan (akin to National Goals #4 and #5) and asserted that the "qualities that count with employers" were valid because employers wanted them. At the same time he inferred objectivity in external standards and examinations.

Like the NEA, the AFT is a lobby, albeit a smaller one.[79] The realities of politics and the influence the AFT can assert on behalf of teachers requires AFT leaders and others to contribute to the corporate metanarrative on schools. Lindblom suggests that "businesses use their disproportionate influence to try to create a dominant opinion that will remove grand issues from politics. They do not press for agreement on the grand issues but for political silence on them. It is here that their participation in polyarchy, even though not always successful, goes furthest toward indoctrination. It short-circuits popular control—that is, renders it circular in significant degree."[80] The AFT, then, is silent as regards the negative effects of corporate involvement in schools. While their silence on this point is replaced by vocal appeals for meeting business interests (achieving agreement in Lindblom's terms), the AFT acquiesces to the larger, singular, corporate narrative. Lindblom again:

> In this activity, as in legitimizing its privileged position, business tends to speak in one voice. It is not much challenged by any other voice. Medium-sized and large corporations in the polyarchies approach a consensus on what we have as the grand issues of politico-economic organization: private enterprise, a high degree of corporate autonomy, protection of the status quo on distribution of income and wealth, close consultation between business and government, and restrictions of union demands to those consistent with business profitability, among others.[81]

Where corporations demand autonomy and reduced government oversight, Shanker was willing to concede teacher and school autonomy to corporate autonomy. What is good for the goose, is *not* good for the gander. This point raises the more intricate dilemma of autonomy and choice that will be explored in more detail in chapter 4. The point for now is that Shanker argued that what is valid for corporate interests *must* be shared by public schools. Again, the purpose of schooling is directed to the advantage of corporations and secondarily, if at all, to students and teachers.

To be sure, the AFT, like the NEA, must combat post-Reagan successes at union-bashing and appear interested in working instead of striking. Joining force with corporations is one way to succeed at this task, even though the *voice* used to "negotiate" AFT interests is, at root, corporatist and consumer materialist. Lindblom offers that "corporate voice is joined by the voice of many government officials [and AFT/NEA voices] and for several reasons. One is that they are caught in a potential crossfire between privileged controls and polyarchical controls. Hence, they would like to remove from politics those highly divisive issues on which businessmen would be loath to yield. Since theirs is the task of seeing to it that business performs, they do not want the fundamentals of private enterprise to become lively political issues."[82]

Yet the fundamentals of private enterprise *are* political issues and are, as seen above, used by the AFT to make training-oriented schooling arguments. Such arguments favor business-desired training-oriented schooling over education-oriented schooling and recast teachers as incompetent semiprofessionals based on commercial versus intellectual criteria. The problem occurs at the point where private enterprise goals and free-market logics subsume pluralistic and democratic goals in the public, not private, sphere. The issue, then, is the private control of public domain. While it is true capitalism is not divorced from the public domain, there is the tendency to think that public spaces should be privately controlled. This, in part, is what makes the NEA and AFT positions so troubling. They sabotage their memberships for the very same private gain that corporations reap when they focus so narrowly on business goals and profit rationales. Of the two, businesses or the NEA/AFT, it might be difficult to see any differences in the ways they operate. Yet if schools were fashioned as democratic *public* spaces, the NEA/AFT would not have to rely on business rationales as goals for their members and for the school about which they are supposed to be intimately connected.

Said differently, corporations are not in business to represent public concerns like equity and ethics. The NEA/AFT, also, are not currently positioned to represent public concerns, but they are better situated than corporations to delineate teacher and student issues that combat the privatized control of public schools. The NEA/AFT are not, fundamentally, capitalist agencies. As with the textbook illustrations from chapter 1, reactionaries may label questions about the validity of free-market capitalism (such as the questions raised herein) as socialist or communist, but the issue is whether schools are public spaces for the critique of the very freedoms that make freedom possible, or whether private enterprise is the only topic given for consideration in corporate-partnered, or potentially privatized, schools.

SCHOOL-BUSINESS PARTNERSHIPS TO CORPORATE PRIVATIZATION

From Campbell's soup-label campaign for computers to DuPont-sponsored chemistry packets to M&M Mars candy company's support of nutrition programs, adopt-a-school and school-business partnerships number over 140,000.[83] They have reinforced the assumption that the purpose of schooling is to meet consumer-materialist desires. The relative absence of critique (in mass media, public schools themselves, etc.) regarding this situation gives the "green light" to continuing the corporate takeover of public schools by privatization entrepreneurs. School-business partnerships are the beginning of the end of public schooling, privatization *is* the end.

Where school-business partnerships represent corporate exploitation of schools for their own market interests, privatization represents schools as markets themselves. Said differently, school-business partnerships use schools as a means of marketing toothbrushes, pizzas, candy, and other products. School is a way *to* those markets. For privatization, however, schools are not the means to a market, they *are* the market.

In privatization plans, schools are pitted against one another such that competition will force some schools "out of business." Where school-business marketing campaigns have students and teachers "choosing" among goods, privatization has parents "choosing" among schools. In this way, consumer materialism is reified insofar as pedagogical understandings are set aside in favor of consumer purchasing power. Schooling is reduced to "client expectations," "saleable goods," "measurable products," and "delivery of chosen services." "Choices," as we will see, are central to privatization arguments. "School choice," "parental choice," and even "student choice" are used by privatization advocates to mask the ulterior results of privatization: control, power, and profit for a few at the expense of many.

NOTES

1. Jeffrey Kane, "Educational Policy, National Intellectual Capital, and the Profits of Childhood," *Holistic Education Review* 9, no. 2 (Summer 1996), 3.

2. Adopt-a-School programs and school-business partnerships are used interchangeably in this chapter. Any differences between the two might be of degree of participation where adopt-a-school programs are only marginally involved compared to school-business partnerships. Marginal involvement is characterized, for

example, by Frito Lay hosting lunch for a local school or by local banks passing out awards at end-of-year ceremonies. See Sharry Shepard, "Thanks, Frito Lay," *Brookhaven Buzz*, August 1997, 14; Ginnie Netherton, "Nimitz School Thanks Sponsors: Execs Attend Reception," *Tulsa World*, 2 May 1997, D3; and Valerie Parker, "Olive Branch Elementary Thanks Teachers," *The Commercial Appeal*, 12 June 1997, DS2. For specific information on Adopt- a-School programs, see such works as Alton C. Manning, *Adopt A School–Adopt A Business* (Bloomington, IN: Phi Delta Kappa Educational Foundation, 1987); and Lowrie A. Fraser, *Adopt-a-School Handbook* (Atlanta: Atlanta Partnership of Business & Education, 1984).

3. See any of the Goals 2000 listings in, for example, *The National Education Goals Report: Building a Nation of Learners* (Washington, DC: U.S. Government Printing Office, 1995), 10-13. The original goals list has been expanded to include a goal for teacher education ("By the year 2000, the Nation's leading teaching force will have access to programs for continued improvement of the professional skills and the opportunity to acquire the knowledge and skills needed to instruct and prepare all American students for the next century.") and parental involvement ("By the year 2000, every school will promote partnerships that will increase parental involvement and participation in promoting the social, emotional, and academic growth of children.").

4. For a similar rationale, see Pierre S. duPont, IV, "A 'GI Bill' for Educating All Children," in *Privatizing Education and Educational Choice: Concepts, Plans, and Experiences*, Simon Hakim, Paul Seidenstat, and Gary Bowman, eds. (Westport, CT: Praeger, 1994), 121-143.

5. Textbooks in marketing and/or communications make this point apparent. See, for example, George E. Belch and Michael A. Belch, *Introduction to Advertising and Promotion: An Integrated Marketing Communications Perspective* (Boston: Richard D. Irwin, 1993).

6. Ibid.

7. Businesses lament, for example, that students graduating from high school do not possess technologically advanced skills to compete in a global economy. The truth of this claim is mitigated by understanding that the rate of technological change renders it impossible to "adequately prepare" students for a future, when that future is perpetually and rapidly changing.

8. Very careful scrutiny reveals that the tassel on the mortar board is on the right side (on the view of the person who wears it). Successful learning, fulfilling necessary requirements, and the achievement of scholarship are indicated when the tassel is moved from the right side of the mortar board to the left. To the possible chagrin of the advertisers who put the flier together, "Partners in Education," apparently, is symbolically unfulfilled.

9. Joseph W. Newman, *America's Teachers: An Introduction* (New York: Longman, 1994). Newman offers an informative and concise interpretation of this dilemma when he distinguishes three conditions necessary for a profession to exist: "(1) A profession performs a unique, essential social service. (2) A profession has a defined, respected knowledge base. (3) A profession has autonomy." (102) Teachers clearly satisfy the first requirement. Given pedagogy and, for example, mathematics,

English, history, etc., persuasive arguments exist that teacher *can* satisfy the second requirement, if they already do not. To achieve autonomy, however, the structure of their (local/county/state) government positions, the generally negative perception of teacher unionism, and/or the lack of collective intellectual agency on the part of teachers must be revised.

10. See *Rankings of the States, 1996* (Washington, DC: NEA, 1996).

11. Joel Spring, *American Education* (New York: McGraw-Hill, 1994), 90. Both of the figures Spring notes are above the national average, but the point is the disparity between areas that are geographically close but distinct.

12. Newman, *America's Teachers*, 275. Newman notes that in many states, property taxes are figured in terms of assessed value of real estate. In these states the percentage of market value can be 10-20 percent but such states have higher rates of taxation. See also, Michael W. Kirst, *Who Controls Our Schools? American Values in Conflict* (New York: Freeman, 1984).

13. Newman, 275. (Italics in original.)

14. Hilary Stout, "Marketing: Firms Learn That Subtle Aid to Schools Can Polish Their Images, Sell Products," *The Wall Street Journal*, 25 March 1991, B1.

15. Jonathan Kozol, *Savage Inequalities: Children in America's Schools* (New York: Crown Publishers, 1991), 80.

16. Ibid.

17. Stout, op. cit. In the final editing of this book, a proofreader (who signed her name as "Linda") attached a note to this section of the book. She wrote, "Just a note on Pizza Hut BOOK IT! program. This is in existence here in Orchard Park. Many parents, myself included, take our kids for the free pizza, but order nothing ourselves. Kids are bribed, but not all parents are." Linda raises a good point: it's possible for a student to be taken to Pizza Hut by his or her parents without parents ordering food. What does it represent, however, when she notes that kids are bribed, but not all parents are? Aside from what has been given (i.e., that some parents may intentionally *not* purchase food), does Linda's note indicate that she condones the bribing of students?

18. Alex Molnar, *Giving Kids the Business: The Commercialization of America's Schools* (Boulder, CO: Westview Press, 1996), 45. See also, David T. Sehr, *Education for Public Democracy* (Albany, NY: SUNY Press, 1997).

19. Kozol, *Savage Inequalities*, 80.

20. *The Singer Company v. The United States*, 449 F.2d 413 (1971).

21. See also, Pat Wechsler, "This Lesson is Brought to You By...: Corporations Are Flooding Schools with Teaching Aids and Propaganda Galore," *Business Week*, 30 June 1997, 68-69.

22. See John Delland, "Is This the News?" in *Watching Channel One: The Convergence of Students, Technology, and Private Business* Ann De Vaney, ed. (Albany, NY: SUNY Press, 1994).

23. Jonathan Kozol, "Whittle and the Privateers," *The Nation*, 21 September 1992. In 1994, K-III Communications Corp. bought Whittle Communications in a deal estimated at $250 million. See "Whittle's Sale of Channel One Completed by K-III," *City Wall Street Journal*, no. 65 (3 October, 1994), B10.

24. Harold Rugg developed a series of social-studies texts that were used in the 1930s and that portrayed the pros *and the cons* of American society. It was radical in the sense that it was a typical celebration of U.S. history, politics, economics, and general life. In fact, The Advertising Federation of America attacked Rugg's series because it raised questions about marketing and consumerism and questioned advertisers' motives. See Frances Fitzgerald, *America Revisited: History Schoolbooks in the Twentieth Century* (Boston: Little, Brown, 1979); and Joel Spring, *Conflict of Interests*, op. cit., 134-136.

25. Chava Willig Levy, "Metropolitan Life Insurance and the American Educator: Partners in Leadership," *American Business and the Public School: Case Studies of Corporate Involvement in Public Education*, Marsha Levine and Roberta Trachtman, eds. (New York: Teachers College Press, 1988), 35.

26. Ibid., 36.

27. W.C. Rappleye, "John J. Creedon: 'Heed the Teacher,'" *Financier: The Journal of Private Sector Policy* IX, no. 11, (November 1985): 40-43.

28. Barbara Gothard, "Burger King Corporation: Education Enriches Everyone," *American Business and the Public School: Case Studies of Corporate Involvement in Public Education*, Marsha Levine and Roberta Trachtman, ed. (New York: Teachers College Press, 1988), 44-45.

29. Ibid., 45-46.

30. According to the *Statistical Abstract of the United States, 1996* (Washington, DC: Government Printing Office, 1996), the number of 16- to 19-year olds enrolled in school and working in the civil labor force was 11,272,000 (p. 398, table #623). The median hourly rate of pay for workers aged 16-19 was $4.99 with males making $5.14 and females making $4.94 (p. 429, table #668).

31. See for example, Svi Shapiro, *Between Capitalism and Democracy: Educational Policy and the Crisis of the Welfare State* (New York: Teachers College Press, 1988), 14.

32. Richard A. Brosio, *A Radical Democratic Critique of Capitalist Education* (New York: Peter Lang, 1994), 278.

33. Rita Kaplan, "Honeywell," *American Business and the Public School: Case Studies of Corporate Involvement in Public Education*, Marsha Levine and Roberta Trachtman, eds. (New York: Teachers College Press, 1988), 14.

34. Ibid., 15. (Italics added.)

35. Kaplan, 16.

36. Ibid.

37. Jeanne Oakes, *Keeping Track: How High Schools Structure Inequality* (New Haven: Yale University Press, 1985); Mihaly Csikszentmihalyi and Rick E. Robinson, "Culture, Time, and the Development of Talent," in *Conceptions of Giftedness*, Robert J. Sternberg and Janet E. Davidson, eds. (New York: Cambridge University Press, 1986); Mara Sapon-Shevin, "Gifted Education and the Protection of Privilege: 'Breaking the Silence, Opening the Discourse,"in *Beyond Silenced Voices: Class, Race, and Gender in United States Schools*, Lois Weis and Michelle Fine, eds. (Albany, NY: SUNY Press, 1993), 33.

38. Sapon-Shevin, 33.

39. David Fetterman, *Excellence and Equality: A Qualitatively Different Perspective on Gifted and Talented Education* (Albany, NY: SUNY Press, 1988), 1.

40. Kaplan, 15.

41. Ibid.

42. Ronald E. Berenbeim, *Corporate Support for Mathematics and Science Education Improvement* (New York: The Conference Board, 1993), 11.

43. Ibid., 11-14.

44. Ibid., 12.

45. Caught up in this is the concern of degrees. Methods and content are important in teaching, but they are seen as foundational requirements *before* teaching can take place and this is simply mistaken. Teaching and learning might be purposive, as Scheffler points out, but they do not require particularistic prefaces. See Israel Scheffler, *The Language of Education* (Springfield, IL: Charles C. Thomas, 1960), 60-102.

46. Ronald E. Berenbeim, *Corporate Support of Dropout Prevention and Workforce Readiness* (New York: The Conference Board, 1993), 24-28.

47. Ibid., 25.

48. Ibid., 24.

49. Ibid.

50. Ibid., 25. Figure 2 is adapted from a chart in the article "Teaching Students the Consequences of Today's Decisions," 24.

51. Ibid., 24.

52. Ibid.

53. Recall the Quality Core Curriculum (QCC) and the Atlanta Public School (APS) requirement that teachers post their objectives each day.

54. Ronald E. Berenbeim, "Helping 'Average' Students Excel," *Corporate Support of Dropout Prevention and Work Readiness*, 16.

55. Brosio, op. cit., 6.

56. Colin Greer, *The Great School Legend: A Revisionist Interpretation of American Public Education* (New York: Basic Books, 1972), 59.

57. Nancy Dalvantes, "JA Hawaii Reaches 30-Year Mark," *Pacific Business News*, 24, sec. 1 (22 September 1986).

58. Ibid.

59. See David G. Armstrong, Kenneth T. Henson, and Tom V. Savage, *Teaching Today* (Upper Saddle River, NJ: Merill, 1997), 19.

60. Dana Phillips, "Showing Kids the 'Power of Work,'" *South Florida Business Journal*, 8 December 1995, 16, sec. A1.

61. Ibid.

62. Ibid., 2.

63. Charles Lindblom, *Politics and Markets: The World's Political-Economic Systems* (New York: Basic Books, 1977), 170-187.

64. Ibid., 175.

65. Daryl Janes, "Construction Groups Team Up On High School Training," *Austin Business Journal* 16, (7 June 1996), 25.

66. Ira Shor, *Culture Wars: School and Society in the Conservative Restoration* (Chicago: University of Chicago Press, 1992), 44-58.

67. Janes, op. cit.

68. Al Ionnone, industry liaison for the Capital Area Training Foundation, quoted in Janes.

69. See, for example, Richard D. Lakes, ed., *Critical Education for Work: Multidisciplinary Approaches* (Norwood, NJ: Ablex, 1994).

70. Charles E. Silberman, *Crisis in the Classroom: The Remaking of American Education* (New York: Random House, 1970).

71. Ira Emery Rodd, "McLunchrooms!" *Nation*, 21 September 1992, 276.

72. Ibid.

73. Ibid.

74. George R. Kaplan, "Profits R Us," *Phi Delta Kappan* (November 1996), K6.

75. Susan Otterbourg, *Bring Business and Community Resources into Your Classroom: A Handbook for Educators from the National Education Association* (Washington, DC: National Education Association, 1991), Appendix D. Given the associated and linked terms "techniques" and "strategies," it appears that "methodologies" should read "methods." Methodology is the larger/broader conceptual study of methods (procedures).

76. Ibid.

77. Ibid. (Italics added.)

78. Albert Shanker, "Where We Stand: Linking School and Work," advertisement in *New Republic* 212, no. 20, 15 May 1995.

79. The NEA has almost 2,200,000 members, the AFT has about 750,000. For more detailed reading on the differences of the unions, see Charles Taylor Kerchner and Douglas E. Mitchell, *The Changing Idea of a Teachers' Union* (London: Falmer, 1988); Marjorie Murphy, *Blackboard Unions: The AFT and the NEA, 1900–1980* (Ithaca, NY: Cornell University Press, 1990); and Wayne J. Urban, *Why Teachers Organized* (Detroit: Wayne State University Press, 1982).

80. Lindblom, op. cit., 204-205.

81. Ibid., 205.

82. Ibid.

83. See *Business Leadership: The Third Wave of Education Reform* (New York: The Conference Board, 1989), xiii; and Kaplan, "Profits R Us," op. cit.

CHAPTER 4

Privatization and the Future of Public Schooling

"While the average American would scream loud and long were some government board to tell him or her which model and color of automobile to purchase, parents willingly renounce their freedom to choose something as significant as education."[1]

Capitalism relies on both production and consumption for its survival. It does this through constructed marketplaces where goods and services are exchanged at rates as high or as low as the market will bear. Competition between producers results in better quality goods and services for consumers who have choices among those goods and services in their respective markets. Capitalist markets are intended to be as free from government intervention as possible and are private, not public, thus primarily accountable to private stockholders and not to the public or its agencies. Private enterprise, not public works or anything akin to them, is the goal of capitalism. As was demonstrated in chapter 3, businesses use schools to promote goods within their markets. They do so, in part, by reinforcing the consumer-materialist assumption that schools are places where students learn how to compete for future jobs. In this process corporations and businesses exploit the consumer materialist assumption by "partnering" with schools in order to profit from a captive student population. Accordingly, businesses and corporations strongly influence the tenor and content of the discussions that take place in schools.

The current critique has thus far hinted that a strict determinism is at work in American schools, but it is not so simple. Strict determinism relies on strict correspondence, which obtains only when "the structure of society at large [is] mirrored in the school system and vice versa."[2] Strict correspondence holds that schools *only* reproduce the status quo and that, given the present case, businesses and corporations have *total* power over students, teachers, and the curriculum. On this view consumer materialism and training-oriented schooling are the only options for school systems. Brosio calls this view the "iron-clad determinism of vulgar Marxism,"[3] but however close the current critique comes to representing *strict* determinism, it is not.

As noted in all of the previous chapters, there *are* teachers who are critically transitive and teach behind closed doors in ways that exemplify arbitration of the consumer-materialist dilemma. There are still others who, for a variety of reasons, consciously critique what they do, even if they succumb to external bureaucratic requirements and reinforce consumer materialism (semitransitiveness?). This is important because the complexities of the lives of students and teachers (and parents, etc.) continually mediate the external corporate influence of consumer materialism. Given this point, students and teachers *nonetheless* demonstrate and reproduce consumer materialism in American schools.

This is the hegemony discussed throughout but it must be understood, if it has not been made explicit before, that students and teachers are not automatons carrying out without *any* question the consumer-materialist expectations of corporate culture. If they did, it would represent *strict* correspondence and, flatly, that is not the case. Shapiro helps us with this point when he notes that "to view education [schooling] as an expression of cultural hegemony means to take seriously the view that dominant forms of curriculum and pedagogy represent, not the imposition of a single class view of those activities, but a complex structure of diverse and sometimes conflicting social practices and ideas."[4] Accordingly, Brosio tells us that, *a la* Gramsci, "hegemony is maintained successfully partly because it is something more than the creation of just one dominant group. Hegemony is mediated as it is imposed by containing symbols, meanings, conventional wisdom, values, hopes and fears that resonate among the persons within the lived culture."[5] Brosio ties the point together by noting that "[t]he mediation of hegemonic imposition is performed to some extent *by those who are themselves manipulated and sometimes controlled.*"[6] Michael Apple puts it this way:

> People. . .have their own interests that they [try] to pursue on their own material circumstances and histories. Many times, these interests will cohere with those of dominant groups, perhaps especially now when capital and the Right are resurgent. At times though, these same people

will mediate, transform, and attempt to. . .set limits on what is being imposed from the outside.[7]

This does not mean, however, that students' and teachers' (and parents', etc.) attempts are not severely restricted by a dominating capitalist discourse wherein correspondence exists, albeit mediated by culture and experiences. Brosio refers to this as "soft" correspondence.

> A "soft version" of correspondence allows us to see that, if the principle of correspondence does not work in a fashion believed by iron-clad determinists, the fact remains that the power of the capitalist economy is paramount in our society and culture. There are powerful consequences which spin off from the dynamic economy, and they do affect the lives of everyone within less powerful institutions such as our schools. Although it is true that various sectors of contemporary culture are relatively autonomous and have a dialectical relationship with each other and the economy, it is not true that these sectors and the actors within them can operate as though those who control the command heights of the economy are not in charge of the rules by which the interaction occurs.[8]

Note that capitalism in the United States (i.e., not theoretical capitalism, but capitalism as practiced in the context of the U.S.), relies on the production of some and consumption of most for its survival. That is, in terms of schooling and the roles of students and teachers, capitalism relies on schools to produce students who are only or primarily consumers. What capitalism can do to secure its success is construct a new market—privatized schools—where students not only consume, but *re*produce the goods and services to be consumed. *Re*production is then distinct from production in that it requires no new knowledge. It means teachers and students are expected to transmit and acquire the *same* "basic" information at regulated paces as everyone else. In this sense, Bacon's famous dictum "knowledge is power" is reversed. Those who control and/or influence the aims of schooling, the curriculum, the tests taken to determine "success," etcetera, are in the proverbial "driver's seat." By restricting the production power of teachers and students, corporate-directed aims of schooling make teacher and student roles reproductive of control, order, and consumer materialism—and have for most of the twentieth century.

It has been argued thus far that consumer materialism's existence in American schools is one of the worst vestiges of capitalism and is detrimental to education-oriented schooling in that it reduces the potentially vibrant roles of students and teachers to noncritical (though potentially enthusiastic) consumers and providers—neither being critically transitive.

It would make schooling a very different process, indeed, were students' and teachers' roles reformed (by students and teachers?) in terms of propositional knowers (or some other version of multiple ways of knowing) and critically transitive agents for democratic pluralism. Were propositional knowing and critical transitivity major purposes of schooling in a democratic public sphere, consumer materialism would be subjected to the kind of critique that would minimize reproduction and keep American capitalism in check. Said differently, because American capitalism relies on oligopoly-controlled production and consumption, the greatest threat to it is critical transitivity and democracy. A critically transitive population is more questioning than accepting (making marketing and sales more difficult) and democracy means responsibility to more people than stockholders (making the oligopoly break down).

Ostensibly, consumer materialism—the approach to existence whereby individuals are intransitive receivers or "getters" of products, services, and information—is capitalism's goal. Note again how this assertion captures only some of the point as American capitalism relies on there being more consumers than producers. When coupled with the current structure and purposes of schooling, American capitalism successfully exploits class distinctions along consumer-reproducer/producer lines by championing consumer materialism in the school's tracking system (more in lower tracks than in upper tracks), curriculum, and general aims of future workforce preparation.

Consider a counter argument, however, as a way of clarifying the point: if consumer materialism really is *the* goal of corporate and capitalist interests, would it not fail of its own success? That is, if consumer materialism came about in the way asserted in this work, it would mean that consumers—not producers—are the outputs of schooling (and in a strict determinist way). Accordingly, capitalism would *not* be served by consumer materialism because there would be a dearth of producers. Yet, the concern misses two points: (1) even if *every* student in the public school were, theoretically, *only* consumers, there would still be enough producers from the influential private-elite schools to maintain hegemonic influence; and (2) in addition to production and consumption, capitalism also relies on *re*production in the form of the principle of correspondence, as just detailed. Recall that correspondence exists when "the structure of society at large is mirrored in the school system and vice versa."[9] While Giroux, Apple, Carnoy and Levin, and others are correct that correspondence is mediated by various contexts and factors,[10] the mediation typically results in figuring out ways to better make do within and in accordance to the status quo. This is not to suggest that contexts, histories, backgrounds, and other factors of difference are unimportant, but to point out that until students and teachers gain control of the sphere in which they work, they remain largely hegemonic pawns in the "acquisitions and accountancy" game of consumer materialism. Corporations, however, are not yet satisfied by this situation. Satisfaction resides on the cornered market and it is to that end—the privatization of public schools—that corporations, businesses, and their allies increasingly focus their attention.

Accordingly, schools are no longer ways nor means *to* markets, they *are* the markets. Furthermore, privatized schools are *deregulated* markets. This is the crux of the problem with privatization and represents part of the detrimental effect corporate interests have on public schools. Advocates of privatization assert that free-market competition among schools will result in increased choices for parents, a better quality of instruction for students, and greater efficiency and cost savings for legislatures. Yet, as Alex Molnar notes:

> Privatization schemes are inevitably advanced in a deregulatory public policy environment, at least in part promoted as cost-saving measures. But their proponents tend to omit the essential element for realizing cost savings from such schemes—rigorous oversight. That isn't as surprising as it sounds. Rigorous oversight is expensive. When the costs of oversight are added to the cost of a private contract, it is likely to mean that not only will there be no net savings, there also may well be increased costs. That's why proponents of privatization prefer to speak loudly (if not clearly) about how private sector "expertise" will ensure quality and how "competition" will ensure efficiency and low cost without the need for "interference" from government regulators.[11]

Molnar is alluding to Chris Whittle's Edison Project and John Golle's Education Alternatives, Inc. These for-profit companies, along with Alternative Public Schools, Sylvan Learning Centers, Eduventures, and Huntington Learning Centers, are interested in making money by privatizing public education. They are doing so by first establishing themselves as "partners" with public schools then launching initiatives at taking over either schools or programs within schools (e.g., Minneapolis, Dade County, FL, Hartford, CT, Wilkensburg, PA, Baltimore, MD).

This chapter explores the meaning and forms of privatization, attempting to clarify what it is and what it is not as connected to the current critique. Ultimately, the point is to link concerns about consumer materialism, corporate influence of student and teacher roles, and school-business partnerships to concerns about making an already commercialized and partly privatized school sphere privately managed and left to profiteers.

PRIVATIZATION: WHAT IT IS NOT

When we talk about privatization of contemporary American public schools, we have to distinguish between a few forms of privatization. Like Russo, Sandidge, Shapiro, and Harris, we are not concerned here with nonpublic, nonprofit schools.[12] Traditionally known as private schools, these include nonprofit religious schools such as those affiliated with the Roman Catholic, Independent Christian, Adventist, and other faiths. Traditional private schools also include the more elite institutions like Choate Rosemary Hall, Phillips Exeter, and Andover. These are not-for-profit corporations that exist for the sole purpose of schooling young people.[13] Neither religious nor not-for- profit schools are our concern unless they are options of corporate-funded privatization plans. Generally, however, they are not our concern because the free-market arguments for competition that are furthered by privatization advocates are not as important to the success of religious and not-for-profit schools as "tradition, church affiliations, wealth, and endowments."[14] Garcia and Garcia note that "[e]ntry into these institutions is carefully restricted to keep out those who do not fit the model of a particular school. Thus, competition is further *restricted* to keep out those who do not fit the model of a particular school."[15] This concern emerges later in a slightly different form: the power and control of privatized schools in selecting their students in a deregulated free market.

Charter schools are also beyond the scope of this chapter insofar as they are funded and established from the public rather than private sector. Charter schools are usually "legally autonomous publicly-funded schools operating under explicit contracts with local school boards,"[16] but there has been some confusion about including charter schools in discussions and considerations of the privatization movement. Russo and his colleagues clarify:

> Another complicating factor in a possible shift toward privatization is that although the term is often associated with not-for-profit, nonpublic, and charter schools, there is no universal agreement on its meaning. An example of the differences between for-profit schools and charter schools may be seen by comparing legislative responses in Minnesota and California (National Governor's Association, 1993). Charter schools in Minnesota, statutorily identified as outcome- based schools (Minnesota Statues, 1994), are legally autonomous public schools, whereas in California (California Education Code, 1994), the school board negotiates not only a charter but also who may hire or dismiss school personnel.

> Additionally, Howard Fuller, the superintendent of Milwaukee Public Schools, offers an interesting perspective. Fuller maintains that Wisconsin's statute is not a charter school law because employees of these schools would be employed by the local board of education rather than a private contractor; thus they are subject to existing state bargaining agreements and statutes (Olson, 1994).[17]

The position Fuller highlights questions control and the larger issue of due process. It is indicative of the degree to which privatization arguments erroneously extend the practice of contracting for goods and services into the realm of teaching and learning. Before we explore this point, however, we should further clarify the boundaries of our use of privatization. We have already excluded religious and not-for-profit private schools from our consideration. Charter schools and magnet schools are *in*cluded, but only to the degree that they represent the same push for free market, for-profit competition that typical privatization arguments make. This is important because not all charter schools or magnet schools represent the same ideology.

As Russo and his colleagues illustrate, charter schools spark confusion. Minnesota charter schools are outcome-based and legally autonomous. California schools, however, have boards that negotiate charters *and* hiring and firing practices. Milwaukee schools, furthermore, are unclear about contractual obligations versus state bargaining agreements in employing teachers. The concerns raised in all three of these illustrations are governance and power. Some charter-school proponents assert that charter schools will begin the reform that will lead to eliminating the monopoly public-school systems currently have. On this view, charter schools are seen as the first step toward competition and choice.[18] Governance and power are moved from educators and bureaucrats in a propped-up sphere to parents and "consumers" in a free-market sphere. This interpretation of charter schools is, for our purposes, part of "privatization" and will not be treated as a separate topic, particularly given the existence of charter school plans that are not directed toward free market, for-profit ends. Similarly, magnet schools are not particularly germane to this chapter's critique. Magnet schools are schools that are "thematic" or offer special curricula, for instance, performing-arts magnets, and science and technology magnets. In these schools, the performing-arts and math and science concentrations are augmented by the nonconcentration areas. That is, math and science are still taught in performing-arts magnets, but they are taught with the performing arts in mind (the science of acoustics, the biology of dance, etc.) such that they "feed" the emphasized curriculum. Magnets have the potential to further privatization, free-market, and for-profit initiatives. The degree to which they do is the same degree to which they will, in this chapter, be critiqued.

In many ways privatization is confusing because of its variance in areas and degrees of application, but schooling has not been (nor will be) simple or unilateral. What should be considered, however, are the various degrees to which charter schools and magnet schools represent the furtherance and spread of free-market entrepreneurship in public schooling. What this means is that privatization already exists in public schools and even though it applies primarily to one area, "hard services," it also threatens the other area, "soft services." Recall Howard Fuller's perspective regarding Milwaukee Public Schools and the laws involved in charter-school initiatives. While we are not focusing specifically on charter schools, the question of *governance* represented in his interpretation is the same as that raised in privatization efforts. Fuller asserted that Wisconsin's statute is not a charter-school law because teachers would be employed by the local school board rather than a private contractor. As a result, private contractors must defer to the state's laws concerning bargaining and related statutes. This is important because it raises questions concerning what services private contractors offer under private-enterprise assumptions (e.g., hiring and firing) that are still regulated by the state. To what degree, in other words, is the free market actually free? To whom (only?) are private contractors accountable, if not responsible?

PRIVATIZATION: WHAT IT IS

The practice of contracting for goods and services *already* exists in public schools. Drucker's midcentury concept of privatization[19] helps us clarify "the practice of public school districts entering into contracts with private, for-profit organizations to deliver a variety of educational goods and services."[20] Accordingly, American public schools already practice a form of privatization. They contract out services to companies or entities that provide school districts instructional media (recall Channel One from chapter 3), books (recall textbook adoptions from chapter 1), food, transportation, custodial services, etcetera.[21] The literature on privatization makes a distinction here, however, between the kinds of services just outlined ("hard services") and those services which require human interaction ("soft services"). This distinction is misleading insofar as "soft" carries a derogatory connotation (as with "hard" versus "soft" sciences and the respect paid to each). The point nonetheless turns on the ease of accountancy represented by the two areas.

To calculate amounts of food, numbers of buses, sums of books, and quantified schedules for maintaining buildings requires the relatively easy task of assessing whether students were fed, buses ran, books arrived, and rooms were cleaned. What makes the service "hard" is really the *ease* of measurement of the topic/process. Differently, "soft" services include counseling and teaching. They are "soft" because they are not easy to assess (standardized-testing assumptions notwithstanding). We should realize that teaching and learning are intricate and multifaceted, not "soft," but the terminology of "hard" and "soft" accurately characterize privatization talk. Herein is a dual, but intertwined, problem with privatization: (1) "soft" services are treated as "hard" services in order to (2) reduce costs and subsume due process and academic freedom under market logics. It is precisely here that privatization becomes transparent.

Privatization is further clarified by noting proponents' arguments for it: privatization brings the efficiency of the marketplace to public schooling;[22] because schools do not keep pace with international standards, they must respond to the competitive demands of the marketplace;[23] and privatized schools would be more accountable, cost-effective, and entrepreneurial in promoting teacher and parent empowerment.[24] Undergirding these arguments is the free-market logic of individualist economics and a Goals 2000–esque competitive fear that other countries might be better at something than the United States. Privatization means eliminating government oversight and dispensing with collective values because government, on the measures of cost and efficiency, is not as profitable as private industry. Kent defines privatization as "the process of transferring functions previously performed by government, usually at zero or below full-cost prices, to the private sector at prices that clear the market and reflect the full costs of production."[25] Add to this definition the desire to make money, and the primary rationale for privatizing American schools emerges: profit for a few at the expense of many.

In broad terms, privatization is distinguished by the governance or control evidenced in different ways.[26] Hunter illustrates the distinction between two notions of privatization where provision is the policy of government and production is the decision of government. He uses case studies of security services to clarify.

Case 1. Both functions are public. The city assigns its police officers to night-time foot patrol in the business district to reduce burglaries. Neither function is private.

Case 2. Production is private; provision is public. The city decides to provide security when high school hockey teams play at the city arena and contracts with Pinkertons to provide the guards.

Case 3. Provision is private; production is public. The government sells a service to private buyers. The hockey team wants security at the sports center and contracts with the city police to have security provided.

Case 4. Both functions are private. A department store decides that it wants uniformed security and employs its own guards. Government performs neither function.[27]

Schools suffer in translations of these kinds because "production" and "provision" are commodified such that the evaluative criteria are restricted to measurement standards that favor businesses. Teaching and learning, as a result, are reduced to processes of production and provision that must meet market goals of transfer efficiency and quality control. Such evaluations *necessarily* favor business interests and privatization efforts because the form of the measurements for learning (standardized, "scientific," "objective") are the same measurements used on durable goods. The problem is that when teaching and learning are reduced to the techniques and procedures that embrace market logics of this kind, they no longer qualify as teaching and learning. They become production-line oriented–processes of transmission of data, retainable by some students, but only those whose cultural capital is valued in the commodified classroom and represented in similarly representative textbooks.

Parenthetically, it is perhaps ironic that Hunter illustrates privatization via security guards. Security provision is so often equated with teachers' roles that "teacher as disciplinarian," "teacher as enforcer of rules and regulations," "teacher as police," etcetera, are accepted metaphors (under the guise of classroom "realities"), reinforced by privatization proponents who see teachers as providers of "hard" services. This becomes bizarre when the dualism breaks down. That is, in Hunter's contracting terminology, teachers as disciplinarians provide a "hard" service at the same time as teaching is categorized as a "soft" service. The dilemma is that teaching is seen in consumer-materialist terms such that "providing the goods of education" is a "hard" service and many teachers and administrators operate on the same assumption. Standardized test scores thus become reinforced as the means of justification for higher pay. Objectivism, scientism, and technorationality are useful, given the underlying competitive market logic of privatization, such that teaching becomes a "hard" service—the worth of which is quantified in terms of output and products.

EDUCATION, INC.

On July 11, 1996, C-SPAN 2 broadcast a symposium at the Center for Business and Government, the Kennedy School, Harvard University. The symposium was "Business Opportunities in Education" and included on its panel Roger Brown, CEO of Motorola; William Bowman, president of Logical Math and Science Software; Michael Perik, president of Softkey Educational Software; Chris Whittle, CEO of Whittle Communications; and Michael Sandler, president and CEO of Eduventures, Inc. The panel discussed the possibilities schools provided for private enterprise. They talked about efficiency and costs, accountability and customer satisfaction, as well as the benefits of management contracts between their businesses and public schools. The bottom line was that schools cannot afford to provide all of the services they are required to provide by law with the funding they currently receive. Instead of arguing for increased funds for public schools, however, the panel argued, quite understandably, for private businesses "helping" schools by providing needed resources. In short, the panel argued for privatizing American public schools. The panel is not alone.

Privatization is recently enjoying increased popularity, begun by conservative reformers in the 1980s. This is described by Peter Cookson and Barbara Schneider.

> In the 1980s these reformers were carried into the mainstream of educational policymaking by a rising tide of conservatism that swept up from the Southwest, where free enterprise and antigovernment sentiment dominated public discourse. There was a loss of faith in public institutions, which were often pictured by conservatives as being expensive, self-interested, and incompetent. . . . The loss of faith in public institutions paved the way for a new belief that drew its inspiration, not from the democratic social metaphor of community and cooperation, but from the market social metaphor of individual interest and competition....Because of the ascendancy of the market faith, by the early 1990s privatizing education became a credible policy in the eyes of certain reformers, newspaper reporters, and educational policymakers.[28]

"Market faith" is another way of agreeing with a kind of social Darwinism, or survival of the fittest, measured by profit-margin comparisons. Privatization *qua* for-profit schools is a corporate desire that enjoys tacit approval from consumer-materialist societies primarily interested in "getting" an "education" (training) that will prepare their students for future work. Accordingly, concerns about profiteering are minimized by and in arguments for "choice" and accepted, intransitively, as "the way our society operates."[29]

Behind this talk is the assumption that ineffective schools deserve the blame for economic competition woes in the U.S. economy.[30] In terms of privatization, some implications are highlighted in the Harvard symposium noted above. When the assembled corporate leaders discussed their reform agendas, the themes undergirding their arguments for privatization were international competition, consumerism, and "future preparation" of students for a technological world. The talk revealed, for example, that William Bowman, president of Logical Math and Science Software, sees teachers "as consumers of products" to be sold on the merits of his software. He lamented that he had to get approval from department chairs, principals, central-office personnel, superintendents, and schools boards in order to sell his product. Michael Sandler, the president and CEO of Eduventures, saw struggling and low socioeconomic schools as "the at-risk market." He reduced the difficulties of at-risk students and their communities to operational market terms, thus subsuming any value of other considerations, such as culture and context, under corporate expectations for business opportunities. Michael Perik, president of Softkey Educational Software, saw students "exceeding and excelling beyond what they've already done," but in terms of technology-oriented goals "so the United States can get ahead of the curve." Accordingly, schools are in competition with world nations and must "beat them" in order to "stay number one."

The terms and ideas represented in the symposium and in conservative attempts at reform conceive of schools as profit centers where teachers are the primary purchasers of goods used to prepare students for future corporate employment. Note the apparent support for teachers. When Bowman lamented about having to go through department chairs, principals, etcetera, he took a popular stand against bureaucracy and seems to be saying that teachers should be deciding the materials and format for their classes. Recall from chapter 1, however, how Texas teachers were swayed by textbook-adoption sales pitches. When technology is a "given," like textbooks, marketing becomes central to its adoption. Teachers "decide" between door-to-door sales strategies that, like textbooks, are not the object of scrutiny, but are accepted in part because of their "given" nature and in part because the "choices" that result from their "given" nature do not include nonadoption. Said differently, teachers would not have, on Bowman's view, the choice *not* to adopt *any* of his technology packages. There is no choice not to choose, only selection from "given" lists.

The Harvard panel only represents some of the talk regarding privatization and public schools, as privatization covers a wide and sometimes confusing spectrum. Some people consider public schooling an evil government monopoly.[31] Others see privatization as a great way to tap into a new market.[32] Like the Harvard group, this group argues for free-market capitalism in the arena of schooling and argues that centralization (as well as the governing bureaucracy that follows from it) should be replaced by decentralized, local control. There are still others who consider public schooling a government monopoly, but instead of calling for corporate-centrist, for-profit private schools, emphasize the kind of free-market choices that would allow family- or home-schooling at the same time as entrepreneurial and religious schools.[33] Other people see flaws in equating business interests with public schooling and argue against corporate-influenced privatization plans.[34] This group sees conflicts of interest between those who purport to have the interests of students in mind, but are involved in school decentralization and privatization because it is a money-making venture. Still others use "teacher choice" as a way of highlighting the flaws of privatization.[35] By looking more closely at some of the extremes represented here, we can better understand the privatization continuum and begin to fashion a different vision of the privatization *qua* choice posture.

EXTREMITIES OF CHOICE

With privatization comes issues of choice, control and power, testing, and profits. At one extreme is a growing number of powerful conservative voices that influence legislatures and politicians to privatize schools on the basis of rugged individualism and "parent choice." We will balance this extreme with the contrasting, and somewhat tongue-in-cheek "teacher choice" argument of Jerry Ellsworth.[36] The issue of choice begins the *non*-exhaustive series of subtopics (including control and power, testing, and profits) that help clarify the problems with privatization.

Privatization is the most recent attempt in the history of education to assert individual control over state control (*viz.*, classical liberalism's focus on the individual over the community[37])in the form of parent "choice." Uneasy about compulsory education or state requirements for schooling, the "individualist-choice" position has much to be unhappy with and a long tradition with which to be concerned. Compulsory schooling (no choice), argued for as far back as 1524 by Martin Luther, was established in Geneva by John Calvin during the early 1600s.[38] The Massachusetts Bay Colony demonstrated its version of compulsory education by enacting the first law mandating reading (The "Old Deluder Law") in 1647.[39] In 1779 Thomas Jefferson's education bill, the "Bill for the More General Diffusion of Knowledge," came before the Virginia legislature. It called for counties to be divided into wards of "hundreds" and each ward would be responsible for providing an education at an elementary school to all "free children, male and female." Schooling would be without charge and the purpose of the school was to provide all citizens with basic literacy including reading, writing, and ciphering. In a similar vein, Benjamin Rush proposed an education plan for Pennsylvania in 1786. His intent was to require (or compel) basic literacy of all citizens in order to achieve "American homogeneity" and a standard of intellectualism that would benefit the country.[40] While states had variations on the compulsory schooling theme, the "common school" movement of the late 1830s and 1840s began the national push for required schooling. Massachusetts enacted the first compulsory school attendance in 1852, Mississippi the last in 1918 thus making the twentieth century the first time the United States saw compulsory schooling nationwide.[41]

Much of the debate over these issues centered around state control versus individual responsibility, and echoes of this debate can still be heard in current discussions about privatization of schools. State control is seen as inefficient, bureaucratic, and so convoluted that individual initiatives and parent/family interests are sacrificed. In extreme instances, state control is even compared to evil government monopolies on par with Nazi and fascist schooling prior to World War II.[42] Supporters of this position think schools should break free from state control and that parents should choose for their children—in a free educational market—which schools are appropriate. This echoes the ninetienth-century arguments for decentralization. In most areas "citizens of states and territories over and over again showed their disdain for strong government by limiting their legislatures and weakening the executive branch," according to David Tyack.[43] He explains, however, that "[d]espite their fear of centralized government, the writers of state constitutions, like most leaders in public education, shared a powerful ideology that linked the survival of the republic to the education of all its citizens."[44] Nonetheless, Lytle exemplifies disdain for compulsory schooling by suggesting that as it became more common "it helped foster the theory that, at least as far as education was concerned, children belong to the government and not to their parents."[45] Such an interpretation continues to exist in the minds of those who dismiss arguments for collectivity and who spurn the idea of public responsibility for others.

Conservatives of this ilk seek a kind of rugged individualist separation from community based on "free-choice" arguments (religious, educational, fiscal, etc.). They disdain government control of schools and, instead, seek "choice" plans that have families controlling their children's schooling. Instead of collective public spheres where different ideas of different people are shared, explored, and critiqued, they argue for a kind of "survival of the fittest" rationale whereby "you take care of you and I'll take care of me." Conservatives of this vein argue that the same kind of constitutional separation of church and state should also apply to school.[46] In some cases, these conservatives make their points by comparing public schools to communist camps for propagandizing students into becoming socialists. Richard Ebeling, the vice president of the Future of Freedom Foundation (FFF), for example, writes that:

> Over the generations, the content of what proper behavior and good citizenship means has changed, with changes in prevailing political and cultural currents in America. . . . The parent has been viewed—and still is viewed—as a backward and harmful influence that must be corrected for and replaced by the "enlightened" professional teacher who has been trained, appointed, and funded by the state. The public school, therefore, is a "reeducation camp" in which the child is to be remade in the proper "politically correct" image.[47]

By characterizing public schools as "reeducation camps," Ebeling demonstrates an "exposure" fear. This is the same phobia some parents have about sending their children into pluralist classrooms. It is a fear that a teacher or fellow student might mention a phrase or idea or argue a point that would contradict the dinner-table talk of the parents. In part xenophobic, in part sociophobic, Ebeling's "reeducation camp" is a misnomer. Additionally, by using the conservative-constructed phrase "politically correct," he culls reactionism from some who listen to him such that by labeling x "politically correct," x is dismissed without consideration.[48] Modern scarlet letters, "pc" is the conservative way to restrict conversations about the ways schools might be run and what schooling might represent in a heterogenous culture.

How, then, do such conservatives see schools functioning? Jacob Hornberger asks and answers the same question and details other aspects of how schools, in his view, operate.

> How does public schooling work? It is run by a political commission, either at the local, state, or national level, by which politicians or bureaucrats plan the educational decisions of thousands, sometimes millions, of children. How is it funded? The state uses its coercive power of taxation to take

money from some, even those who do not have children, to fund the
schooling of others—a perfect embodiment of the Marxian principle,
"From each according to ability, to each according to need." What do
students learn? They learn official, approved doctrine from
government-approved schoolteachers who use government-approved
textbooks. How do public schools get their customers? Through
compulsory attendance laws by which adults are commanded to deliver
their children at age six to these government-approved institutions.[49]

Note the apparent Marxophobia. Like Ebeling's use of "politically correct,"
Hornberger's labeling *x* Marxist means not considering notions that very
well might be more than just capitalism—albeit according to different
criteria than Hornberger would allow.

David Kirkpatrick demonstrates another theme in the extreme
conservative position when he argues that separation of school and state is
more important than the separation of church and state.

Millions of Americans belong to no church at all. Other millions belong
only on a nominal or occasional basis. Even active churchgoers may
average only a few hours a week in religious or church-related activity.
Furthermore, there are hundreds of denominations from which to choose,
and a person may move from one to another with relative ease. This is a
result of the fundamental right of religious freedom in our society, which
includes the right to refrain as well as to participate. Given that argument,
should not the right of educational freedom be even more fundamental?[50]

Make no mistake, schooling and educational policy were (and are)
constitutionally state concerns. Constitutional requirements for schooling are
state (local) requirements as the federal Constitution makes no extant
provision for schools.[51] But what Kirkpatrick reinforces, like Ebeling and
Hornberger before him, is a separatist choice posture. It is based on a
libertarian individualist resentment of community that values keeping to
one's self or separating one's family from others. Theirs is not an academic
argument for choosing not to choose, it is the initial, though masked,
demonstration of fear: fear of difference, fear of loss of control, and fear of
ideological discussions that negatively critique capitalism.[52] Furthermore, the
comparison between religions and "educational freedom" is flawed. Religion
relies on revelation, faith, and acceptance of doctrine. Education-oriented
schooling relies on reason, argument, and multiple interpretations.[53] To
accept the extreme of Ebeling, Hornberger, and Kirkpatrick is to embrace
(however minimally) the privatization of public schools for much of
privatization's justification rests on the same disdain for professional

teachers, school taxes, and heterogeneity for which Ebeling, Hornberger, and Kirkpatrick argue.

Compare the foregoing position, though, with Jerry Ellsworth's position. In a 1992 *Newsweek* editorial, Ellsworth, a teacher for eighteen years, asks readers to picture his vision of a "choice" school.[54]

> Many Americans on the national, state and local levels are calling for parental choice or open enrollment as a way to improve the educational system. The argument is that when our schools are forced to compete for students, the quality of education will improve. Parents will be able to choose from among schools, both private and public, and funding will accompany the child through some sort of voucher system. The school that best sells its program will reap the profits of the highest enrollment. The parental-choice approach calls for applying American competitive practices to our schools. In the business world the profitable businesses will succeed while those who cannot attract customers will go out of business or change.[55]

Ellsworth then goes on to note that "choice is a good idea, and just as doctors, lawyers and other professionals can choose their clients, so also I, as a public-school teacher, want some choice for my school."[56] Ellsworth would, in his tongue-in-cheek scenario, choose children whose parents are professionals with stable jobs. Parents who are shift workers or in service jobs cause "scheduling confusion for children." Ellsworth would choose children that are well-dressed, well-nourished, and whose families only have one parent working outside the home. Well-dressed children will fit in, he reasons, students with fetal alcohol syndrome or students who were crack babies will "bring down our test scores." Ellsworth would choose children who live in the same home and area for over two years. High turnover rates "negatively affect. . .test scores." He would choose children who do not have special needs. Students with physical or mental exceptionalities "need special schools or institutions. . . .It's too expensive to educate them." Ellsworth would choose students who have a computer in their home. Students who are "computer ignorant won't fit well into our. . . progressive society." He would choose students who go home to caring families. He notes that "latchkey kids who go home to empty houses are an embarrassment. Another school can take them and provide after-school activities to keep them busy." On the way to ending his long list of "choice" criteria, Ellsworth would choose only those students who are proficient in English. His school would not "tolerate any of this bilingual nonsense. The American way is best, and that means English. Those other schools can teach those foreigners. We're going to keep our schools American." Finally,

Ellsworth would choose students for his school who attended a good preschool. "Those Head Start kids can be so difficult. They can go to the other schools. Besides, those kids will be happier with their own kind."

Ellsworth substitutes the traditional players in the choice and privatization game (conservative think-tank pundits *qua* parents) and, in so doing, reveals how flawed the initiative is. When left to their own devices, in a free market, privateers will be accountable to their constituency—only. He outlines the likely ramification of deregulated choice: race, class, gender, sexual-orientation bias and other forms of discrimination based on difference. This point was alluded to earlier in the chapter. Where not-for-profit schools rely primarily on traditions, church affiliations, wealth, and endowments, privatized for-profit schools—in the ideal sense (i.e., free from government oversight and based on parental choice)—are positioned to preclude difference. Such preclusion may be based on bias and xenophobia, but it would, as Ellsworth illustrates, be masked in terms of capitalist-supported reasons: competition, test scores, and discipline/control/order.

WITHIN THE BOUNDARIES OF EXTREMES: DIFFERENCES STILL EXIST

Importantly, extremists are not the only ones calling for reform under the banner of privatization. When Hornberger complains about schools being mired in political commission partisanship, bureaucracy, and overly-influential government, he is not alone. But his interpretation is more akin to procorporate, proprivatization consumer-materialist arguments than it is to any other kind of argument. There are those, differently, who are concerned about political-commission partisanship, bureaucracy, and overly-influential external controls (government, school board, administrators, etc.), but because political-commission partisanship, bureaucracy, and external controls are corporate and consumer materialist. They are critical of the degree to which current schools use corporate models, emphasize standardized testing, and promote rugged-individualist competitiveness.[57] In an effort to move away from what they see as negative aspects of schooling, this group only somewhat ironically offers arguments that business-oriented privatization advocates also *seem* to offer: more parental involvement, more responsibility for teachers,[58] more local control. This is, in part, what makes the issue so problematic.

When Terry O'Conner, for example, talks about the "walls" to overcome in order to talk to his child's teachers, he is, like John Holt, John Dewey, and George Wood, lamenting the structure of contemporary schools and arguing for smaller, more locally governed schools.[59] At a glance this is the same argument given by Bowman when he lamented going through different levels of bureaucracy to reach teachers. It also appears to be the same argument advanced by John Chubb and Terry Moe when they indict schools for serving too many masters and being barricaded behind a heavy bureaucracy that disallows easy access.[60] For all of the apparent similarity between these positions, however, the two views could not be more disparate.

The difference is one of *kind*. The kind of choice O'Conner, Dewey, Wood, and others, desire is democratic choice. The kind of choice Chubb and Moe, Myron Lieberman, Rinehart and Lee, and others, desire is economic choice.[61] One outlook sees schools as democratic public spheres where students actively engage in democracy, where the process is both the means and ends at the same time, and where English, mathematics, history, science, etcetera, are areas of study in which to discern, debate, and question even the makeup (i.e., what is considered part) of the courses themselves. The other outlook sees schools as corporate ventures where students "choose" (i.e., *select* among givens) a deterministic track and a specialized course of study in order to "cover" "basic," "useable" material. On this view, the process is linear and sequential such that the means are separated from the end and where English, mathematics, history, science, etcetera, represent dominant cultural expectations for producing productive workers for corporate jobs. Courses, or the canon, are not open to reformation or rejection. Like rugged individualism and social Darwinism, the economic-choice perspective has parents and students as customers over citizens, consumers over participants. In this way, a sort of "divide-and-conquer" strategy is employed with skill.

Chubb and Moe exemplify this when they appeal to the mass public sensibility that parents not only have the right to choose which school, which teachers, and which curriculum their children will "have," but that such choices are *individual* choices rather than individual *and* collective ones. If the "choices" were collective, that is, if they were open to scrutiny by more than one person, they risk being critiqued as suspect or questionable choices. To say, for example, that a parent has the right to choose the curriculum for his or her child moves pedagogy into the narrow economic sphere where process means efficiency and product means quality control. In such a case, choice is economic in kind and curricula are reduced to widgets. Once reduced in this way, pedagogy restricts teaching and learning in terms of the mere transfer of (controlled and controlling) information. Marketing agents within the corporate sphere win the day because, by asserting economic choice as a parent's right regarding schooling, they set up a distinct power relation that favors corporate interests and consumer materialism. The guise of parent choice is a euphemism for parents as consumers, in other words. When parents utilize the consumer or economic-choice perspective, they are *reactive* agents to profit- minded, marketing-oriented, privatization franchises (schools), thus reducing schooling, teaching, and learning to commodified and commodifiable processes and purposes. Not only is learning for the sake of learning beyond this perspective, it goes against the very teacher autonomy that advocates of privatization say teachers would enjoy in the first place.[62]

Furthermore, the parent/consumer-choice position assumes that parents will, *de facto*, make informed and wise choices regarding privatized schools. This point is important because as part of a "divide-and-conquer" strategy, privateers like Pierre S. duPont IV suggest that anti-privatization arguments are elitist insofar as they question parents' abilities to make pedagogical decisions.[63] Like Ebeling, duPont believes that anti-choice arguments represent disrespect for parents as teachers. Ebeling, recall, thinks the "parent has been viewed—and still is viewed—as a backward and harmful influence that must be corrected for and replaced by the 'enlightened' professional teacher." Ebeling and duPont are banking on parents to confuse the point, put here in the form of a question: Can all parents make choices for their children regarding school and schooling? Even if the answer is "yes," it confuses the issue. If schools are reducible to soup cans, cars, or computers, parents *can* make such choices. That is, if schools are lessened in scope and intricacy and offered as merchandise in sound-bite fashion to "choice checklists," parents can pick what they want. The problem is in the reduction and who does it.

If privatization were widespread, schools, on the choice/free-market/capitalist-competition view, would advertise themselves. Like breakfast cereal and tuna fish, parents who care would look at labels and costs and make choices. Still, at least two problems exist: (1) the measures that equate to food labels for schools are standardized tests; and (2) the potential stratification of those who can afford filet mignon versus those who can afford hamburger means that those who "have" will continue to have, while those who do not have will remain without. Though duPont eschews the idea, it remains the case that succeeding at being a parent, that is, having children, does not equate with being a good parent. Similarly, succeeding at having choices does not mean good choices will be made.

TOWARD ILLUSTRATING THE PROBLEM

By narrowing the discourse on schooling in economistic ways and focusing attention on market expectations, parents are lulled into a false sense of security that simply does not exist in schooling. As Robert Almeder points out, those achievements (even of knowledge) we embrace in the name of security and/or certainty are only temporarily conclusive.[64] Note the direction of the initiative, though. Privatization advocates suggest that open, free choice will lead to *more*. Importantly, however, the determinants and procedures they champion actually result in *less*.

Recall, for example, Chubb and Moe's and Lieberman's arguments for school choice. They have parents as consumers, teachers as more autonomous than they are under the current bureaucracy of schooling, and students as achievement-oriented products. Under their plans, parents and students would choose between private schools (i.e., independently governed versus state-run). They would take a voucher with them to the school they select and be guaranteed, on the basis of intra-school competition, that the services provided will come with quality-control guarantees. Set aside for the moment concerns such as parents' ability to decide pedagogy, sheer space for students, the dollar amount of the voucher, what happens to students who are in schools that go "out of business," what happens to special-education students, and the general dilemma of transportation to different schools. Consider, instead, who gains what from privatization and whether privatization means *more* or *less*—and in what ways.

Privatization advocates repeatedly stress that *choice* and *accountability*, not profit, are the primary rationales for privatizing public schools.[65] They point to over 140 school districts that, in the early 1970s, were "privatized." By this they mean that delivery of instruction ("soft services"), parent choice (usually in the form of vouchers), and governance (in the form of private, for-profit companies) were intended to shift the public organization of the school to private management. These experiments nonetheless lay the groundwork for recent efforts at privatizing public schools where profit *is* the motive. Compare and contrast the following illustrations. The first three are experiments from twenty-five years ago. The remaining illustrations are much more recent.

TEXARKANA

Carol Ascher points out that the early efforts at privatization have their roots in the positivism and appeal to behaviorism of the Defense Department. During the Vietnam War, the Defense Department wanted to gain "greater control over the skyrocketing costs of military products."[66] In the Office of Education, she notes, Leon Lessinger, an engineer who served as associate commissioner of education, "was shocked to find that there was no accountability for productivity or quality in his new field."[67] Desegregation in Texarkana was Lessinger's opportunity to privatize instruction. The city counted 60,000 residents at the time, 75 percent white and 25 percent black. It was felt at the time that most blacks and some whites needed extra help getting "up to grade level."

With a grant from the Elementary and Secondary Act of 1965 (ESEA) the Texarkana school district hired Dorsett Educational Systems, Inc., an audiovisual company from Oklahoma. According to Ascher,

> The contract called for the [350] students to gain one grade level in both reading and math after 80 hours of instruction, for which Dorsett would earn a base payment. If the students gained more than a grade level or reached grade level in less than 80 hours, Dorsett would earn extra payment. In addition, Texarkana promised to buy Dorsett's learning technology at the end of the performance contract.[68]

In addition to the profit Dorsett would enjoy, consider the link to student learning and the "delivery of instruction." Dorsett installed carpeted trailers with air conditioning and outfitted each trailer with what they called "Rapid Learning Centers." Students identified for the program were taken from their regular classes for two hours each day. The emphasis, recall, was on reading and mathematics. Ascher explains that

> students sat in front of [behaviorist] teaching machines that used filmstrips synchronized with sound. Built on a stimulus/ response model, the machines prompted students to answer questions by pushing buttons. When the answer was correct, the filmstrip moved to the next frame. Because the students proceeded at their own pace, the program was defined as fostering the educational innovation of "individualized instruction."[69]

Further, Dorsett utilized other crude behaviorist reinforcement techniques. "[N]ot only was learning to proceed by responses to stimuli, but concrete rewards were offered to increase the motivation of students. Dorsett offered Green Stamps and radios for completed lessons, and a television set was promised to the outstanding student at the end of the year."[70]

The program has the air of consumer materialism and technorationality all around it. A for-profit company uses machines it sells to streamline and sterilize the messy, humanistic process of teaching and learning in order to meet predefined numerical success ratings. In order to achieve cash bonuses, the company offers bribes as "motivations" for learning, then calls it "individualized instruction." This is an example of privatizing *part* of a school, in this case "delivery of instruction." The ultimate failure of the initiative was evidenced after three more years of the experiment: *in*creased dropout rates and just 38percent of students meeting predefined "grade level" expectations. It was a hard lesson to learn, but Dorsett's failure at "hardening" the "soft" service of teaching and learning has not halted the push for privatization.[71]

ALUM ROCK

While Texarkana illustrates problems with privatizing "delivery of instruction," Alum Rock illustrates the intricacy of vouchers and "parent choice." The Alum Rock experiment officially began in the 1972–1973 school year and intended privatization in the form of vouchers. It was one of the first voucher plans tried that was not tied intimately with the *Brown v. Board of Education of Topeka* decision of 1954. This is important because the history of "choice" plans includes efforts after *Brown* to continue segregation based on "choice" proposals.[72] Alum Rock was nonetheless an attempt to use monetary vouchers to represent parent choice. Daniel Weiler explains how the process works.

> In an education voucher system, parents are given cash vouchers that they are free to spend to enroll their children in public or private schools of their choice. The vouchers are redeemable in public funds. Because vouchers follow the students and because they constitute the schools' most important source of funds, schools must compete for students in the academic marketplace. The ones that attract many children can expand; others may be forced to reduce their operations or even go out of business. Voucher proponents claim that this process of selection and competition will enable parents to choose the schooling best suited for their children, will motivate the schools to respond to the demand for diversity, and will otherwise improve the quality of education.[73]

The Alum Rock experiment was sponsored by the Office of Economic Opportunity (OEO) under the Nixon White House, an administration interested in reducing the costs of public schools and moving the public sphere into the private sector. Alum Rock, however, was not a voucher program in the purest, free-market sense. Under a true voucher program, all schools—public *and private*—would vie for students and the money that comes with them. Additionally, under the rules (or lack of them) of free markets, schools could cease to exist.

In 1970 Alum Rock was a medium-sized California school district of around 15,000 students in 25 schools. It was tapped because of a variety of factors: William Jefferds, the school superintendent, was interested in extricating the district of financial difficulties it suffered prior to his arrival in 1969; a vocal community group alleged that the schools were failing their children; and the OEO awarded a grant to Alum Rock in order to experiment with school choice—both private and public.

Because the California legislature failed to pass laws permitting private schools to be part of "choice" programs, the Alum Rock voucher experiment only included public schools.[74] Further, the government guaranteed the rights of the faculty and staff within those schools. "It was therefore known as a 'transition' voucher model which was to look toward the inclusion of private schools in the future."[75]

In order for the experiment to prove the worth of privatization, "complex interrelated changes had to occur in the organization and operation of the school district. Schools had to develop diverse programs so that parents could have a choice, budgeting systems had to be developed so that dollars could follow students, and authority had to be decentralized so that school administrators and staff could create autonomous programs."[76] Levinson concludes that the program, after three years of implementation, failed to achieve the basic changes privatization advocates had hoped. "Specifically, the decentralization of budgetary decision making to the school and minischool level was gradually being eroded, competition among minischools for students had decreased, and total schools, rather than autonomous minischools, were again beginning to operate as the main organizational units. Private schools had not become part of the demonstration, and parents had not been as assertive as had been hoped for in exercising their choice."[77]

What this indicates, generally, is that the overt simplicity of "parent choice" is actually far from simple and might be illusory.[78] Consider three points: (1) parents already have choices within the public system; (2) that race, class, gender, and other differences are necessary outcomes of "choice" programs (recall Ellsworth); and (3) the irony that "choice" and "free educational markets" will only come about, if they ever do, as a result of powerful, centralized government initiatives.

For (1), parents already have choices and ultimate power in the form of sending their children to magnet schools, charter schools, minority/majority transfer programs, etcetera—all within public systems. While this text ultimately questions the success of such initiatives in terms of education-oriented schooling, the choices nonetheless exist. Moreover, though unrealistic for many families, the choice has always existed for parents to move to different districts. Getting a voucher for $3,000, however, positions middle- and upper-middle-class families in better positions of "choosing" than it does poor families. The gap widens, in other words, between the "haves" and the "have nots" when families that already have resources act. Those who do not have, continue not to have until—*and if*—they amass enough to act. This does not preclude "choice" programs, but it eventually means that those who already have less will be forced to have *even less* and at a much later time.[79]

For (2), that race, class, gender, and other differences are necessary outcomes of choice, Ellsworth conceptualizes the negative effects of "choice" as it implies sanctioned re-segregation. Historically, as has been indicated above, "choice" plans were used in certain areas of the country as a means of continuing segregation. It was the "choice" of some to distance themselves from difference. Ellsworth reminds us not only of this history, but warns of the dangers of "choice" plans that appear to be based on "equal opportunity" arguments, but that result in continued stratification.

For (3), "the irony that 'choice'. . . will only come about . . .as a result of powerful, centralized government initiatives," Alum Rock illustrates the irony of "parent choice" and "local control," as it required the federal Office of Economic Opportunity and the entire Alum Rock school system to govern the experiment. Beyond this, however, Alum Rock was the first serious effort at privatizing public schools. Privatization advocates resented the fact that teachers and principals gained power and control over their schools, vis à vis parents, and not the reverse. In their view, the attempt was doomed from the start because the essential free-market forces were restricted.[80] Another experiment at another time in another part of the country, however, would test vouchers and "parent choice" again.

NEW HAMPSHIRE

After the Alum Rock experiment, a voucher experiment was crafted for New Hampshire schools. Vouchers are not novel to New Hampshire because, while not of the same kind, some New Hampshire districts had already been using vouchers for years, well before Alum Rock.

> These particular local districts had, and still have, school boards that allocate funds, raised mostly though local taxes, to primary and secondary education. Such funds are not allocated to purchasing paper, pencils, and

chalk; to hiring teachers, janitors, and coaches; or to heating and lighting buildings. Instead, they are used to give local parents the choice of any public elementary or secondary school anywhere in the state or in another state, as long as such schools are approved by the New Hampshire State Board of Education.[81]

Menge clarifies the difference between the elementary and secondary school vouchers: "The value of an elementary school 'voucher'. . .is limited to the New Hampshire state average cost per pupil of current expenses of all New Hampshire public elementary schools, or the current expense of the particular receiving school plus a 2 percent rental charge for the capital investment of said district, whichever is less."[82] The secondary school voucher is different. The sending district, or the district from which a student comes, has to pay "full tuition at whatever public New Hampshire or other approved public high school the parents choose, even when it exceeds the state average, subject to the statutory provision that no receiving school may charge more than the school's per pupil current variable costs plus a 2 percent rental fee."[83] This is important when one considers the Hanover school district. Given that Dartmouth College is in Hanover, the local public school tuition is higher "than that charged by all but a few of the most prestigious private schools in the East."[84] With this backdrop, New Hampshire considered a voucher test in September 1974. The test, according to Menge, was simple. There were twelve steps.

1. An Education Voucher Authority would be established.
2. Once approved by everyone, it would operate for seven years, the last two for phasing out federal funding.
3. A local Voucher Review Committee would recommend voucher values to local districts; the first year based on each district's current cost per pupil. Afterward, vouchers could vary according to community wishes.
4. Vouchers would be provided to every district-resident parent/legal guardian for each eligible child.
5. Parents/legal guardians could cash the voucher at any school (anywhere in the U.S.) that would accept it.
6. Schools that accepted the voucher would have to certify that they were qualified to accept the funds for educational services provided.
7. Given existing state statutes, no-fee transportation would be provided to any contiguous district.
8. Local districts would have to continue existing levels of funding to support the district. Additional costs due to the implementation of the voucher test would be absorbed by the National Institute of Education (NIE).

9. A one-time-only grant equal to 30% of districts' total appropriation for the school budget for the past year would go to each district as an incentive to participate.
10. Parents could transfer their children at any time.
11. Schools would operate on the voucher funds plus any additional funding voted by the school district annually.
12. Schools could operate multi-grade schools, but they would qualify as one option for parental choice. At least one alternative would have to exist in each district.[85]

On this plan, parents who would choose to send their child to a more expensive school could do so, but they would have to pay the difference. In the case of parents who would choose to send their child to a less expensive school, the receiving district would have more funds to spend in their school district.

Menge, a supporter of voucher programs, laments that as detailed and visionary as the plan was—and even though it continued to be discussed well into 1976—it was never tried. Sixteen targeted school districts decided not to test the plan, so the experiment failed. Menge concedes that "Apparently most parents didn't care much one way or the other—few turned out, in many instances less than 1 percent of the eligible voters. Those few who were motivated to cast their ballots wanted no part of the New Hampshire free market voucher test program."[86]

FROM SAN ANTONIO TO INDIANAPOLIS

All three of the previous attempts at privatization, in the form of parent "choice"/vouchers, happened about twenty-five years ago. This does not mean, however, that efforts have dwindled. The increase in conservatism and disgust with federal oversight from the 1980s fueled new initiatives, or breathed new life into already existing attempts. San Antonio, Indianapolis, and Milwaukee are only three of the most recent efforts; each a "choice" program, but each emerging out of different coalitions. The San Antonio and Indianapolis experiments began with wealthy businessmen who used corporate rationales to persuade other large corporations to contribute to the program.[87] Milwaukee saw political advocates for the poor join forces with corporate interests in putting forward its choice plan. All three efforts, however, illustrate the renewed interest in vouchers and the degree to which corporations provide the consumer-materialist rationales for privatizing public schools.

In San Antonio, for example, James Leininger spearheaded the effort to include private schools in Texas legislation concerning school-choice initiatives. Leininger is "a physician and chief executive officer of Kinetic Concepts, a large medical supply company "headquartered in San Antonio, Texas."[88] His primary concern was that the employees he hired were not performing as he desired and he blamed the public schools for their perceived shortcomings. This is not surprising given Leininger's longstanding disappointment with San Antonio public schools.

> Dissatisfied with the public and private choices available, Leininger opted for home schooling. After many frustrating efforts to get his son to focus on learning, the father discovered the behavioral reinforcement value of M&Ms—if his son answered correctly, he got an M&M. If not, dad got the M&M. Experience teaching his son deepened Leininger's interest in education.[89]

When Martinez, Godwin, and Kemerer illustrate Leininger's understanding of teaching, they reveal the reduction of it to behaviorism (not unlike the Dorsett company in the Texarkana illustration of twenty-five years ago). In other words, one of the primary foundations of Leininger's understanding of the problem of education boils down to M&M provision. "Experience teaching his son deepened Leininger's interest in education." As though teaching is reducible to S =>R conditioning, such an oversimplification of the process is a shaky foundation upon which to build an argument for school choice. Leininger, however, added to his teaching perspective his understanding of corporate need. As a result, he fashioned a choice argument that would yield him better workers.

Because he was the CEO of Kinetic Concepts, Leininger was concerned about the "products" schools were providing him for his labor force. "Leininger noted in the mid 1980s that increasing numbers of applicants for employment in his company were functionally illiterate despite having high school diplomas."[90] Part of the blame for the situation as he saw it was that public schools did not have competition. If families—particularly poor families—had the means to choose a school, the overall quality of schools would not only improve (according to M&M measures?), it would mean better workers in Leininger's factory because free-market competition demanded it. Martinez and her colleagues clarify:

> In addition to his company's own substantial financial contribution, Leininger involved the chief executive officers of the USAA Federal Savings Bank and the *San Antonio Express-News* in setting up a $1.5 million tuition scholarship fund to enable low-income San Antonio families to attend private or out-of-district public schools over a three-year period. Concerned about what its publisher termed "the postliterate age," the San

Antonio newspaper provided the necessary publicity to launch the program and gave it editorial support.[91]

The message is not too mixed. Poor families are targeted by large corporations as the primary beneficiaries of a privately funded "choice" program. A public-relations coup, wealthy businesspeople appear to demonstrate philanthropy and egalitarianism. The ulterior motive is still evident, however: public schools are targeted to either increase the already large amount of corporate-influenced teaching and learning that goes on there, or risk competing with schools that do not have to meet the same responsibilities public schools do. Private schools do not, for example, have to meet federal requirements for special-needs or special-education students. Such schools also do not typically require certification for their faculty, nor do faculty usually enjoy collective bargaining. With lower teacher salaries and expensive programs gone, private schools in San Antonio are not competing on the level playing field of privateer's free-market dreams, they are oligopoly-subsidized efforts that "succeed" by excluding groups and eliminating justifiable costs that public schools cannot exclude or eliminate. In fact, in the San Antonio experiment private schools are comprised of "approximately 60 percent enrolled in Catholic schools, 30 percent in Baptist and other Protestant schools, 9 percent in other denominational schools, and 1 percent in nonsectarian schools."[92]

Such is the truly interesting part of the San Antonio plan: it is privately funded and modeled on the Indianapolis initiative called the Golden Rule Program. Leininger fashioned himself as the Texas version of J. Patrick Rooney, the chairman of the Golden Rule Insurance Company, based in Indianapolis. Rooney established the Educational Choice Charitable Trust, a large-scale, privately funded "choice" program ostensibly designed for low-income families.[93] The assumption of the trust fund is that "increased access to private schools increases the families' choices about and control over where and how to educate their children."[94]

Through the trust program, Rooney attempted to achieve two distinct goals. The explicit goal was to provide greater access to private schools for a limited number of children from low-income families. (Although trust grant recipients can send their children to any school located in Marion County—private or public—all have selected private schools.) A second implicit and subordinate goal was to assess the efficacy of private educational vouchers as an educational policy.[95]

In other words, private conglomerates use needy families to fashion public policy that furthers consumer materialism and the oligopoly from which, cyclically, the conglomerates ultimately benefit.

At the heart of this dilemma is the corporate hope that private schools will do a better job at instilling consumer materialism than public schools are doing. It is ironic that public schools *are* succeeding at instilling the very consumer materialism businesses want. What businesses cannot see is that the problem is in both the "instilling" and the "product" (consumer materialists). Instead of getting out of the way of innovative and critical teaching, they even more ardently influence policy that reinforces teacher and student roles as subordinate to economic rationales, content, and procedures. The offense is that business interests use the most vulnerable, though enthusiastic and interested, echelon of society to achieve hegemony. This point is, perhaps, best illustrated by the Milwaukee experiment.

MILWAUKEE ... NOW OR NEVER?

In 1990, Milwaukee enacted the Milwaukee Parental Choice Program (MPCP). In the city-wide school system of 100,000 students, 70 percent of the students are African American. The drop-out rate is, according to Hetland, somewhere around 50 percent.[96] In order to successfully pass the legislation allowing the Milwaukee initiative, a unique coalition was built between conservatives and legislators representing the urban poor. Annette (Polly) Williams was the leading advocate and architect for the choice initiative. She "concluded that underfunded, problem-ridden urban school systems had become a barrier to [African American] children's upward social and occupational mobility."[97] Williams had been at odds with the school system for years and eventually pulled her children out of public school and placed them in a private school. While she was able to "make ends meet," other parents—particularly the urban poor—could not. Vouchers became the answer to the problem.

Originally, the law limited the voucher experiment to about one thousand low-income students "who could attend—at state expense—private, non-sectarian schools within the city that were willing to participate in the program."[98] The voucher was equal to about $2,500. Note the difference between Alum Rock, San Antonio, Indianapolis, and Milwaukee. In Alum Rock, private schools were not part of the experiment (in part because of geography—private schools were not close to Alum Rock schools); and in both San Antonio and Indianapolis they were (because the initiatives used private funds). In Milwaukee, private schools were options, as long as they were nonsectarian.

Choice schools had to meet only one of four educational requirements: (1) At least 70 percent of the pupils in the program had to advance one grade level each year; (2) the average attendance rate had to be at least 90 percent; (3) at least 80 percent of the students had to demonstrate significant academic progress, or (4) at least 70 percent of their families had to meet parent involvement criteria established by the private school. Choice schools did not have to accept children with exceptional needs, and they did not have to meet the financial disclosure or other record-keeping requirements placed on the public schools.[99]

In order to participate in the "choice" program, students could not be enrolled in private schools or in public schools outside the Milwaukee Public School (MPS) system. "The income restriction is close to the eligibility requirement for the reduced-lunch program (185 percent of the poverty line) and higher than the qualification for the free-lunch program (135 percent of the poverty line). Approximately two-thirds of MPS students qualify for free or reduced-price lunches, with 90 percent of those students qualifying for the free-lunch program."[100]

The players in this choice game, then, are low-socioeconomic-status African Americans who have the seemingly odd but strong support of wealthy, white, conservative businesspeople. Businesses, their advocates and representatives, used carefully chosen research findings as fuel for pro-choice arguments pertaining to legislative action, but with such impeccable timing as to not arouse suspicion. The concern here stems from evaluations of the choice program.

The Milwaukee plan underwent four annual evaluations. John Witte, a political-science professor at the University of Wisconsin, was in charge of the evaluations—in accordance with the law. As Molnar notes, however, none of the evaluations "was able to find statistically significant differences in the achievement of students attending choice schools and that of a comparable group of students attending the Milwaukee Public Schools. The evaluations did find a high degree of parental satisfaction with the choice schools. However, more students left the choice schools each year than changed schools in the comparable group of public schools students."[101] Witte was not the only person to do research, though, and it is here that timing and business interests arouse suspicion.

Researchers from Harvard University and the University of Houston released a study which asserted that students in the Milwaukee program did "substantially" better than students who had applied to the program, but were rejected.[102] Molnar, Farrell, Johnson, and Sapp reveal that the "results were released just as the national Republican convention was getting underway in San Diego and on the eve of a widely anticipated August 15 court hearing in Madison, Wisconsin, that was intended to determine whether or not an injunction blocking expansion of the Milwaukee choice program would be lifted."[103] Add to this the fact that two of the authors of the study, Greene and Peterson, editorialized in the *Wall Street Journal* on August 14, 1996:

> The political value of the new study quickly became apparent. During an August 22 appearance on "Newshour with Jim Lehrer," Lamar Alexander, former governor of Tennessee and secretary of education under the Bush Administration, repeatedly referred to the "Harvard study" as proof of the wisdom of Bob Dole's campaign pledge to provide low- and middle-income parents with "opportunity scholarships" that they could use to send their children to private schools.[104]

What is important is that the battle between Witte's research and the research of Greene, Peterson, and Du was used in Milwaukee political circles to advantage business interests for privatization. "The. . .effort to keep Wisconsin legislators abreast of internecine battles in educational research was launched courtesy of Timothy Sheehy, president of the Metropolitan Milwaukee Association of Commerce (MMAC). Sheehy began his cover letter to the legislature: 'School choice programs are working in Milwaukee and should be expanded. Milwaukee employers have made it their number one legislative priority.'"[105]

This point is important because of the ulterior motives of business interests in privatizing schooling. When Sheehy announces that employers in Milwaukee have made school-choice programs their "number one legislative priority," it is not because Milwaukee employers are interested in community service. Their interest is production and profit. Whatever they can do to influence the business-friendly legislature to expand choice plans, they are happy to do. But why? They may use low-SES African Americans as the test case to appear to take a "high-road" posture regarding equal opportunity, but it is a strange partnership indeed. Molnar, Farrell, Johnson, and Sapp put it this way:

> The strategy of [business-backed school choice] advocates appears to be to exploit the dissatisfaction of poor, predominantly minority parents who have been left behind by our economy in order to achieve the goal of creating a publicly funded private school system free of public control and oversight. If achieved, this alternative system will inevitably reproduce and legally sanction the doctrine of "separate but equal" on a grand scale, with the primary beneficiaries being middle- and upper-class families. In other words, the politics

of private school choice now resembles a high-stakes version of the old "bait and switch" scam.[106]

By revealing the potential for public-school oversight to become private, Molnar and his colleagues also reveal the racist and classist underpinnings of such an initiative. On the surface, as noted earlier, the effort appears to mean *more*, as in more choice, more opportunity, and more control. Ultimately, however, it means *less* of all three and the corporate takeover of public spheres by private interests. This point is perhaps best illustrated by looking at for-profit companies that are hired to run public schools. Such companies represent the kind of privatization that has public oversight replaced by private profit expectations.

EDISON'S DIM BUT GLOWING BULB: BOSTON

In addition to Chris Whittle's Channel One school-business partnership (see chapter 3), he also developed a company that is separate from Channel One. Whittle Schools and Laboratories is the private, for-profit company created by Whittle as the corporate home for the Edison Project, his initiative to develop two hundred for-profit, technology-laden schools.

On May 15, 1991, Whittle detailed his plan. It called for building for-profit schools from the ground up. These schools would be technology-based and would cost no more per pupil than what public schools spent. As outlined by Alex Molnar,

> The Edison Project team would be recruited through the remainder of 1991, and it would create the blueprint for the new American school in 1992 and 1993. From 1994 to 1996, it would raise capital, develop the necessary technology, and construct schools for the first 200 campuses. In the fall of 1996, the first 200 schools would open, serving 150,000 students (probably ages 1 through 6). In 1997, it would begin adding one age unit per year and marketing the entire system and its technology. It would start opening additional campuses in 1998, achieving an enrollment of 2,000,000 by 2010, at which time the system would be copied nationwide either in full or in part.[107]

Whittle enlisted the help of Lamar Alexander, former Tennessee governor and secretary of education under George Bush, in advancing the idea of for-profit schools. Alexander and Bush were enthusiastic supporters of the idea and were pleased to know that the Edison Project would include prominent names. Benno Schmidt, the former president of Yale University was wooed away from Yale in part by a reported salary of $800,000 to $1 million (plus stock options).[108] The "team" also included conservative Vanderbilt University professor and former under-secretary of education Chester Finn, Brookings Institute member and voucher proponent John Chubb, and the former managing editor of *Newsweek*, Dominique Browning. Unfortunately for the Edison Project, the grand early vision of two hundred schools with state-of-the-art technology stations for each of the estimated 150,000 students by 1996 never materialized. Instead of $2.5 billion to begin nationwide for-profit schools, Whittle managed to attract investors who put in only $12 million over a three-year period.[109] The result was that Whittle began running four schools, instead of two hundred, in 1995. Only one of these four schools, the Renaissance Charter School, held some potential at making money for the Edison Project. Located in Boston, the potential success of the school came about, according to Molnar, *not* because the free market supported it, but because conservative Republican governor William Weld arranged a state loan of $12 million to renovate the former University of Massachusetts building the school would occupy. Along with the loan, the state provided a lease deal at an estimated $1.5 million below the property's market value. The Renaissance School also receives money from the Boston Public Schools for each child who attends Renaissance. "By one estimate," concluded Molnar, "the school will be the beneficiary of $52.4 million over the five-year term of its charter school contract."[110]

Given these conditions, Whittle might turn a profit, but it remains a large question as to whether a government subsidy demonstrates the free-market argument so fervently made by Whittle and his privateer allies. According to the *Boston Globe*, Renaissance received almost "$1,000 more per pupil in tax funds than the average Boston public school."[111] Governmental legislative help, government subsidies, and government tax breaks are antithetical to the Adam Smith arguments repeatedly put forward by corporate leaders. Less means more where less is government and more is profit. In the Boston case, however, more means more for some (those at Renaissance and Edison) and less for most (the average student in Boston public schools).

What is vital to note here is the for-profit motive. While Whittle ultimately failed his own test,[112] privatization advocates see the effort as the wave of the future for American schools. Privatization advocates, to be sure, are not limited to Republican stakeholders (as illustrated in the Edison Project). John Golle agrees with this point and his efforts with Dade County, Florida, and Baltimore, Maryland, schools illustrate the bipartisan aspect of the for-profit motive.

DADE COUNTY, FLORIDA, AND BALTIMORE, MARYLAND: PRIVATIZATION'S LINK TO PROFIT

Education Alternatives, Inc. (EAI) is Golle's project and its ultimate role in the privatization of Baltimore schools underscores the concerns of this text.[113] Briefly, EAI began in 1986 as the brainchild of former Xerox salesman John Golle. Golle acquired part of Control Data Corporation in an effort to set up a series of computer-oriented schools. He called the program Tesseract, which is the name of the fantasy world in Madeline L'Engle's *A Wrinkle in Time* children's book. After establishing two schools, one in Eagan, Minnesota and one in Paradise Valley, Arizona, Golle gave up the idea of developing a network of computer-oriented schools and went on to develop EAI.

> The idea behind EAI was to offer Golle's Tesseract program and an assortment of management services to public schools. EAI first drew national attention when it signed a five-year contract to run South Pointe Elementary School in Dade County, Florida, in June 1990. The signing of the South Pointe contract raised interest in the company among school districts around the country. That interest, in turn, helped the company generate almost $6 million on the stock market when Golle took EAI public in April 1991.[114]

EAI is a private, profit-making firm that runs public-school systems. The Dade County, Florida experiment required the Dade County School Board, EAI, and the United Teachers of Dade to agree to a contract that "established South Pointe as a public school, staffed and managed by public school employees, governed by a school-based management cadre, and supported by the teachers' union (which approved waivers to the union contract)."[115] Ostensibly the role of EAI was to procure private funding for South Pointe while also having a major say in the hiring of faculty and staff. Additionally, the program instituted by EAI, Tesseract, was the foundation for the "integrated" curriculum.

Ultimately, Dade County did not renew the contract with EAI. While Parham and Peeler put a standard administrator-like "good face" on the initiative, EAI failed to live up to the promises it made.

> Dade County officials say attendance and test scores improved during the five years of the contract, but test results were no better than at a comparable school. Also, EAI raised $1.5 million in private and corporate donations for South Pointe, a sum $1 million less than the company had said it would raise in the contract goal.[116]

The separation was congenial, as separations go, but EAI considered the experiment a necessary step in developing itself as a profitable private management firm. Recall the public offering of EAI stock. After Dade County, Florida, EAI signed a five-year, $135 million contract with Baltimore schools to run eight elementary schools and one middle school.

At the time, EAI stock was performing reasonably well. "EAI made its first public stock offering in 1991 and raised $5.7 million. A second offering in 1992 brought in an additional $1.9 million. And a third offering in 1993 raised $31 million."[117] Consider two major points in determining the merits of EAI's for-profit structure: (1) the way EAI operates and is financially managed; and (2) the success of EAI in educational *and* fiscal terms. Richard Hunter described EAI's operations in an article for *Education and Urban Society*.

> EAI has structured contracts with Baltimore to minimize operating costs. According to the contract, they receive money for salary costs and other operating expenses from the city of Baltimore on a predetermined schedule of payments. EAI is able to invest the money and return its principle to the city of Baltimore, who in turn pays the salaries of the employees and other operating expenses. This accounting practice has created some mistrust with the public about EAI. The pass through receipts from the city of Baltimore that are used to pay the salaries of the teachers and employees of the city of Baltimore have been reported as revenue for EAI. This accounting practice increased EAI's annual sales by approximately $26 million and portrayed to some Wall Street investors that EAI had achieved miraculous growth.[118]

Hunter goes on to clarify that the vast majority of the $26 million goes back to Baltimore, so it is deceptive to think that the $26 million represents financial success. It results in inflated stocks.[119] This is a problem when one considers who stands to gain the most from the privatized, for-profit schooling effort.

In fact, it was considered a major problem by two EAI stockholders. They filed a lawsuit alleging "EAI has issued statements and used accounting methods that paint an overly positive picture of its current and future financial position. . . .The suit claims that stock prices were pushed to artificially high levels by the accounting methods that exaggerated the company's size and by Mr. Golle's predictions of company growth that had 'no reasonable basis.'"[120] Commenting on the stockholders' lawsuit, Molnar notes that "[a]lthough the suit was subsequently dropped, both Golle and former St. Paul, Minnesota, superintendent of schools David Bennett, who was president of EAI from April 1991 until his resignation in July 1995, had contributed to the suspicion that EAI was an overhyped proposition, a bubble that was about to burst."[121] Molnar continues:

> In autumn 1993 when EAI stock was riding high, [Golle and Bennett] each exercised stock options that brought them huge profits. Bennett realized a profit of $460,000 by exercising options on 14,860 shares of common stock for $5.69 each and selling them for between $36.50 and $36.75 each on September 23, 1993. Bennett's sale of stock represented his entire interest in EAI at the time. Golle reaped a profit of $1,758,500 when he exercised options for 50,000 shares of common stock at $3.08 each and sold them for $38.25 each between September 29, 1993 and October 8, 1993. When Golle completed his sale, he still retained 377,102 shares of common stock.[122]

While such profit-taking may not be surprising, it is nonetheless indicative of the fundamental problem with privatized, for-profit schools. Those who already "have" and stand to gain will "have" more and will gain more; those who have less will supply those who "have," or be accounted for in such a way as to symbolically supply those who "have," with the "more" they ultimately get. On the view of privateers, however, profits such as the ones realized by Bennett and Golle are appropriate rewards for jobs well done. But was the job well done?

In a study by the American Federation of Teachers, EAI was highly criticized for a number of problems: its failure to fulfill the instructional/testing goals it had set out, unaccounted for Chapter I funds, redefining special-education students' needs in order to reduce costs, and diverting funds from classrooms to overhead, lawyers, corporate travel, and profit.[123]

The report was based "exclusively on testing, staffing, and financial information obtained by the AFT from the Baltimore City public schools."[124] Some of the findings include:

*The EAI contract was initially based on an estimated per-pupil average cost in all Baltimore schools of $5,549—a routine calculation that does not count preschool children in the pupil count. The school district, however, paid EAI for preschool students.
*EAI received funding for 4,815 FTE students; when, in fact, fewer than 4,600 were counted in an official state audit.
*EAI cut most Chapter I teaching positions and then used money to finance low-paid interns, training, technology, facilities maintenance, and contract administration.
*Public and private schools account differently for their use of Chapter I funds, with private schools permitted to charge administrative and overhead costs to Chapter I. EAI appears to have handled Chapter I funds as though its schools were

private—rather than public—by improperly charging administrative and maintenance costs off against Chapter I funds.

*During the second year of EAI's contract, EAI's repayment to the district for central support services was reduced from a fixed amount of $3.4 million to 7 percent of the contract, effectively adding $1.4 million of new funds to EAI's coffers.

*In its first two years of operation, EAI reduced the number of self-contained special education classes by one-half.

*The certified teacher-to-pupil ratio in EAI elementary schools rose from 1:18.5 before EAI, to 1:25.3 in 1993–94.

*An Arthur Anderson audit of the EAI contract revealed that EAI made at least $2.6 million in profits, while cutting staff, increasing class sizes, and reducing services to students.

*Financed by cutbacks in regular education, special education and Chapter I programs, EAI accounted for $2.9 million in "enhancement expenditures" by calling the $1.1 million spent on interns and the $700,000 spent on wiring and cabling for computers "enhancement."

*More than $225,000 was spent on training materials for staff development—much of it purchased from EAI itself.

*Between spring 1993 and fall 1993, both reading and math scores decreased at every grade level.

*In EAI schools, attendance rates declined from 91.9 percent in 1991-92 to 91.6 [percent] in 1992-93.[125]

In sum, EAI makes money by spending less than the value of the contract it signed in Baltimore. This is different from the promises Golle made in 1994. At that time he asserted that "schools funds are reallocated from noninstructional areas to instructional areas wherever possible."[126] The audits paint a different picture.

The difference is attributable, again, to privatization's major weakness: reducing teaching and learning to commodified procedures and individualist profit. Privatization arguments about efficiency and accountability simply do not hold up when judged by their own criteria. Even with this reality, arguments for privatization continue. Accordingly, the task is to meet each privatization argument with a counterargument and to broaden the critical discourse to include those most vulnerable to privatization's consequences—teachers and students.

RECONSIDERATIONS

Let us focus again, then, on the necessary outcome of privatization and the metanarrative of reduction, which is antithetical to the foundation of privatization plans. In other words, let us reconsider the idea that privateers promise more, but deliver less. Golle and Whittle made such promises, even though Molnar called such guarantees "glib slogans" and "false promises."[127] Again, where privatization asserts that it means *more*, it actually results in *less*. Privatized schools compete to provide their customers the best services and products they can. Cost-efficiency means offering only those programs that will earn the school a profit and risks putting programs, like those in the arts for example, in positions of constant "market defense."[128] Marketing campaigns between those schools (businesses) intent on luring more and better students to their school become requirements for survival. Glossy fliers tout the very reduction that is the point: hyper-vocationalistic specialization and test scores.

The problem, of course, is that the potential still exists under privatization plans for alternative schools. Magnet schools and charter schools, for example, could focus on music or literature or on alternative forms of instruction that ostensibly deny the relevance of standardized tests. The reality of American society, however, is that test scores drive upward mobility. What this means is that privatization plans disguise elitism and essentialism by proclaiming choice and entrepreneurial opportunity. Since alternative schools could exist, nobody can argue that choice is not inclusive of *more* (people, schools, etc.), so the privatization argument goes. Developing demographic niches and selling to those niches means, however, specializing in increasingly narrow ways and eliminating those "extras" that reduce profit margins. This is another example of the *more*-means-*less* ruse played out by corporatists arguing for privatization.

Under the guise of choice, programs that are marketed to meet students' needs will use standardized tests as comparative measures set against competing schools' scores. Just as with selective testing, where certain students are conveniently excused from Iowa Test of Basic Skills (ITBS) testing, a larger, consciously executed exclusion of programs means increasing test scores, "competitive edges," and profits.[129] The argument for "choice" is predicated on the hope that certain areas of study and groups of people will find a common link somewhere else, over in another place, where they can do what they "choose" to do, so long as they attract enough students (and vouchers) to stay in business. Inclusivity is mouthed, but it does not follow from privatization. Moreover, since success in capitalist America rests on supply-and-demand exclusivity, the *more* people who are left out of increasingly elite privatized schools, the *less* competition there is for the very people who tout the virtue of competition in the first place. The game is fixed, in other words. Those who are in privileged positions will gain the most because privatization already fits their sociocultural proclivity.

In part, the problem is the kind of community that results from specialized, for-profit private schools: restricted, isolated pockets of sameness that fit marketer's demographic data bases, parents' intentions to break into the status quo, and real estate agents' sensibilities for profit. Privatization is thus the means to achieve increased capital on all fronts, or at least on those fronts that are able to capitalize on new markets. Competing with the economic sphere, however, is the sociopolitical one that claims to be a pluralist democracy. The degree to which self-serving competition exists is the same degree to which collective emancipatory action does not. Pluralist democracy requires the latter, American capitalism the former.

Ironically, the Harvard symposium noted earlier asserted, as did Chubb and Moe, and Lieberman, that economistic individual choice necessarily results in increased possibilities for social justice and is more egalitarian than current schooling because it provides equal opportunity.[130] Similar to the assumption that privatized choice in schools means *more*, equal opportunity suffers in application. Some people, to echo Gramsci and Illich, are more equal than others.[131] When you wish upon a star, notes McLaren, it makes a difference who you are.[132] We might suggest that current schooling practice, dominated as it is by false economic imperatives, already divides students into predestined classes under the guise of choice, and results in classist reification. The tracking that goes on in contemporary school is, for example, aligned with privatization's theoretical base: homogeneous grouping by means of competition with the appearance of choice at the outset.[133] Community identities are forged in this process and are reproductive of communities of sameness (class/caste). Lost, of course, are oppositional voices or the kinds of critical questions that require justification of the unspoken consequences of privatized markets (e.g., marginalization of groups of difference, hence increased racism, homophobia, gender bias, etc).

The Harvard symposium did not address questions of this sort, due in part, perhaps, to the fact that the panel consisted only of corporate advocates. Oppositional voices simply were not there.[134] The void or amnesiatic pallor of the discussion called to mind Tyack's illustration of educational reformers waking up as "modern-day Rip Van Winkles," unaware of the arguments for privatization and current arguments for reforming educational governance. They "wake up" to find a new world order to which they contrast their ideas:

> Horace Mann discovers that many key policy makers, including the president of the United States, think that schooling should be part of an open market where parents, as consumers, choose where to send their children. What happened, asks the evangelist for the common school ideal, to the notion that public education is a common good? Do not all citizens

have a stake in the civic and moral instruction of the next generation? Has education become merely a consumer good in 1991? . . .

A school board member of a one-room school of the 1890s, one of almost a half million lay trustees of America's schools, the most numerous class of public officials in the world, awakens to find that there are fewer than one thousand one-room schools and that districts have been consolidated until there are fewer than sixteen thousand. The ranks of school trustees have been decimated. He discovers that few lament the loss of this traditional form of democratic governance. In fact, he notes that in policy talk about reforming education, people discuss roles for the nation, the states, and the individual school staff and parents—but rarely for school trustees. . .

Pierre S. duPont awakens to discover that businessmen today denounce centralization as bureaucracy gone mad and call for "restructuring" in education as in business—by which they usually mean decentralization of decision-making to the school site. Do they know nothing about the value of scientific management, economies of scale, consolidation, and coordination? . . .

A U.S. senator who fought federal aid to education for thirty years, from 1932 to 1962—because control, he believed, followed the dollar—is startled to learn that the president and all fifty governors are now advocating a national curriculum and national standards, all to be policed by national examinations. They had the gall to call this idea "A Jeffersonian Compact"—an insult to that great advocate of states' rights. Have the Russians taken over the government, in the guise of the Charlottesville 51? Does no one recall that one hundred congressmen were so bothered by federal control that they voted to name the U.S. Commissioner of Education the Commissar of Education? . . .

John Dewey, who encouraged children and teachers to create a distinctively democratic form of social learning and who believed that education had no goals beyond itself—surely no targets of achievement imposed from the top down—is alarmed. Now national leaders assume—they do not have to prove—that the central purpose of education is to make the United States economically competitive. In a Darwinian world of survival by test score, autocratic Korea becomes a country to beat and centralized Japan a nation to emulate.[135]

Part of the point of this text is to avoid waking up after the fact to find even more corporate influence than is currently evidenced in public schools. In fact, much of the point here is to argue for a repeal of corporate influence and lessening the reductionism that characterizes American schools and talk about American schools. One way to argue this point is to focus on the language used to talk about education.

A LANGUAGE OF ECONOMICS AS CULTURE: KICKING THE TIRES TO QUALIFY SCHOOLS

Mimicking complexity is one of the most revealing aspects about privatization and another is the way schools are regarded by privateers as merely a commodity. Automobiles are a recurring comparison, uniquely asserted by several privatization advocates as a correlate to schooling and school choice. Rinehart and Lee state the case this way: "While the average American would scream loud and long were some government board to tell him or her which model and color of automobile to purchase, parents willingly renounce their freedom to choose something as significant as education."[136] When discussing the problem of parents' abilities to evaluate the quality of schooling, Lieberman appears to differ with Rinehart and Lee over the reductionism inherent in their claim, but ultimately compares automobile warranties to schools. Lieberman addresses the issue this way:

> Choosing a school is more like choosing a career than like choosing a necktie. In the former, some of the most important information about the wisdom of the choice is not available until years after the choice is made. Although the same problem may arise with respect to products, it can usually be resolved by warranties. For example, in buying a car, maintenance costs are an aspect of quality but are not known when the car is purchased. Even so, buyers can factor in the cost of a warranty, so the uncertainty factor is not so critical.[137]

Lieberman is, indeed, advocating some kind of school warranty. He goes on to offer reasons why public schooling *sans* free-market choice is a problem, or perceived to be a problem, but he ultimately rejects concerns such as how diagnoses of student learning will meet the hyper-specific demands of warranty programs. Instead, he sees how school warranties could guarantee paying customers that the product they purchased will not fail during a given time frame. The problem with this perspective is that it denies humanity and pedagogy, where humanity is not static and pedagogy is not inert. Automobiles are assembled from parts and are guaranteed to run for x years or y miles, whichever comes first. They are moving compilations of inert matter, only. If the metaphor used by Lieberman and Rinehart and Lee stands, automobiles are students (product), teachers are the assemblers, and bits of information are the parts to assemble (schooling process). The larger, connected point is that consumers (parents) of the schooling process have the right to have the process warrantied.

This is the foundation of free-market ideology and it works in specific ways in terms of automobiles, but students are neither inert nor static. They continue to be regarded as such, however, as when they are subjected to "quality-control" measures such as standardized achievement tests and Goals 2000-esque expectations. Such controls, however, do not even meet the standard of the automobile. Tests for bumper strength can be conclusive, standardized testing can not. Comparing schools to automobiles is simply part of privatization-advocates' larger point: schools and schooling are reducible to markets. In this way, education is narrowed in terms of accountability (warranties), autonomy (customer choice), and achievement (competition).

"Skills" are another way to reduce schooling and at the same time reinforce the technorational, economistic point that the primary purpose of teaching and learning is future workforce preparation. This next section of the chapter argues for the deletion of the word "skills" from the English language and attempts to reveal the reductionism inherent in the terminology used to talk about schooling. Consider this section only partly "tongue-in-cheek," as the point is to highlight the degree to which corporate utilitarianism influences the ways in which we talk about schooling and the results, goals, and purposes we expect of schooling.

SKILLS, SKILLS, SKILLS: THE LANGUAGE OF CORPORATE REDUCTION

Educational arguments are replete with the term "skills." It buttresses the end of a point, as in "listening *skills*" and "cooperation *skills*," and serves as a post-detail interjection. Well-intentioned people use "skills" to further a purpose, such as literacy projects, but its continued over-appropriation by noncritical readers in education circles makes it symbolic of the economic reductionism of privatization. By using the term as part of a tautology, "skills" has become an exemplified non sequitur where its purpose is shrouded in vague assumptions.

Using the term has become a part of the language of technocrats and consumer materialists: those within society seeking to market their ideas by alluding to educational intent for ulterior, economically motivated purposes. A recent issue of *The Wall Street Journal* reported the dilemma faced by consumer materialists this way: "If children don't know math skills, they won't be able to acquire technical skills. If they don't have those skills, U.S. economic competitiveness will decline in the increasingly technological marketplace."[138]Note the technorational, linear-sequential argument. "Skills" becomes the focus in place of mathematics and is a necessary condition for marketplace success. Indeed, mathematics, in this case, becomes the vehicle by which "skill" acquisition is furthered.

Robert Carkhuff, David Berensen, and Richard Pierce titled their text *The Skills of Teaching: Interpersonal Skills.*[139] In it, they devote four major sections to "Attending Skills," "Responding Skills," "Personalizing Skills," and "Initiating Skills." Their purpose is to focus attention on what they call "content development skills" and "teaching delivery skills."[140] As though teaching and learning are relevant and substantive when reduced to a set of techniques or methods, the authors, similar to the other consumer materialists, reinforce "skill" acquisition as the purpose of schooling (in this case, training-oriented) in both elementary/secondary situations *and* teacher preparation programs in colleges and universities.

William J. Stewart's text suggests that "decision-making skills" not only can and should be taught, but that teachers can and should be taught "how to" teach them.[141] A two-fold problem exists. First, Stewart suggests that teachers should accept nonpropositional, "how to" roles that emphasize method. Second, what is transmitted (via obligatory overhead projector presentations?) is teeming with the term "skills." In this case, decision-making has "skills" leeched to it, presumably giving the phrase integrity.

The link to corporations is clear. "Companies have always depended on schools to provide their future employees not only with knowledge and *skills*, but also with attitudes and critical abilities equally important to functioning within the work force."[142] When Richard Haayen reveals the link schools have to businesses, he is using terminology illustrative of the larger point. Haayen uses "skills" in a reductionist way but he also uses "knowledge," "critical abilities," and "attitude" in the same way. They all become qualified means to a corporate end ("functioning in the workforce").

Haayen is not alone. John Nidds and James McGerald argue that corporate leaders are the best sources of information regarding what schools should be doing. They surveyed corporate leaders of Westinghouse, Gillette, Ford, Mobil, American Cyanamid, Chrysler, and Pfizer. Of the five questions they asked the business people, four had "skills" as the focus. "What academic skills should our schools teach to prepare students for the 21st century?" "What social skills should our schools teach to prepare students for the 21st century?" "What academic and social skills do you see lacking in students entering the workforce today?" "What leadership skills should we teach to prepare students for the 21st century?"[143] The questioners make three dubious assumptions: (1) "skills" are the reductionistic focus of schools; (2) teaching and learning is preparatory, in this case for the oft-cited "21st century"; and (3) corporate leaders are qualified to evaluate pedagogy.

Even the widely touted Paideia Program has bought into the notion of skill accumulation.[144] Mortimer Adler argues for a three-columned approached to reformed schooling. His second column "is devoted to developing the intellectual skills of learning. These include the language skills necessary for thought and communication—the skills of reading, writing, speaking, and listening. They also include mathematical and scientific skills; the skills of observing, measuring, estimating and calculating; and skills in the use of the computer and of other scientific instruments."[145]

What is actually meant here is that intellectualism depends, in part, on language, communication, reading, writing, listening, etcetera. Why inculcate "skills"? Aside from the merit of Adler's overall position, the use of the term "skills" betrays his own point: that intellectual competence and learning depend on clarity and accuracy.

These examples are not isolated ones. Replete with "skills" nomenclature, teachers unwittingly demonstrate their hypertensive need to gain respect as a viable part of American society by naively utilizing a technorational language to further normative purposes. It is a paradox. On one hand teachers are usually interested in a process of learning that encourages students to actively seek answers to questions and apply the developmental knowledge to their lives and experiences. On the other hand, in order to bureaucratically notate objectives "met," teachers face a technorational, corporate hierarchy that qualifies their intent and requires them to reflect a language of economics. "Skills" seeps into educational jargon as businesses continue to advocate schools meeting their needs alone.[146] Rarely interested in questions of social justice or intellectualism (which, ironically, may surpass businesses' own expectations in the marketplace), business leaders and other consumer materialists saturate teachers and the public-at-large with a language of schooling rife with "skills." Repeating, *ad nauseam,* well-worn phrases advocating "skill" acquisition for "competitiveness in the twenty-first century," we further a corporate world-order paranoia.[147]

The problem, of course, is not with those teachers who recognize the language dilemma as one of semantics and instigate their own processes in their classroom usurping the "skills" mentality in favor of the needs of their students and a critically transitive posture. Instead, the problem is situated with the increasing number of teachers who do not make the distinction between schooling as an ebbing and flowing process of engaged inquiry and schooling as a linear-sequential process for consumption of information. These nondiscriminating teachers become full-fledged consumer materialists when they accept and utilize banner phrases and trendy additions to already substantive notions. If the point is to teach reading and writing, teachers should research whole language and phonics and decide for themselves and *with* their students which avenue holds the most potential in their classroom context. The point is reading, not reading "skills." Teachers must go beyond the glib acceptance of *a priori* notions of reality and begin to develop themselves as transformative intellectuals in their classrooms. Linking student experiences with their experiences and a curriculum that is investigative of society, not immediately accepting, would indicate the kind of critical transitivity for which this work ultimately argues. In part this means teachers assuming roles that critically review and question seriously any notion decorated with "skills." In short, something akin to transformative intellectualism means teachers realizing their potential to become scholars in the classroom and takes as its starting point a view of schooling as emancipatory. The first step toward emancipation is to rid education of the pervasive "skills" lingo.

The point may seem exaggerated, but the frequency of use and pervasiveness of the term "skills" is indicative of the reductionism of privatization advocates. Note the brief compilation of some of the generic terms exploited by consumer materialists: Basic skills,[148] Communication skills,[149] Language acquisition skills,[150] Study skills,[151] Teaching skills,[152] Math skills,[153] Thinking skills and critical thinking skills,[154] Job skills and technical/non-technical skills,[155] Life skills,[156] Writing skills,[157] Play skills,[158] Social skills,[159] Problem-solving skills,[160] Decision-making skills.[161]

While overuse is an understatement, the result of the overuse of "skills" is, at best, the generation of platitudes and, at worst, the destruction of intellectual clarity. "Skills" as a concept, has died a prolonged and painful death and it's time for the funeral. Sadly, there may not be enough pallbearers to inter the dearly departed term as consumer materialists continue to practice a form of linguistic necrophagia. In other words, marketwise privateers feed off the term "skills": parents believe the success of their child is contingent on learning "skills" in a linear-sequential fashion; textbook publishers have a broader understanding of exploitive marketing and continue to flood the field of education with volumes of "skills" and "skills"-related texts.

The point, of course, is to recognize the extent to which people allude to the term "skills" in an attempt to add credibility to their proposals by sticking it at the end of their suggestions. In the process, paradoxically, they achieve the opposite. By sloganeering "reading skills" to market literacy textbooks, vague assumptions may be reinforced, but meaning and substance are lost. Significance is gone. Depth is impossible. In their places emerges a crabgrass of the mind. Plentiful but annoying, "skills" has been seeded in the vocabulary of noncritical citizens and, particularly, noncritical teachers.

Much of the difficulty rests with the assumptions inherent in "skills" phrases. As though everyone is supposed to know the reference, "skills" signals a type of ubiquitous nod of nebulous approval. It is similar to regional and national teacher conferences when one person banters about "higher-order thinking skills" and five hundred listeners begin bobbing their heads in unison. Five hundred assumptions become fixed and accepted. The problem, of course, is that within the group of five hundred, no two assumptions are exactly alike. But why assume in the first place? What is it about the security attached to the term "skills" that has made its usage so pervasive? What purpose is being served by promoting "skills"?

Perhaps a technorationale is at work that encourages the torrent of "skills" phrases. Technorationality, recall,

> reveal[s] lawlike propositions about certain curriculum design, implementation, and evaluation that can either be factually proven or disproven. Theory is thus reduced to an empirical explanatory framework for social engineering. From [a] critical perspective, theory appears incapable of stepping outside of its empirical straight jacket in order to raise questions about the nature of truth, the difference between appearance and reality, or the distinction between knowledge and mere opinion. Most importantly, theory in the dominant curriculum paradigm appears unable to provide a rational basis for criticizing the "facts" of a given society.[162]

There is a literal capitalization of the term. The purpose exists for the generation of revenue and teachers hegemonically *re*produce corporate cultural capital. Furthermore, those *semi*transitive teachers who realize the problem but refuse to act—because the political climate is intolerable or because they see the problem as a "given," impervious to change—are at fault. Fault? Perhaps fault is too strong, but the point is to focus on teacher rights and responsibilities and not deflect obligations elsewhere. Only when teachers emerge as the powerful enclave they *can be* will "skills" reductionism and consumer materialism be widely and influentially reconsidered. To comply with the promotion of "skills" terminology leads to student acceptance of a vision of schooling that subordinates them to a linear-sequential, programmed set of consumer-materialist "skills" assumptions.

There are two further points here: (1) by not actively renouncing and rejecting "skills" gibberish, consumer-materialist teachers stigmatize learning as a set of pre-formed skills-acquisition tests; and (2) students come to view school as an inert place where their experiences, questions, and knowledge are made ancillary to objectives lists fraught with "skills" outcomes. In the larger picture, the United States is jeopardizing its future as a democracy: not because "skills" are not being "learned," but because merely accumulating "skills" hinders clear understandings of what schooling and democracy are about—namely, inquiry and participation (a.k.a. "citizenship skills"?). Indeed, this line of reasoning is imbued with a distinct vocabulary normally seen in annual market reports of major businesses.

A language of economics is utilized to advance the idea that schools should supply businesses with qualified workers. Aligned with conservatives and reductionists, the promotion of economics is masked by a vocabulary of culture. Included in this vocabulary are phrases such as "choice," "free markets," "core curricula," "accountability," "cultural literacy," and "competency testing."[163] Such ideas are seeded in popular vocabulary by those who believe that the success of the American culture is based mainly on the United States' ability to be a competitive leader in the world economic marketplace. The California Business Roundtable, for example, joined others to lobby lawmakers in their state resulting in a major education bill, SB-813, calling for reform.[164] Their generalized recommendations are representative of the language of economics with which this essay is concerned. The Roundtable of Chief Executive Officers called for, among other things, the adoption of the following aims for education; "establishing *accountability* based on *performance* and *choice*, upgrading instruction, and *capitalizing* on diversity."[165]

Chubb and Moe demonstrate the confusion between culture and economics when they use democratic individuality as a mask for "choice" and "competition" in the public-school arena.[166] As though democracy is capitalism, language confuses sensibilities. After appealing to populist zeal about the cultural hues of "choice," the shift is quickly made to capitalist materialism. The culture(s) of school becomes trivialized in brochures touting test scores and "organizational effectiveness" in order to lure more and more parents into demonstrating their right to "choose" a privatized school. Hegemony is the result: large numbers of citizens consciously demonstrate and champion a language of economics as culture. What makes such a demonstration hegemonic is not only the consciousness of those involved, but the effects of reducing culture to simplified "effectiveness" schemes. Purchasing a phonics "package" via television commercials characterizes the larger point. "Owning" and "having" the package equates to cultural acceleration and success. "Having" more—recall Maxine Greene—is equated with "being" more.

THE END OF INTENTIONAL PUBLIC DOMAINS?

The ultimate point, of course, is to consider the role and purpose of public school in America. What we have seen, however, is where school-business partnerships are the beginning of the end of public schooling, privatization *is* the end. School-business partnerships reduce the idea of community to markets and materialism; for-profit and free market privatization plans institutionalize the reduction. They do so by appealing to rugged-individualist fears about cooperation and collective action and, instead, focus on capitalist expectations for competition and selfishness. As a result, privatization uses market logic to coopt difference, pluralism, and liberal (that is, broad and critical) study. By touting "choices" (as in tracks, vouchers, for-profit specialized schools, etc.) privateers *appear* in favor of difference and pluralism, but the "choices" available are only available as long as they are profitable. If school *X* is a for-profit school, for example, programs in the arts must shift their emphasis away from the study of the arts and toward the marketing of the program to yield profit. School bands and orchestras must literally pay for their existence. This is consistent with free-market entrepreneurship, but it also means that the musical selections students study and perform must be "sellable." The result is that bands and orchestras face restricted repertoires and limited knowledge because of "bottom-line" expectations.

Importantly, arguments against privatization do not, *de facto*, represent tacit acceptance of current schooling practice. In other words, arguing against privatization is not a defense of the current bureaucracy of schools. Instead, arguments against privatization reveal that contemporary American public schools *already* embody much of the ideology of privatization (ironically, perhaps, not by choice). That is, the tilt of contemporary American public schools toward comparable test scores, competition models for international economic production races, and classist hierarchies of tracking *already* mimic the assumptions of for-profit and free-market privatization plans. To intentionally take schools further toward private enterprise is to reinforce the flawed assumption that the primary purpose of schooling in the United States is for individual competitiveness, vocationalism, and consumer materialism.

Herein recurs the twisted irony: because current schools *already* promote consumer materialism, "going back" to nonprivatized schools means going very far back indeed to see anything akin to a democratic vision for U.S. schools. The point is not to appeal to a past that was better, for if we were somehow magically transported "back" to the times during which schools were seen in terms of democracy and citizenship, we would find ourselves in a classist, sexist, and racist society worse in many ways than the classism, sexism, and racism we currently face. The point is to define a vision of public schools as education-oriented, pluralistic sites that provide authentic opportunities for participating in the betterment of the life of those who live in schools as well as the ultimate change of schooling and society.

Such a vision is very different from privatization plans that are training-oriented, tracked sites that offer excellent opportunities for some at the expense of others. Most current schools are already close to the privatization vision, as demonstrated in their stratified, deterministic, and reductionistic approaches to teaching and learning. Recall, also, that this situation is not the fault of teachers or students. Their roles are defined by consumer-materialist expectations held up for them by policymakers, parents, and corporations. What must be crafted, then, is a very different vision of schools as democratic public spheres where critical transitivity is the broad goal and student experiences are central to learning. A different purpose, therefore, also means different roles for teachers and students. Chapter 5 attempts to clarify what these different roles require and how they might come about.

NOTES

1. James R. Rinehart and Jackson F. Lee, Jr., *American Education and the Dynamics of Choice* (New York: Praeger, 1991), 4.

2. Kathleen P. Bennett and Margaret D. LeCompte, *How Schools Work: A Sociological Analysis of Education* (New York: Longman, 1990), 15.

3. Richard Brosio, *A Radical Democratic Critique of Capitalist Education* (New York: Peter Land, 1994), 266.

4. Svi Shapiro, *Between Capitalism and Democracy: Educational Policy and the Crisis of the Welfare State* (New York: Bergin & Garvey, 1990), 75.

5. Brosio, 264.

6. Ibid., (Italics added.)

7. Michael W. Apple, *Teachers and Texts: A Political Economy of Class and Gender Relations in Education* (New York: Routledge, 1986), 25-26.

8. Ibid., 266-267.

9. See Bennett and LeCompte, op. cit.

10. See Henry Giroux, *Ideology, Culture and the Process of Schooling* (Philadelphia: Temple University Press, 1981); Michael W. Apple, *Education and Power* (Boston: Routledge & Keegan Paul, 1982); and Martin Carnoy and Henry M. Levin, *Schooling and Work in the Democratic State* (Stanford, CA: Stanford University Press, 1985).

11. Alex Molnar, *Giving Kids the Business: The Commercialization of America's Schools* (Boulder, CO: Westview Press, 1996), 80.

12. Charles J. Russo, Rosetta F. Sandidge, Robert Shapiro, and J. John Harris, III, "Legal Issues in Contracting Out for Public Education Services," *Education and Urban Society* 27, no.2 (February 1995): 127-135.

13. See Frank Brown and A.R. Contreaus, "Deregulation and Privatization of Education: A Flawed Concept," *Education and Urban Society* 23 (1991): 144-158.

14. George F. Garcia and Mary Garcia, "Charter Schools—Another Top-Down Innovation," *Educational Researcher* 25, no.8 (November 1996), 34.

15. Ibid. (Italics added.) Garcia and Garcia continue: "In essence that is what Smith and Meier (1995) found when they studied private school enrollments in Florida during the 1980s. Private schools were picked by customers not because of the poor quality of the public school but because of religious preference or because public school enrollments were growing in minority students. Racial and religious segregation were the primary motivators for private school choice rather than competition for a quality education" (24). Note, even here, the consumer language that has parents as customers. See also, K.B. Smith and K. Meier, "School Choice—Panacea or Pandora's Box?" *Phi Delta Kappan* 77, no. 4 (December 1995): 312-316.

16. Russo et al., 128.

17. Ibid., 129. Russo et. al., cite the National Governor's Association, *Strategic Investment: Tough Choices for America's Future* (Washington DC: National Governor's Association, 1993); Minnesota Statutes, § 120.064 (1994); California Education Code, §§ 47600-47615 (1994); and L. Olson, "Varied Laws Raise a Question: What is a Charter School?" *Education Week* (19 January 1994), 14.

18. K. McGree, *Charter Schools: Early Learnings. Insights . . . on Educational Policy and Practices. No. 5 Policy Brief* (Austin, TX: Southwest Educational Development and Laboratory, 1995).

19. See Peter F. Drucker, *The New Society: The Anatomy of Industrial Order* (New York: Harper & Row, 1962).

20. Charles Russo et al., " Legal Issues in Contracting Out for Public Education Services," *Education and Urban Society* 27, no. 2 (February 1995): 127.

21. See Alex Molnar, "Education for Profit: A Yellow Brick Road to Nowhere," *Educational Leadership* 52, no.1 (1994): 66-71; C. Devarics, "Weighing the Contract Option," *American School Board Journal* (September 1993): 42-44; P. Schmidt, "Fairfax to Probe Troubled Bus-Privatization Experiment," *Education Week* (15 June 1994); and G. Miller, "Maintenance and Custodial Services: Getting the Most for the Money," *School Business Affairs* 59, no. 7 (1993).

22. John E. Chubb and Terry M. Moe, *Politics, Markets, and America's Schools* (Washington, DC: The Brookings Institution, 1990).

23. Russo et. al.; See also, Paul T. Hill, *Reinventing Public Education* (Santa Monica, CA: Rand/Institute on Education and Training, 1995).

24. Chubb and Moe, op. cit.; and Myron Lieberman, *Privatization and Educational Choice* (New York: St. Martin's Press, 1989).

25. Calvin A. Kent, "Privatization of Public Functions: Promises and Problems," in *Entrepreneurship and the Privatizing of Government*, Calvin A. Kent, ed. (New York: St. Martin's Press, 1989).

26. See T. Kolderie, "Two Different Concepts of Privatization," *Public Policy Review* (July/August 1986)" 286-290.

27. Richard C. Hunter, "Private Procurement in the Public Sector and in Education," *Education and Urban Society* 27, no. 2 (February 1995):138.

28. Peter Cookson, Jr. and Barbara Schneider, "Why School Choice? A Question of Values," in *Transforming Schools*, Cookson and Schneider, eds. (New York: Garland Publishing, 1995), 560.

29. See for example, David W. Kirkpatrick, *School Choice in Schooling: A Case for Tuition Vouchers* (Chicago: Loyola University Press, 1990); Myron Lieberman, *Privatization and Educational Choice* (New York: St. Martin's Press, 1989); and Simon Hakim, Paul Seidenstat, and Gary Bowman, eds., *Privatizing Education and Educational Choice: Concepts, Plans, and Experiences* (Westport, CT: Praeger, 1994).

30. G. Kaplan, "Scapegoating the Schools," *Voices from the Field: 30 Expert Opinions on America 2000, the Bush Administration Strategy to "Reinvent" America's Schools* (Washington, DC: Commission on Work, Family and Citizenship, William T. Grant Foundation, 1991).

31. See Sheldon Richman, *Separating School and State: How to Liberate America's Families* (Fairfax, VA: The Future of Freedom Foundation).

32. Terry Moe, ed., *Private Vouchers* (Stanford, CA: Hoover Institution Press, 1995); and Chubb and Moe, op. cit.

33. See John Taylor Gatto, *Dumbing Us Down: The Hidden Curriculum of Compulsory Schooling* (Philadelphia: New Society Publishers, 1992); and Daniel McGroarty, *Break These Chains: The Battle for School Choice* (Rocklin, CA: Prima Publishing, 1996).

34. See, for example, Edward S. Herman, *Triumph of the Market: Essays on Economics, Politics, and the Media* (Boston, South End Press, 1995); Alex Molnar, "The Emperor Has No Clothes," in *Social Issues and Education: Challenge and Responsibility*, Alex Molnar, ed. (Alexandria, VA: Association for Supervision and Curriculum Development, 1987); Stanley Aronowitz and Henry A. Giroux, *Education Still under Siege* (Westport, CT: Bergin & Garvey, 1993); and Alex Molnar, *Giving Kids the Business: The Commercialization of America's Schools* (Boulder, CO: Westview Press, 1996). Molnar gives a scathingly accurate and detailed analysis of the flaws of corporate influences on schools.

35. Jerry Ellsworth, "Keep Schools Open to All," *Newsweek* (16 March 1992): 16.

36. Ibid., Ellsworth offers a not-so-tongue-in-cheek illustration of the potential dangers of choice, opening that racial discrimination would be unavoidable.

37. See Nel Noddings, *Philosophy of Education* (Boulder, CO: Westview Press, 1995), 160-178.

38. David W. Kirkpatrick, *Choice in Schooling: A Case for Tuition Vouchers* (Chicago: Loyola University Press, 1990), 17-21. It is perhaps ironic that Calvinism represented pluralism at the time of its rise as well as control over those who subscribe(d) to it. The irony is the Protestant argument for "freedom" of religion but dominant control regarding compulsory schooling. Pluralism and freedom on one hand, strict control and authority on the other.

39. See Nathaniel B. Shurtleff, ed., *Records of the Governor and Company of Massachusetts Bay in New England* (Boston: William White, 1853), II, 6-7, 203. It is ironic that many of the current arguments for reducing compulsory schooling come from the same conservative circles that take little umbrage at requiring biblical reading akin to the 1647 colony law. See Wayne Urban and Jennings Wagoner, Jr., *American Education: A History* (New York: McGraw-Hill, 1996), 69-92.

40. The reference here is to Revolutionary ideas of general education. Jefferson, Webster, Rush, etc., were all leaders in advocating a version of education that emphasized citizenship through the "general diffusion of knowledge." Given this reference, however, it should be clear that the ideas espoused by Jefferson, Webster, and Rush were inconsistent. On one hand they argued for democratic citizenship, on the other hand their plans were hierarchical and classist. See, Urban and Wagoner, op. cit., 42-43.

41. Given the strong individualism of the South, perhaps best represented by the Agrarians in *I'll Take My Stand*, southern states were the last to enact compulsory education laws: Louisiana in 1910; Alabama, Florida, and South Carolina in 1915; Georgia in 1916; and as noted in the text, Mississippi in 1918. See Edward A. Krug, *Salient Dates in American Education, 1635–1964* (New York: Harper & Row, 1966), 77-79. Krug notes that South Carolina, Mississippi, and Virginia ultimately repealed compulsory attendance laws in 1955, 1956, and 1959, respectively.

42. See for example, Richard Ebeling's Introduction to Sheldon Richman, *Separating School and State: How to Liberate America's Families* (Fairfax, VA: The Future of Freedom Foundation, 1995), xviii-xix. For an analysis of choice programs in the UK, see Geoff Whitty, Tony Edwards, and Sharon Gewirtz, *Specialisation and Choice in Urban Education: The City Technology College Experiment* (London: Routledge, 1993) and Geoff Whitty, "The 'Privatization of Education," *Educational Leadership* (April 1984): 51-53.

43. David Tyack, "School Governance in the United States: Historical Puzzles and Anomalies," in *Decentralization and School Improvement: Can We Fulfill the Promise?*, Jane Hannaway and Martin Carnoy, eds. (San Francisco: Jossey-Bass, 1993), 9.

44. Ibid.

45. R.J. Lytle, *Liberty Schools* (Farmington, MI: Structures Publishing, 1975), 17.

46. Stephen Arons, *Compelling Belief* (New York: McGraw-Hill, 1983).

47. Ebeling, xiv-xv.

48. See Henry A. Giroux, "Pedagogy and Radical Democracy in the Age of 'Political Correctness,'" in *Radical Democracy: Identity, Citizenship, and the State*, David Trend, ed., (New York: Routledge, 1996), 179-193.

49. Jacob G. Hornberger, Preface to Sheldon Richman, op. cit.

50. David W. Kirkpatrick, *Choice in Schooling: A Case for Tuition Vouchers* (Chicago: Loyola University Press, 1990), 30.

51. See *Pierce v. Society of Sisters of the Holy Name of Jesus and Mary/Pierce v. Hill Military Academy*, 268 U.S. 510 (1925); *Wisconsin v. Yoder*, 406 U.S. 205 (1972); Urban and Wagoner, op. cit., 218-220; and Arval A. Morris, *The Constitution and American Education* (New York: West Publishing, 1979), 75-146.

52. Recall the Gablers of Texas from chapter 1. They, according to Joel Spring, were central figures in getting the Texas legislature to pass the law stating that "Textbooks shall not contain material which serves to undermine authority." See Spring, *American Education* (New York: McGraw-Hill, 1994), 254. Spring notes that "Gabler and his wife are always vigilant for any sign of anti-Americanism, attacks on free-enterprise economics, and suggestions that federal controls might be needed to protect the environment" (254).

53. See David Lugan, "A Theological Argument against Theopolitics," *Philosophy and Public Policy* 16, no.1 (Winter 1996): 10-15.

54. Jerry Ellsworth, "Keep Schools Open to All," *Newsweek* (6 March 1992): 16.

55. Ibid.

56. Ibid. All other quotes in this section are Ellsworth's.

57. See Richard Brosio, "One Marx, and the Centrality of the Historical Actor(s)," *Educational Theory* 35, no. 1 (Winter 1985): 73-83; H. Svi Shapiro, "Capitalism at Risk: The Political Economy of the Educational Reports of 1983," *Educational Theory* 35, no. 1 (Winter 1985): 57-72; and Samuel Bowles and Herbert Gintis, *Democracy and Capitalism* (New York: Basic Books, 1986).

58. While the extremist position worries about professional teachers contaminating the minds of the young with suggestions, arguments, or information that critique their deeply held assumptions, corporate arguments for privatization give the appearance that teacher responsibility and autonomy are valuable. Further, John Chubb and Terry Moe go as far as to suggest their version of privatization means more teacher power. See Chubb and Moe, *Politics, Markets, and America's Schools* (Washington, DC: The Brooking Institution, 1990), 49-53; 202-205.

59. Terrence O'Conner, "Dewey Day: Prognosticating Philosophy of Education's Spring," paper presented at the annual meeting of the Ohio Valley Philosophy of Education Society, October 26, 1996, Cincinnati, OH; John Holt, *How Children Fail* (Surrey: The Gresham Press, 1970); John Dewey, *The Child and the Curriculum* (Chicago: The University of Chicago Press, 1902); and George Wood,

Schools That Work: America's Most Innovative Public Education Programs (New York: Plume, 1993).

60. Chubb and Moe, op. cit.

61. Ibid.; Myron Lieberman, *Public Education: An Autopsy* (Cambridge, MA: Harvard University Press, 1993); James R. Rinehart and Jackson F. Lee, Jr., *American Education and the Dynamics of Choice* (New York: Praeger, 1991).

62. See Chubb and Moe, op. cit., 49-53; 202-205.

63. See Pierre S. duPont, IV, "A 'GI' Bill for Educating All Children," in *Privatizing Education and Educational Choice: Concepts, Plans, and Experiences*, Simon Hakim, Paul Seidenstat, and Gary W. Bowman, eds. (Westport, CT: Praeger, 1994), 121-135.

64. Robert Almeder, *Blind Realism: An Essay on Human Knowledge and Natural Science* (Lanham, MD: Rowman & Littlefield Publishers, 1992).

65. See, for example, Lieberman, *Privatization and Educational Choice*, op. cit.; Terry Moe, ed., *Private Vouchers* (Stanford, CA: The Hoover Institute, 1995); and Paul Hill, *Reinventing Public Education* (Santa Monica, CA: Rand Corporation, 1995).

66. Carol Ascher, "Performance Contracting: A Forgotten Experiment in School Privatization," *Phi Delta Kappan* (May 1996), 615-616.

67. Ibid., 616.

68. Ibid.

69. Ibid. See also, Polly Carpenter, A.W. Chalfant, and George R. Hall, *Case Studies in Educational Performance Contracting: Texarkana, Arkansas; Liberty-Elylau, Texas* (Santa Monica, CA: Rand Corporation, 1971); R.F. Campbell and J.E. Lorion, *Performance Contracting in School Systems* (Columbus, OH: Charles Merrill, 1972); and George R. Hall, et. al., *The Evolution of Educational Performance Contracting in Five School Districts, 1971-1972* (Santa Monica, CA: Rand Corporation, 1972).

70. Ascher, 616. She goes on to note: "The discouragement, even disgust, of students who had worked all year to improve their performance became evident when many failed to pick up their radios and the prize television lay unclaimed."

71. Witness Sylvan Learning Centers, Eduventures, Inc., Huntington Learning Centers, and the technorationale of prescriptive standardization. Additionally, we should be aware and wary of reinforcing positivism in critiques of this kind. Specifically, when Dorsett failed, it was because they tried to "harden" the "soft" service of teaching. Pointing out increased dropout rates and low percentages of "grade level" achievement risks representing teaching only in terms of successful outcomes of this kind.

72. Alex Molnar writes: "The earliest voucher plans in the United States were in the South. In 1956, the Virginia legislature passed a 'tuition-grant' program and in 1960 a 'scholarship' plan that provided students with tax dollars they could use to pay the tuition at any qualified nonsectarian school in their district. The express purpose of the Virginia laws (and other 'freedom of choice' plans like them passed by southern legislatures) was to help maintain segregated school systems in the wake of the 1954 U.S. Supreme Court's *Brown v. Board of Education* decision." Alex

Molnar, *Giving Kids the Business: The Commercialization of America's Schools* (Boulder, CO: Westview Press, 1996), 118. See also, Jeffrey R. Henig, *Rethinking School Choice: Limits of Marked Metaphor* (Princeton: Princeton University Press, 1993).

73. Daniel Weiler, *A Public School Voucher Demonstration: The First Year at Alum Rock, Summary and Conclusions* (Santa Monica, CA: Rand Corporation, 1974), v.

74. Eliot Levinson, "The Alum Rock Voucher Demonstration : Three Years of Implementation," paper presented to the American Educational Research Association, San Francisco, CA, 19 April 1976, 7.

75. Weiler, v.

76. Levinson, 1.

77. Weiler, op. cit.; Evaluation concerns also plagued the program. Student achievement scores were supposed to improve, but this point was the object of much debate. See Paul M. Wortman, Charles S. Reichardt, and Robert G. St. Pierre, " The First Year of the Education Voucher Demonstration: A Secondary Analysis of Student Achievement Text Scores," *Evaluation Quarterly* 2, no. 2 (May 1978): 193-214.

78. As directly relates to Alum Rock, see James A. Mecklenburger and Richard W. Hostrop, *Education Vouchers: From Theory to Alum Rock* (Honewood, IL: ETC Publications, 1972).

79. See Mary Erina Driscoll. "Thinking Like a Fish: The Implications of the Image of School Community for Connections Between Parents and Schools," in *Transforming Schools* Peter W. Cookson, Jr., and Barbara Schneider, eds. (New York: Garland Publishing, 1995), 209-236.

80. See John Menge, "The Evaluation of the New Hampshire Plan: An Early Voucher System," *Privatizing Education and Educational Choice: Concepts, Plans, and Experiences*, Simon Hakim, Paul Seidenstat, and Gary W. Bowman, eds. (Westport, CT: Praeger, 1994).

81. Ibid., 166.

82. Ibid.

83. Ibid., 167.

84. Ibid.

85. Ibid., 168-169; see also, New Hampshire State Board of Education, "New Hampshire Educational Voucher Project: Revised Feasibility Study," 14 November 1974.

86. Menge, 171.

87. Valerie Martinez, Kenneth Godwin, and Frank R. Kemerer, "Private Vouchers in San Antonio: The CEO Program," in Terry M. Moe, ed., *Private Vouchers* (Stanford, CA: Hoover Institution Press, 1995), 74.

88. Ibid.

89. Menge, 171.

90. Ibid.

91. Ibid., 75.

92. Ibid., 76.

93. See Patricia Farnan, " A Choice for Etta Wallace: The Private Voucher Revolution in Urban Schools," *Policy Review* no. 64 (Spring 1993): 24-27.

94. Michael Heise, Kenneth D. Colburn, Jr., and Joseph F. Lamberti, "Private Vouchers in Indianapolis: The Golden Rule Program," in Terry M. Moe, ed., *Private Vouchers,* op. cit., 100.

95. Ibid., 101.

96. See Thomas Hetland, "The Milwaukee Choice Program," in *Privatizing Education and Educational Choice: Concepts, Plans, and Experiences* Simon Hakim, Paul Seidenstat, and Gary W. Bowman, eds. (Westport, CT: Praeger, 1994), 183-193.

97. Alex Molnar, Walter C. Farrell, Jr., James H. Johnson, Jr., and Marty Sapp, "Research, Politics, and the School Choice Agenda," *Phi Delta Kappan* (November 1996), 242. The authors also cite Annette (Polly) Williams, et al., "Manifesto for New Directions in the Education of Black Children in the City of Milwaukee," paper distributed by the office of State Representative Annette (Polly) Williams, October 1987; Derrick Bell, "The Case for a Separate Black School System," *Urban League Review* 11, nos. 1 & 2 (1987-88): 136-146.; and A. Polly Williams, "Education Is Not Just for the Privileged Few," *Education Week* (7 February 1996): 33-35. See also, Gary R. George and Walter C. Farrell, Jr., "School Choice and African American Students: A Legislative View," *Journal of Negro Education* 59, no. 4 (1990): 521-525.

98. Molnar, *Giving Kids the Business,* 122.

99. Ibid.

100. John F. Witte and Christopher Thorn, "Who Chooses? Voucher and Interdistrict Choice Programs in Milwaukee," *American Journal of Education* 104 (May 1996), 190.

101. Molnar, *Giving Kids the Business,* 122.

102. See Jay P. Greene, Paul E. Peterson, and Jiangtao Du, "The Effectiveness of School Choice in Milwaukee: A Secondary Analysis of Data from the Program's Evaluation," paper prepared for presentation before the Panel on the Political Analysis of Urban School systems at the annual meeting of the American Political Science Association, San Francisco, August-September, 1996.

103. Molnar, Farrell, Johnson, and Sapp, 241.

104. *Ibid.* Molnar, Farrell, Johnson, and Sapp also cite "Newshour with Jim Lehrer," WMVS-TV, Channel 19, Milwaukee, 22 August 1996; See also, Jay P. Greene and Paul E. Peterson, "School Choice Date Rescued from Bad Science," *Wall Street Journal* (14 August 1996): A14.

105. Molnar, *Giving Kids the Business,* 123. Molnar cites the following: Letter from Timothy Sheehy, president of the Metropolitan Milwaukee Association of Commerce, to all members of the Wisconsin legislature, January 28, 1995. Molnar also adds: "It is impossible to know what Sheehy meant when he said Milwaukee's choice program was 'working.' What does seem clear is that there was a high level of coordination among conservative supporters of vouchers and the MMAC. In fact, Sheehy's letter to the legislators was sent at least four days before the Peterson critique was officially released" (123). See Paul E. Peterson, *A Critique of the Witte*

Evaluation of Milwaukee's School Choice Program, Occasional Paper 95-2 (Cambridge, MA: Harvard University Center for American Political Studies, 1995).

106. Molnar, Farrell, Johnson, and Sapp, op. cit., 243.

107. Molnar, *Giving Kids the Business*, 86. See also, *Whittle Schools and Laboratories* (Knoxville, TN: Whittle Communications, May 16, 1991), 8.

108. Tom McNichol, "Chris Whittle's Big Test," *USA Weekend* (18-20 September 1992).

109. Molnar, *Giving Kids the Business*, 94.

110. Ibid., 95. Molnar also cites David I. Rubin, "Whittle School is Questionable Investment," *Boston Sunday Globe*, 2 April 1995.

111. Ibid.

112. Molnar notes, "By the time Edison had found enough cash to open a handful of schools, Whittle had lost his communications empire. And in a development heavy with irony, given the rhetoric of privatization, even his former headquarters building in Knoxville, Tennessee, had been sold—to the federal government. The building, a noncolonial edifice he spent $55 million constructing in 1991, was purchased by the U.S. General Services Administration. The selling price was $20.4 million, out of which Whittle had to pay the city of Knoxville $7.1 million to pay off bonds issued by the city to help finance the building originally. This was hardly an illustration of the kind of performance that was likely to save many schools." (94). Molnar also cited, "Whittle Building To Be U.S. Courthouse," *(Memphis) Commercial Appeal*, 12 January 1995.

113. Alex Molnar, *Giving Kids the Business: The Commercialization of America's Schools* (Boulder, CO: Westview Press, 1996), 96-115.

114. Ibid., 96. Molnar also cites Joe Rigert and Carol Command, "Education Firm Oversells Its Record," (Minneapolis) *Star Tribune*, 4 June 1994.

115. Patricia Parhan and Thomas Peeler, "A New School of Thought in Public/Private Partnering," *The School Administrator* 49, no. 7 (August 1992), 16.

116. "Dade County Says Good-bye to EAI," *The American School Board Journal* 182, no. 7 (July 1995), 46.

117. Molnar, *Giving Kids the Business*, 99. Molnar again cites Joe Rigart and Carol Command, "Education Firm Oversells Its Record," (Minneapolis) *Star Tribune*, 4 June 1994.

118. Richard C. Hunter, "Privatization of Instruction in Public Education," *Education and Urban Society* 27, no. 2 (February 1995), 180.

119. G. Putka, "Fast Learner: Do For-Profit Schools Work? They Seem To for One Entrepreneur," *Wall Street Journal* (1995), 1.

120. Peter Schmidt, "E.A.I. Fiscal Health at Issue in Suit by 2 Stockholders," *Education Week*, 9 March 1994, 6; cited in Molnar, *Giving Kids the Business*, 99.

121. Ibid., 100.

122. Ibid. Molnar also cites news items from the (Minneapolis) *Star Tribune* for October 10, 1993 and November 22, 1993, respectively.

123. *The Private Management of Public Schools: An Analysis of the EAI Experience in Baltimore* (Washington, DC: The American Federation of Teachers, 1994).

124. Ibid., i.

125. Ibid., i-ii.

126. John T. Golle, "You Must Take Care of Your Customers," *Education Week*, 22 June 1994, 44-45. Note how Golle reduces teachers, students, and parents to mere customers.

127. Alex Molnar, quoted in "Whittle, Molnar to Spar on Privatization," *Connections: The National Conference on Education* (Arlington, VA: American Association of School Administrators, July 1994), 1.

128. Programs in the arts are under constant attack in current public schools as well. For privatization advocates, however, the continuation of such programs is only due to "vested interests" (that is, teacher unions, central-office personnel) that bureaucratize schooling. Privatization advocates, however, offer a solution: develop a school for the arts and attract paying students, much like arts magnet schools do, in order to stay in business. If such a reality comes to pass, it means eliminating music classes in schools that see their "business" as providing only x, y, or z specialization (engineering, business, science magnets, etc.). It is in this way that *more* is actually *less*.

129. Witness the recategorization of special-education students in the EAI/Baltimore experiment.

130. See Chubb and Moe, *Politics, Markets, and America's Schools*, 30-68; and Lieberman, *Privatization and Educational Choice*, 118-151.

131. See Ivan Illich, *Deschooling Society* (New York: Harper & Row, 1971); and Antonio Gramsci, *Prison Notebooks* (New York: International Publishers, 1971).

132. McLaren, *Life in Schools*, op. cit., 158.

133. For an extensive treatment of tracking, see Jeannie Oaks, *Keeping Track: How Schools Structure Inequality* (New Haven: Yale University Press, 1985).

134. Except when Howard Gardner, author of *Frames of Mind*, was critical of the "entrepreneurial and capitalistic flavor of the panel." On the related point of multiple intelligence and how narrow choice programs (via magnet schools, specialized charter schools, etc.) might dismiss difference, see Howard Gardner, *Frames of Mind: The Theory of Multiple Intelligences* (New York: Basic Books, 1993).

135. David Tyack, "School Governance in the United States: Historical Puzzles and Anomalies," in *Decentralization and School Improvement: Can We Fulfill the Promise?* Jane Hannaway and Martin Carnoy, eds. (San Francisco: Jossey-Bass, 1993), 21-23.

136. Rinehart and Lee, op. cit.

137. Lieberman, *Privatization and Educational Choice*, 134.

138. David Stipp, "Reinventing Math," *The Wall Street Journal*, 11 September 1992, B4.

139. Robert R. Carkhuff, David H. Berensen, and Richard M. Pierce, *The Skills of Teaching: Interpersonal Skills* (Amherst, MA: Human Resource Development Press, 1977).

140. *Ibid.*, ii.

141. See William J. Stewart, *How to Teach Decision-Making Skills to Elementary and Secondary School Students* (Springfield, IL: Charles C. Thomas, 1988).

142. Richard J. Haayen, "Preamble," *Labor Force 2000: Corporate America Responds* (New York: Allstate Forum on Public Issues, 1989), 1.

143. John A. Nidds and James McGerald, "Corporate America Looks at Public Education," *Principal* (March 1995), 22-23.

144. Mortimer Adler, "The Paideia Proposal: Rediscovering the Essence of Education," *The American School Board Journal*, (July 1982).

145. Ibid.

146. See Lauren H. Vicary, *An Annotated Bibliography of Research on Basic Skills in the Workforce and Related Issues* (Washington, DC: The Southport Issues of Policy Analysis, 1990).

147. See, for example, The Secretary's Commission on Achieving Necessary Skills, *What Work Requires of School: A SCANS Report for America 2000* (Washington, DC: U.S. Department of Labor, 1991) and William J. Bennett, *What Works: Research about Teaching and Learning* (Washington, DC: U.S. Department of Education, 1987). Educators pander to this lead by producing textbooks of support. See, for example, Joyce S. Choate et al., *Assessing and Programming Basic Curriculum Skills* (Boston: Allyn and Bacon, 1987), 3.

148. See Robert E. MacDonald, *A Handbook of Basic Skills and Strategies for Beginning Teachers: Facing the Challenge of Teaching in Today's Schools* (New York: Longman, 1991); most recent of 78 books listed.

149. See Marilyn Penovich Friend, *Interactions: Collaboration Skills for School Professionals* (New York: Longman, 1992); most recent of 101 books listed.

150. See Paul S. Anderson, *Language Skills in Elementary Education* (New York: Macmillan, 1988); one of the most recent of 118 books listed.

151. See Thomas G. Devine, *Teaching Study Skills: A Guide for Teachers* (Boston: Allyn and Bacon, 1981); one of the most recent of 251 books listed.

152. See David D. Dill and Associates, eds., *What Teachers Need to Know: The Knowledge, Skills, and Values Essential to Good Teaching* (San Francisco: Jossey-Bass, 1990); most recent of 280 books listed.

153. See Robin Spizman, *Bulletin Boards* (Carthage, IL: Good Apple, 1984); one of the most recent of 9 books listed.

154. See Gary A. Woditsch, *The Thoughtful Teacher's Guide to Thinking Skills* (Hillsdale, NJ: Erlbaum Associates, 1991); most recent of 36 books listed. Also see the CD-ROM from Heartsoft, Inc., "Thinkology, The Guided Tour: A Software Resource for Teaching Critical Thinking Skills," (Broken Arrow, OK: Heartsoft, 1997).

155. See Steven J. Bennett, *Playing Hardball with Soft Skills: How to Prosper with Non- Technical Skills in a High-Tech World* (New York: Bantam Books, 1986); one of the most recent of 18 books listed.

156. See Carol Mullins, *Life Skills Reading* (New York: Educational Design, Inc., 1987); one of the most recent of 76 books listed.

157. See Jerry D. Reynolds, *English Ninety-Three: Lessons in Basic Writing Skills* (River Forest, IL: Laidlow, 1984); one of the most recent of 26 books listed.

158. See Bruce Baker, *Play Skills* (Champaign, IL: Research Press, 1983); one of the most recent of 7 books listed.

159. See Johnny L. Matson, *Enhancing Children's Social Skills: Assessment and Training* (New York: Pergamon Press, 1988); one of the most recent of 133 books listed.

160. See Michael Eisenberg, *Information Problem-Solving: The Big Six Skill Approach to Library and Information Skills Instruction* (Norwood, NJ: Ablex, 1990); more recent of 15 books listed.

161. See Eugene McGregor, *Strategic Management of Human Knowledge, Skills, and Abilities: Workforce Decision-Making in the Post-Industrial Era* (San Francisco: Jossey-Bass, 1991) more recent of 10 listed.

162. Henry Giroux, *Teachers as Intellectuals: Toward a Critical Pedagogy of Learning* (Granby, MA: Bergin & Garvey, 1988), 13-14.

163. William Lind and William Marshner support the idea of a "core curriculum" because it allows schools to "reinforce and inculcate [cultural] virtues such as punctuality, impulse control, respect for legitimate authority, and sound work habits." The idea of "cultural literacy" is promoted by E.D. Hirsch, who seeks a more efficient method of communication among business executives. Culturally literate individuals would, according to Hirsch, have common backgrounds from which to convey ideas and thoughts in economical, effective ways. Along with "basic skills" and "cultural literacy," competencies are advocated by those who claim they have the knowledge base and ability to note what is needed by subordinates in corporations and students in schools. Businesses support this orthodoxy because it maintains the authority of corporate leaders to dictate standards that mainly benefit their situations. See William Lind and William Marshner, *Cultural Conservatism: Toward a New National Agenda* (Lanham, MD: Free Congress Research and Education Foundation, 1987), 48; and E.D. Hirsch, *Cultural Literacy: What Every American Needs to Know* (Boston: Houghton-Mifflin, 1987).

164. Paul Berman et al., *Restructuring California Education: A Design for Public Education in the Twenty-First Century . . . Recommendations of the California Business Roundtable* (Berkeley, CA: Berman, Weller Associates, 1988), 3.

165. Ibid. (Italics added.)

166. Chubb and Moe, op. cit.

CHAPTER 5

Critically Transitive Teachers

"No matter how carefully he deliberates, how artfully he develops alternative modes of instruction, the teacher is forever involved in constituting meanings. This act of forming applies to perspectives on the teaching act, on education viewed as intentional undertaking and as social enterprise. It applies to the perspectives through which persons are seen, knowledge structures apprehended, ethical problems resolved. Also it applies to questions touching on dissent, reform, and the transformation of cultural institutions; it applies to the methods chosen for responding to the inhumanities of the time. The teacher can not assert that the schools should or should not 'dare to change the social order.' He must choose the part he will play in such an effort."[1]

In an age where "world-class standards" are the focus of public schooling, teachers find themselves consistently relegated to positions of intellectual insignificance in favor of competitive corporate goals, content, and markets. In his 1997 "State of the Union" address, Bill Clinton reinforced these themes by asserting, among other things, that "every state should give parents the power to choose the right public school for their children. Their right to choose will foster competition and innovation that can make public schools better."[2] As though trying to stage an Alum Rock revival, the president implied that the "choice" would be between public schools, but he nonetheless reified free-market capitalism and consumer materialism by maintaining the corporate position for competition. Consequently, the president called for the very national standards and national testing that perpetuate the idea that schooling is centrally a preparatory process for information gathering. National standards and national testing are far-removed industrialized (or technologized) engines that drive teacher roles and responsibilities. Note that teachers are not in the driver's seat of such a project. As the AFT advertisement illustrated in chapter 3, businesses are in the driver's seat when it comes to standardization, testing, goals, and as a result, the roles of teachers. Accordingly, teachers and students are *objectified* by such calls and evaluated in terms of GNP, international test comparisons, and workforce readiness. The president's speech illustrated these elements when he pointed to his idea of a twenty-first century "knowledge industry," the Third International Math and Science Study, and his G.I. Bill for American Workers.

Teachers are pawns in such an economistic, quasiscientific game of power and money played by politicians and businesspeople in search of "the" model for ultimate corporate profit. It is a game, in other words, for oligopolies who use quantitative measures not only as evidence of success, but as the means for compartmentalizing (hence accounting) for teaching and learning. By so doing, the oligopoly reinforces the impression that mathematics and science are the best indicators of human interaction and that success is the sum of "proven" methods and/or "met" standards. Teachers are faced, again (perpetually?), with external mandates regarding how they should teach, what they should teach, and which tests are "acceptable" measures to "account" for their teaching and the "success" of student learning.

It should be noted from the outset of this chapter that there are teachers who consider such cook-book teaching acceptable. There are also those teachers who embrace the corporate/oligopoly logic and see schools as places for preparing students for future jobs. There are still other teachers who, for a variety of reasons (heard it all before, near retirement, hoping for tenure, etc.) find an alternative vision is one that is best left for people other than themselves to consider and debate. The intention of this chapter, nonetheless, is to build an argument on the previous chapters that reveals to as many teachers and supporters of teachers as possible the intransitive or semitransitive positions they appear to maintain. The general thrust is to suggest multiple, varying, and "in-need-of-contextualization" aspects of critically transitive teacher roles. Pluralist democracy requires these conditions if it is ever to overtake the current oligopoly and come into being.

To the point, then; teachers must become transformative educators asserting that which is, at root, the case. Teachers and students are interested and interesting people who inquire into areas *not* easily quantifiable, accountable, or generalizable. They do so in diverse settings that hold the possibility of democratic engagement and they are best able to achieve critical transitivity by critiquing consumer materialism, capitalism, and private corporate involvement—not embracing and perpetuating it.

What is missing from most conversations about schooling, particularly those that begin with assumptions about the twenty-first century and the transcendent virtue that science, business, and technology have in it, are teacher positions that are critically transitive. Teacher positions exist, to be sure, but they are rarely critically transitive. There are teachers who parrot preparatory language and teachers who truly believe their role is to transmit essential raw data into passive receptacles (students) in order to stay "time on task" and in order to show numerical increases on standardized test measures. These characteristics are, note astute teachers, "real-world" expectations and their positions reflect "reality." The truthfulness of such a claim is not in dispute here; the issue is whether the truth of testing expectations, textbook reliance, state and national curriculum requirements, etcetera, should and can be changed.

This chapter asserts that the realities that face teachers should and can be changed, but that such change will only come about when teachers are the primary, collective agents responsible for educational initiatives—not businesspeople and legislators. The claim is that more and more teachers must assume roles that are concerned less about acquiescence to oligopoly control, standardization, consumer materialism, training-oriented schooling and nonpropositional knowledge and concerned more with initiating democratic citizenship, critical transitivity, education-oriented schooling, and multiple ways of knowing. It is on these grounds (among others) that external expectations from ill-informed or selectively informed legislators and businesspeople will be challenged and critiqued. Challenge and critique, after all, are hallmarks of a free(er?) society. Challenge and critique, however (recall the "responsible consumer thesis" from chapter 3) are precisely what businesses loathe because they confront the deeply entrenched expectation that schools are the perfect places to foster consumer materialism and future corporate profit. Challenge and critique are also inimical to legislators whose campaigns are financed and/or whose pockets are filled by the very corporations that market "school reform." To transform the roles of teachers and the aims of schooling (and student roles) consumer materialism must become the target of schooling, not the goal of it. This does not come about by increasing external demands like national testing and national standards. Indeed, as has been illustrated, national testing and national standards are the very formats for the replication, expansion, and perpetuation of economistic, consumer-materialist expectations.

A central focus for teachers must be in developing an expanded world view in which schooling is seen as a pluralistic form of democracy. Such an alternative approach, according to this new breed of teacher, would see the development of knowledge and social practices that encourage students to think and act critically—staving off the worst features of training-oriented, capitalist schooling. Accordingly, teachers and students redefine their roles as *autonomous* ones, which, in part, confront social problems in order to transform political and economic inequalities.[3] This point is, perhaps, much more problematic than it appears.

AUTONOMY OR AUTOMATON?

Studying and understanding the role of teachers in American schools reveals that *autonomy* is an artificial construct when given as an indicator of the degree of power teachers have over their efforts to do what it is they do.[4] Yet, in the process of mulling over the arguments in favor of autonomy, it is a struggle to defend the aura of the idea. The problem is two-fold and paradoxical: (1) on one hand, autonomy, as an idea, tends toward the type of rugged individualism that sanctions separated and isolated efforts (something that teachers not only should not, but, in truth, cannot accomplish as schooling is a social activity[5]); and (2) on the other hand, the converse of autonomy (acquiescence, consumer-materialist status-quo reproduction, hierarchical corporate power structures, business-influenced curricular/academic confinements), is so entrenched in school practice that it is politic to argue *for* the anti-Deweyan position of rugged individualism if only to swing the pendulum of thinking from the current reality of anti-autonomy to a different point on the continuum—one closer to what is ultimately proposed—collective autonomy.

What further complicates the dilemma is that autonomy is intimately linked with the notion of freedom and freedom finds its definition in the negative. In *Autonomy and Schooling*, Eamonn Callan puts it this way:

> The most straightforward use of the word "free" occurs when we speak of a subject which might have a certain property or exist in a certain relation, but does not. This use normally carries the suggestion that it is far more desirable that the subject does not have the property or exist in the relation than that it does. For example, we speak of skies free from clouds, streets free from litter, and so on.[6]

For teachers to be autonomous, then, they must define their identity in the negative: teachers free from Dow, Hershey, and Nike curricula,[7] free from Channel One commercial programming, free from corporate-style management objectives and goals lists, free from technorational "modeling" procedures, free from behavioral and statistical accountability schemes, free from ITBSs, CATs, SATs, APs, and free from consumer-materialist expectations regarding job preparation and service-oriented vocationalism. Such a "free-from" characterization may be laudable, but there is something about working in the negative that makes the task of gaining autonomy such a daunting one that its possibility is diminished at the outset, as teachers see that more work—above and beyond the mounds and mounds of work they already face—is necessary to achieve a state of being that may, itself, require even more work to sustain. Said differently, the reality in current schools is already given. In a study of teachers, Cheryl Sattler found that the everyday lives of teachers are layered with external power and authority that constrain their ability to fulfill many of the requirements for teaching that are currently critiqued, both in the popular press and in scholarly literature on education (e.g., disciplinary actions and testing). External power and authority is directed through both structure and social organization in schools. Regarding her interviews with these teachers, Sattler wrote:

> One teacher, Betty, remarked during an interview that "we probably don't supervise anybody but children's lives as closely as we do teachers'. I mean even construction workers get time off for lunch and—they've got a union that says you probably don't have to work on your lunch hour, but teachers do." This results in . . . one of the contradictory positions that teachers occupy; while they are expected to maintain control over their classes, they have little control over their own working environments.[8]

Dee Ann Spencer, author of *Contemporary Women Teachers*, adds that:

> Classrooms are social settings in which teachers hold the most powerful positions. Teachers are expected to gain and maintain control over students, and students are expected to comply with rules and obey their teachers. . . . However, within the context of the school or school system as an organization, teachers take a subordinate role to administrators. . . . Although administrators expect teachers to keep their classes under control, teachers are often treated in infantile ways. Principals can assign teachers to such duties as monitoring restrooms or detention rooms, can enter and observe classrooms without notifying the teachers, and can schedule meetings without consulting teachers.[9]

Spencer's argument illustrates the hierarchy of school organizations, but a necessary consideration for understanding this hierarchy more completely is gender. Women predominate in the classroom, but men hold the majority of administrative and supervisory positions in schools.[10] Men also hold the majority of school-board seats, superintendencies, and legislative posts.[11]

Michael Apple and others argue that this results in the proletarianization of, or control over, teachers' lives and their work environments and is partially a result of the gender stratification of the teaching profession. Apple argues that "it is nearly impossible to understand why curricula and teaching are controlled the way they are unless we understand *who* is doing the teaching [and who is controlling it]."[12]

What is given, then (behavioral objectives, management techniques, curriculum outcomes, discipline programs, testing deadlines and expected levels of achievement, etc.), are the hurdles to overcome, or at least the tensions to balance. If overcome, in Callan's sense of "negative" overcoming, the consequence is an unknown that, because it is unknown is so daunting that it is easier to acquiesce to what *is*, rather than move toward uncharted ground.[13] All of this is not to induce descending minor third exhalation, but to acknowledge that *what is* and *what was* powerfully constrains *what could be*. Teachers are positioned at the center of this nexus of power and, as such, are severely constrained in an educational system that has been shown to be inflexible and repressive of transformative ideas.[14] This is especially true given the manifestation of corporate ideology in the power hierarchy of the school, the curriculum, and the general aims of schooling.

The point, then, is to focus on what is philosophically normative in terms of teaching, autonomy/power, democracy, the general aims of schooling, and the roles colleges of education might play in fostering the critical abilities of teachers. Autonomy is seen in terms of the tension between the definitional extremes of rugged individualism and social interactionism. Consequently, teachers must struggle as a group for contextualized representations of power in order to develop (not perpetuate) democratic citizenship via themselves and their students: individuality, yes; individualism, no. Put another way, critical transitivity and *collective* autonomy are necessary conditions for democratic schooling, but critical transitivity and collective autonomy are not understood, either in popular culture or in teacher-education programs, as vital components of the role of American teachers.

CRITICAL TRANSITIVITY AND COLLECTIVE AUTONOMY

Recall, again, how Freire outlines transitivity in three phases: intransitivity (which repudiates the power of individuals to change their existences—"I can't speak out about teaching-to-the-test because I might lose my job . . . that's the 'real world' and I can't do anything about it."); semitransitivity (individuals see the world as changeable, but see the world in unrelated segments such that semitransitivity is two dimensional and short term—groups feed the hungry without asking why hungry people exist in a society with yearly food surpluses); and critical transitivity (demonstrated when individuals make, according to Shor, "broad connections between individual experience and social issues. . . . In education, critically [transitive] teachers and students synthesize personal and social meanings with a specific theme, text, or issue."[15]).

Critical transitivity is both the product and the process of individual philosophical, conceptual, historical, and sociological analysis. Like democracy, critical transitivity is a struggle between the dual nature of power and with the material conditions of teachers' lives.[16] The degree to which one scrutinizes the world via ontological, epistemological, and axiological lenses is the degree to which one demonstrates critical transitivity. Stanley Aronowitz has characterized the point this way:

> The issue is the capacity for theoretical or conceptual thought itself. When people lack such competence, social action that transcends the struggle for justice within the empirically given rules of social organization and discourse is impossible. . . . Since critical thinking is the fundamental precondition for an autonomous and self-motivated citizenry, its decline would threaten the future of democratic, social, cultural and political forms.[17]

If teachers are to be *collectively* autonomous, therefore, they not only have the responsibility, but the obligation to make sense of enigmatic and multifarious ideologies. The converse of anti-intellectual, critical transitivity requires a form of literacy that is a "cultural action for freedom . . . a process through which [people] who had previously been submerged in reality begin to emerge in order to re-insert themselves with critical awareness."[18] For teachers this means linking their classroom experiences with conceptual problems in such a way as to "shake up" the perceived, the "given."

Reinserting critical awareness means taking personal experiences for what they are (valuable, important, but not generalizable to all classrooms and all teachers) and, through the type of critical discourse to which Aronowitz alludes, making connections with not only theory and practice, but with other teachers as well. This last qualifier is the primary one supporting collective autonomy and keeping *laissez faire* individualism in check, because it requires a throwing off of the yoke of rank libertarianism in favor of social empathy. The converse would be the type of separatist, isolationist perspective represented by Kirkpatrick, Ebeling, and Hornberger (see chapter 4) that "makes it possible to replace social compassion with an insistence on each person's capacity and responsibility (and freedom) to 'make it' on his or her own."[19] Links between teachers are, in fact, an artifact of political (in addition to critical) transitivity, as Casey revealed in her 1993 work.[20] Similarly, Kreisberg makes the point that enhancing power also requires this link, and cannot be found in or by acting alone.[21] Enter democracy and coalitions for democratic pluralism.

DEMOCRACY IS A RADICAL IDEA

Democracy is used so frequently in popular discourse that it suffers from overgeneralization. That is, democracy comes to mean either *only* one person, one vote, or, as Eli Zaretksy notes, a kind of "direct democracy" that "allows people to bypass the representative aspect of democracy entirely" (best illustrated by the phenomena of talk shows).[22] "In recent times," notes George Wood, democracy "has been stripped of its participatory basis, as voting and representation come to replace the active involvement of citizens in making public policy and community decisions."[23] Wood goes on:

> The consequences of this weak, shadowy notion of democracy are all too obvious: voter turnout continues to decline; political debate over difficult issues is reduced to shouting matches; and an individualistic notion of freedom dominates political debate, leading to more and more programs to privatize life rather than to facilitate community values. . . . In private life, similar signs of decay are apparent. From Wall Street lawyers and brokers to school officials, the search for private advancement replaces any sense of public service.[24]

As described by Zaretsky, Alexis de Toqueville saw democracy as a symptom of human narcissism.

> If we read de Toqueville, we will understand one of the recurring conundrums in much . . . thinking today: the link between political democracy and market capitalism. Both satisfy the narcissistic needs of modern men and women. It is not greed that led people to welcome the market system . . . ; nor was it rationalization, the desire for control, as Max Weber believed. It was narcissism: the desire to see themselves, their products, their achievements, in the world outside the self. The same impulse led them to prefer to keep their politicians ordinary, their political sentiments lofty and vacuous, and their statues of politicians short and unimposing.[25]

Yet even as interesting as the claim of narcissism is, it presupposes that democracy already exists (for whatever reasons). Democracy is a radical idea that, as yet, has not come into being. Like teachers as critically transitive agents for change, democracy is still made problematic by the oligopoly all too present in the United States.

Democracy, after all, has been defined as government by discussion,[26] a process to protect the masses,[27] and the collective pursuit of common goals.[28] Who is in the discussion, which process actually protects whom, and which goals are pursued as "common" are the concerns. In terms of schooling, teachers are not in important discussions, tracking secures protection for *a* mass instead of *the* masses, and the common goals are all too easily found in states' objectives lists and Goals 2000 reports. Corporations are perpetually included in discussions concerning education and are very present in goals lists and preparatory mission statements. It is not democracy, however.

Democracy requires, as Dewey argued, a specific mode of associated living. It requires freeing individual potential in the context of social interaction—individu*ality* not individual*ism*. Individual*ism* is separated, disconnected, and egotistical while individu*ality* is linked to the purposes of the larger society while still distinguishable and unique among a crowd. "Freedom for Dewey," notes Tony Johnson, "meant releasing and fulfilling the unique potentialities that each individual possesses. As social beings, this potential is best released or more fully achieved through interaction with others, and the quality of that interaction is dependent upon the quality of the communities individuals inhabit."[29] The quality of the interaction is what is in question. Because most communities are, most of the time, consumer materialist in orientation, freedom is contingent on corporate expectations for the standard of living (status-quo expectations). Teachers and students are not only not immune to the effects of this influence, their role identities perpetuate it.

In fact, given that individuals inhabit inescapable capitalist communities, Dewey's position is best updated, modified, and furthered by using the experience of capitalism as the object lesson for democracy. Put in terms of the school sphere, Joe Kincheloe reveals the un-democratic nature of schooling this way:

> It is interesting that administration is taught only to people who serve at the head of the administrative structure and not to people who are to be administered. Ideas about democratic forms of management are not concepts that are typically discussed between principals and teachers or teachers and students. Without the awareness produced by such

discussion, the social ambience of the school remains within an authoritarian [and oligopolistic] frame. The ideological web formed by this authoritarianism produces a curriculum that teaches teachers and students how to think and act in the world. Both teachers and students are taught to conform, to adjust to the inequality and their particular rung of the status ladder, and to submit to authority. Teachers and students are induced to develop an authority dependence, a view of citizenship that is passive, a view of learning that means listening.[30]

Since it is true that individuals cannot escape the social milieu that surrounds them and since, accordingly, the social milieu surrounding Americans is consumer materialism, the best hope for democracy comes when the oligopoly (and the authority configurations that support it) becomes the object of reform. Standing in the way of such reform, however, are the deeply ingrained assumptions regarding schooling that perpetuate the oligopoly and frustrate democracy. Preparation for future life is but one example of this frustration that directly impacts schooling and the roles of teachers and students.

THE MYTHICAL PROPORTION OF PREPARATION FOR FUTURE LIFE

The accepted aim of contemporary American schooling (that students are to be prepared for future work) assumes that means and ends are separate. Goals are established, standards are noted, and objectives are written in order that procedures and techniques will be crafted to see to it that the ends will result. Goals 2000, Quality Core Curriculum (QCC), Standards of Learning Objectives, etcetera, all indicate establishing the ends first. The "strategies" for "successfully" or "effectively" completing the goals follow. Such an approach assumes that preparation for future life is not only possible to an extensive degree, but is plausible in terms of classroom instruction.

By separating the means from the ends, teaching necessarily relies on Cartesian logic and linear-sequential reasoning. This is more than a problem, it is the bastardization of growth, experience, and childhood. Dewey puts it this way:

> The traditional scheme is, in essence, one of imposition from above and outside. It imposes adult standards, subject-matter, and methods upon those who are only growing slowly toward maturity. The gap is so great that the required subject-matter, the methods of learning and behaving are foreign to the existing capacities of the young. They are beyond the reach of the experience the young learners already possess. *Consequently, they*

must be imposed; even though good teachers will use devices of art to cover up the imposition so as to relieve it of obviously brutal features.[31]

The underlying point is what it means to grow and how schooling must recognize the natural capacities of students. "Our net conclusion," Dewey notes, "is that life is development, and that developing, growing, is life. Translated into its educational equivalents, that means (*i*) that the educational process has no end beyond itself; it is its own end; and that (*ii*) the educational process is one of continual reorganizing, reconstructing, transforming."[32]

To better understand how these ideas relate to current schooling practice, and to contrast traditional (current) educational aims and methods with those that indicate transformation and self-actualization on the part of students and teachers, consider the following story originally told by Richard Nelson, and paraphrased here.

> Johnny and Susie are in the fourth grade. On their way to school one morning they come across the broken shells of robins' eggs. Inquisitive, they each take a piece of a shell and hurry to school to show their respective teachers. Johnny approaches his teacher, Ms. Jones, and eagerly shows her his exciting find. She tells him that it is very interesting and commands the attention of the rest of the members of the class. When all are quiet, Ms. Jones tells the students that Johnny has found a robins' egg shell and will walk around the room so that everyone can see it. She further instructs that there will be no talking and no touching of the eggshell. Johnny is told to walk around the room with the shell in the palm of his hand for everyone to see. As he does so, Ms. Jones instructs the class to get out their workbooks, turn to page 12, and begin working on the new section. Susie takes her eggshell to Ms. Morgan. When approached by Susie, Ms. Morgan calls the students to gather around the front desk to view the egg shell. One student inquires into why the shell is blue. Another questions what actually comes from the eggshell. These questions are followed by others and lead to a project dealing with birds. Included in this project are topics ranging from habitat to identification of types of birds to studying the physical makeup of birds to drawing birds to making plastic models of birds. Ms. Morgan and the students spent three days on this idea.[33]

According to current educational policies, mandates, and techniques, Ms. Jones would be considered an "excellent" or "effective" or "master" teacher. She acknowledged the interest of the students while exercising proper classroom management "skills" and keeping the class "on task." On the other hand, Ms. Morgan, while acknowledging the students' interests, let her classroom-management "skills" suffer by allowing students to leave their seats during class. Furthermore, by exploring the idea of birds with her class, she is now three days behind the other class with respect to standardized objectives.

One question raised by this contrast concerns the intellectual role of the teacher. Is Ms. Morgan allowed to allow? That is, does Ms. Morgan have the intellectual freedom (and wherewithal[34]) to guide the interests of students, or does she have a specific task-oriented, corporate-influenced, externally prescribed (legislative?) agenda that directs and constrains her role? Note that the question is not whether Ms. Morgan had "CHOICERCISE" choices or choices from among a preapproved list of "choices." The question is whether Ms. Morgan has the intellectual freedom (and wherewithal) to guide emergent, student-interest-focused learning and knowing. The ultimate question raised by this predicament, of course, is, "What should the aims of schooling be?"

Lather, Giroux, Dewey, Wood, McLaren, Lankshear, Senese, Fraser, Johnson, Greene, Carlson, Kincheloe, McNeil, among others, hold that schools should be viewed as democratic public spheres.[35] Schools, accordingly, are public places where students learn and know what it means to live in a democracy as opposed to an oligopoly. Learning and knowing are understood here as means/ends in the Deweyan sense. That is, means and ends are the same thing. When separated, as with modernist, Cartesian reasoning, they are removed from experience and fail more times than not in achieving knowledge.[36] This should *not* be interpreted to mean, however, that there exists a pre- ordained, completed list of skills and objectives that, upon successful observation, signifies basic competence. Giroux notes:

> Instead of defining schools as extensions of the workplace or as front-line institutions in the battle of international markets and foreign competition, schools as democratic public spheres are constructed around forms of critical inquiry that dignify meaningful dialogue and human agency.[37]

Ms. Morgan allowed critical questions raised by inquisitive students to contribute to the intellectual life of the classroom. Criticality and personal interpretations were fostered in an interactive environment. It should be understood that Ms. Morgan likely prepared a lesson plan for the day. Further, the lesson fit nicely with the standardized learning objectives for her local and state school systems. Yet, the important issue is not that she had a lesson plan, but whether she assumed a critically transitive role by setting aside the lesson plan in favor of guiding and directing student's interests such that multiple ways of knowing emerged. In traditional discourse, the question is whether Ms. Morgan was allowed by her administrator to assume a different posture. Such an expectation, to be clear, misses the point as it reinforces the power and control *over* teachers. Allowing someone to allow in this context means having more control and power—the antithesis of the overall point.

Interestingly, it is Ms. Jones who represents the rewarded educator in current society. Her name would be published as an "effective" teacher and she would be the one to rise to the top of career ladders. This is a major part of the problem. Teaching is so greatly influenced by corporate "models" of "effective" information transmission that Ms. Jones gets the kudos. Disney crystal apple awards, presidential recognition for having the highest student test scores on the Third International Math and Science Study,[38] and Shell Oil Teaching Awards[39] reinforce the expectation that teachers (72 percent of whom are women[40]) act and perform in certain ways. It calls to mind, of course, John Locke's *tabula rasa*, in which students have a blank tablet for a mind and teachers are to write "necessary," "basic" information on the slate. (And in the modern age, that information is sanctioned by corporations rather than teachers and students.) It also calls to mind B.F. Skinner's "learning machines," computers, and chickens at county fairs that "play" piano. It further calls to mind Paulo Freire's criticism of education as "banking." He laments that traditional expectations for teachers deal with depositing data into a vault others call the mind. This allows the teacher to withdraw the same information when he or she deems it appropriate.[41] Usually, the power of the teacher and school administration is enforced and pointed to as "effective" when the tool of testing is utilized in this manipulative manner. Indeed, what better way to "prove" students learned? The effectiveness and efficiency with which standardized and fill-in-the-blank tests are administered and graded serves to categorize and stratify students very effectively.[42]

What makes Ms. Morgan different is that she allowed and encouraged the instigation of primary questions without the threat of testing or pressure. That is, she did not ask students to raise their hands with answers as to why the shell was blue or list the qualities of a robin's egg within a specified time frame so as to practice for upcoming ITBSs or CATs. The students discovered for themselves and instigated teacher guidance. Ms. Morgan acted to transform the potentiality into reality through intellectual leadership. The proposal, then, takes on a wider scope. Why has current society "bought into" the emphasis on SAT scores, ITBS scores, CAT scores, international comparisons, grade point averages, corporate-modeled hierarchies, classroom management "skills," and business-promoted "basics"? Consider, briefly, four reasons: (1) the quest for certainty; (2) sequential reasoning; (3) learning as knowing; and (4) preparation for future life.

For (1), there exists in American society a nagging desire for certitude. As though there are structural plateaus of attainment, we fixate on "completed" tasks, rarely recognizing that "completion" is at best temporal. That is, as soon as one task is "completed," there will always be something else (often related) to consider or labor over. Home maintenance illustrates the point. As soon as the carpet is vacuumed, there is dusting, then straightening, cluttering, and cleaning again. Schooling is no different. There will always be new problems to consider and new connections to make. Ultimate knowledge exists at the end of infinite inquiry, goes the paradox.

Still, society attributes to ITBS scores the kind of certitude that results in claims such as "students aren't learning what they need to know." The link to (2), above, is between the expectation of certainty (a diploma equals x) and how society ensures that certainty: break learning into its most basic, componential parts and structure separated information in the form of a linear equation. The alphabet is before words, words before sentences, sentences before paragraphs. Students *can* learn this way, but many students *do not* learn this way. Still, because society is in search of scientistic "models" (certainty) for learning, most students, most of the time, in most schools, are subjected to such routine.

Additionally, when this linear, sequential process is finished, learning is claimed to have occurred *and* is equated with knowledge. This is (3) from above. A student can claim to have learned, for example, a Shakespeare soliloquy or Kwaanza precepts. She recites, "I do much wonder that one man, seeing how much another man is a fool when he dedicates his behaviors to love, will, after he hath laughed at such shallow folly in others, become the argument of his own scorn by falling in love . . . " She has learned. But she does not *know* until she explains the sentiment, interprets the terminology, and makes meaning of the passage. Other recitations can be inserted here, as can memorization of multiplication tables. They are techniques of instruction that overwhelm multiple ways of knowing. They are used, so often, as pieces of the preparation puzzle most schools currently represent. This is (4), above, and is the hallmark of America's expectation for its schools. It is because preparation for future life is so deeply ingrained as the purpose of schooling, that the other three concerns have such wide appeal and are demonstrated as much as they are.

This is what Dewey meant when, as noted earlier, he claimed that there was no end beyond itself. When he notes that schooling is its own end, he means to debunk the myth that schools are places where students learn the necessary "skills" to compete in a future world. If they are to *know* anything, students must connect the experiences they already have with new (not always intentional or contrived) experiences—in the present, not some distant future—in order to make meaning, develop implications, and solve problems. The meaning, however, is not certain, contrary to the hopes noted before. Contexts change, students change, and "skills" even change. Instead of dealing with the *present*, however, scientistic prediction is relied on (because of the quest for certainty?) as the rationale for static, unchanging basics, that, to be learned for such a purpose (predictive control?) are also best dominated by linear, sequential procedures.

The link to business and corporate interests should be painfully apparent. If marketing agents can predict student test-score increases because of the "application" of *x*, *y*, or *z* computer program or prepackaged curriculum, international ranking "problems" will be solved. Eager to exploit the educational market, companies develop videocassette packages with "teacher guides" that purport to satisfy the quest for certainty. "Brighter Futures Through Partnerships," for example, is one such package produced by Hughes Electronics. It claims that "schools working to improve their science, math, and technology programs would do well to enlist the help of technology businesses. These firms have the expertise and the facilities that schools need and they have a stake in the math-science education of the future."[43] Not only does this reinforce the problem of school-business partnerships illustrated in chapter 3, it reveals two underlying assumptions: (1) math, science, and technology are the panacea of the future; and (2) businesses see schools as experimental markets for industry-influenced expectations. Ultimately, this results in authority expectations for teachers that both reinforce (for teachers) and are reinforcing of (for students and teachers) acquiescence to consumer materialism.

Indeed, consumer materialists have seized the initiative and argue that a loss of authority and a loss of accountability are the causes of current crises in public education. The call for a reconstituted authority along corporate-conservative lines is coupled with the charge that the crisis in schooling is in part due to a crisis in the wider culture, which is presented as a "spiritual-moral" crisis.[44] Diane Ravitch argues the traditionalist point when she contends the "loss of authority" stems from confused ideas, irresolute standards, and cultural relativism.[45] Bill Clinton argues for order, discipline, curfews, and tougher truancy laws.[46] Elbert Hoppenstedt argues for more classroom management, external control, and accountability.[47] He is not alone. Bunzel, Doyle, and Finn also argue for the kind of standardization that results in control and accountability. [48]

Hoppenstedt, for example, typifies and perpetuates the concern about accountability when he suggests:

> No builder would, under any conditions, attempt to build a house unless he first had access to a set of blueprints supplied to him by an architect. So too, no teacher can possibly hope to successfully complete a year's unit of subject matter without a "blueprint" to guide him.[49]

The language represented here suggests that teachers are (and should be) compliant with *a priori* content. Moreover, the hierarchy implicit in the metaphor (the architect has done the thinking, the builder now executes the instructions) indicates more closely the hue that colors the current role of teachers. "Blueprints" not only provide steps to follow, they also serve as an accountability mechanism. For teachers this not only means that the "blueprint" is required to execute lessons, it also provides a clear measure of accountability should there be deviation from the plan.

Finn represents the accountability position, too, when he suggests higher standardized test scores will indicate school success. Arguing for "outcomes-based" accountability, Finn finds the key to unlocking the mystery of who is doing their work as a teacher and who is not. For Finn, standardized test-score comparisons are the means to justify the end.[50] Comparing such measures, in or out of context, means that those teachers who do not meet statistical norms are identified as doing something incorrectly. Because the purpose of the comparison is to hierarchically rank schools, teachers within those schools must, so the logic goes, account for "deficiencies." Similar notions of accountancy exist within voucher plans, such as those advocated by Chubb and Moe, when free market economics and competitive marketing campaigns decide the continuation or the extermination of any given public school.[51] The argument suggests that those schools that are accountable will be the ones to succeed and profit. Implicit here is a form of social Darwinism and crass capitalism where the "fittest" schools survive, but where "fit" is a construct defined by the very positivist logic that espouses such competitiveness in the first place.

In contrast, Giroux confronts the consumer-materialist view by arguing the following:

> As a form of legitimation, this view of authority appeals to an established cultural tradition, whose practices and values appear beyond criticism. Authority, in this case, represents an idealized version of the American

Dream reminiscent of the nineteenth-century dominant culture in which "the tradition" becomes synonymous with hard work, industrial discipline, and cheerful obedience. It is a short leap between this view of the past and the new conservative [consumer materialist] vision of schools as crucibles in which to forge industrial soldiers fueled by the imperatives of excellence, competition, and down-home character.[52]

Callahan is similarly concerned about what he calls the "cult of efficiency" wherein reading, writing, and comprehending are reduced to component parts.[53] By reducing schooling in this way, hegemony is able to take root because the component "skills" are unconsciously replicated and reinforced as "givens" such that accounting for them becomes the "obvious" focus of teaching. Kincheloe puts it this way:

The taken-for-granted, the common sense nature of the dominant cultural fictions of modernism constitute the essence of their power. The most powerful fictions are not only unquestioned but unarticulated. How often, for example, do school leaders or teachers even speak of the possibility that school teaches anything other than positive academic skills? One can go through an entire career as an educator including pre-service and in-service education and a graduate degree and never even hear an allusion to such a possibility. This is how hegemony operates. A student in a modernist school, for example, most likely will never be exposed to an idea that challenges the conception that achievement is a result of ability plus effort.[54]

Giroux also describes

the technocratic interests that embody the notion of teachers as clerks is part of a long tradition of management models of pedagogy and administration that have dominated American public education. More recent expressions of this logic include a variety of accountability models, management objectives, teacher-proof curriculum materials, and state-mandated certification requirements.[55]

Importantly, R.W. Connell reminds us, again, of the dimension of gender in the overall critique by suggesting that languages of technique and accountancy rationales are closely linked to paternalistic hierarchical schemes.[56] Since schools are largely staffed by women, inherent contradictions of power and privilege are revealed. McNeil found, in her study of four high schools, that teachers actually "reinforced [institutional] goals of order with the justification that doing so was the only way they could protect themselves from . . . institutional pressures."[57]

One can therefore argue in favor of or in opposition to accountability and control, since both exist.[58] Understanding *only* that both realities currently exist would be intransitivity, just as McNeil's findings suggest. Understanding that both realities symbolize and define the role of contemporary teachers would come closer to semitransitivity if those who understand the situation desire to change it. The point, however, is to achieve critical transitivity. The difference between semitransitivity and critical transitivity, recall, is that semitransitive teachers might be interested in defining teacher roles differently, but may go about it via hegemonic means (e.g., arguing for control over the teaching "profession" by [re-] establishing professional regulations). On the other hand, critically transitive teachers would distinguish between the current reality and, instead of replacing an old model with a new one, would engage (individually and collectively) in Freire's notion of conscientization.[59] By conscientization, Freire means "the deepening of the attitude of awareness characteristic of all emergence."[60]

TO QUESTION OR NOT TO QUESTION

At what point do individuals consider it appropriate to question the corporate influence over public schooling? Do we ask questions of teachers, principals, school boards, and politicians about corporate influence? Or is it more likely we ask questions of those same figures regarding how we should *increase* their "practical," vocational applicability?

The idea of education-oriented schooling as an ongoing and never-ending process aimed toward critical transitivity and democratic responsibility does not permeate current American society. Instead, schools are seen by businesses, business advocates, and consumer materialists as the place for children to "get" an education (training) in order to "get" a job allowing businesses to compete and profit in international markets. Further, businesses use schools as captive markets where they can test new merchandise, advance their public relations and appear philanthropic by "donating" materials and funds to schools, and where they influence what goes on in terms of the aims and purpose of "getting" a diploma. Parents perpetuate the general aim by expecting increased scores and the kind of "concrete" results that numeracy and statistics supply, regardless of their relation (or nonrelation) to pedagogy. Teachers, as a result, are forced to garner answers by requiring students to raise their hands *to* questions instead of allowing and encouraging students to raise their hands *with* questions. All too often educators bemoan lack of student interest in classrooms. The belief is that in those very classrooms, the discipline and management techniques are so rigid and finely tuned that students have no idea that they should be asking, probing, and initiating. After all, their role has been to receive information (not knowledge) from the teacher. When the majority of teachers finally complete their lectures, do they really expect students to ask questions? To the student, the teacher "covered" all possible questions.[61] There is no "choice" to seek more.

Indeed, it must be made clear that a call for education-oriented schooling, multiple ways of knowing, and critical transitivity should not be associated, to any degree of seriousness, with superfluous references to student choice in current classrooms. In present classrooms, students many times "choose" between booklets from Time, Inc., or the advertisement-riddled Channel One programming station. To paraphrase Jonathan Kozol, current schooling may answer the charge of promoting antidemocratic values by pointing to the aforementioned "choices," as well as to their learning centers, baby rabbits, and three-thousand-dollar vouchers. This is offered as evidence of freedom. But is it? Kozol refutes the claim:

> They have the right to choose without constraint among a thousand paths of impotence, but none of power, the right to demonstrate their sense of ethical surrender in ten different innovative "resource areas" and at twelve separate levels of proficiency. Like first class passengers on board a jet flight to a distant city, they have their choice of any drink or food or magazine or padded seat they prefer; but they are all going to the same place, they are all going there at the same rate of speed, and the place that they are going is a place neither they, nor you, nor I, but someone else they do not know has chosen for them. They have no choice about the final destination. They have no choice about the flight, the price, the pilot or the plane; but they can stretch their legs, and walk along the aisle, and select their magazine, and they can call this freedom.[62]

The desire is to fashion a view of teaching and learning that legitimates schools as democratic, public spheres and teachers as critically transitive intellectuals who work toward social justice, multiple forms of knowing, and a critical consideration of the merits and demerits of capitalism. The need is to broaden the definition of teachers, authority, and ethics to include and legitimate educational practices linking democracy, intellectualism, teaching, and practical learning. Giroux contends the substantive nature of this task takes as its starting point the ethical intent of initiating students into a discourse and pedagogical process that advances the role of democracy within the school while addressing those instances of suffering and inequality that structure the daily lives of people in the United States and the world.[63]

Calling for increased "professionalism" as some have done (e.g., the NEA and the AFT) only distinguishes teachers as accountants in their classrooms. Critically transitive teachers go beyond roll calls, bathroom monitoring, and cafeteria patrolling. They also go beyond the acceptance of Madeline Hunter techniques, Lee Cantor–prescribed discipline programs, and business-aligned national goals—all of which have become characteristics of "professionalism" in traditional schools. Instead, critically transitive educators distinguish themselves by linking a critical understanding of business influence with the actions they take in their school bureaucracies and in the questions they pose to and with their students.

The argument for critically transitive teachers is aided by Stengel's notion of pedagogical knowing. She claims that educators have a distinct knowledge base that requires a unique epistemology. They must develop "knowledge-for-teaching." "It is a truism," Stengel writes, "that one learns a subject by teaching it. Teaching 'deepens' one's knowledge, we say; we understand more thoroughly. I would take the (radical) step further to say that knowledge-for-teaching is actually taken on initially in the practice of teaching."[64] It appears that her claims represent a paradox, not unlike Meno's:[65] if the teacher is to teach x, she must already know x, not come to know it in the process of teaching. Stengel counters:

> In fact, this puzzle rests on a false assumption. It cannot be stated definitively that the teacher must know x if he or she hopes to bring another to know x. The x in question is the product of negotiation, of the relationship between a particular teacher and particular student(s) in a particular context. It is surely true that the teacher must know a great deal about a great many things before forming the intention to teach anything. It may even be true that the teacher must have the loosely formed intention to have students come to know what (and how) [they] know. But the focused formulation of teaching x to y seems more a fiction constructed of teacher as technician and behavioral objectives run amok than an accurate description of what actually happens in any case of teaching. The x actually taught and learned is rarely the x expressed in the lesson plan objective. While some may bemoan that as an indicator of ineffective teaching, I argue that it is the inevitable consequence of a process that involves human negotiation.[66]

Stengel's notion of pedagogical knowing, therefore—along with Giroux's notion of the teacher as transformative intellectual, Shor's explication of critical consciousness, Ellsworth's questions for teacher interpretation, Kincheloe's arguments for a critical politics of teacher thinking, and McLaren's and Dewey's notions of democratic involvement of teachers in public schools—clarify and support the larger point.[67] To be clear, Dewey's differentiation between individu*alism* (separated, disconnected, egotistical) and individu*ality* (linked to the purposes of the larger society, while still distinguishable and unique among a crowd) justifies teacher coalitions as autonomous within and as a part of the larger democratic society within which teachers are situated. To achieve such an understanding and to make such links is to demonstrate the type of critical transitivity Freire and Shor advocate.

GETTING OVER THE HURDLE: FROM SEMI-TRANSITIVITY TO CRITICAL TRANSITIVITY

The pessimist may claim that American teachers, because they are marginalized from substantive decision making and are perpetually subjected to corporate goals expectations, to testing, and measurement, and to nondemocratic representation, are still at the intransitive stage. If so, teachers see no possibility to change their existence or the aims of public schooling, much less their role as a teacher. But there are increasing numbers of educators who are becoming aware of the detrimental effects of intransitivity. They yearn for change, and therefore find themselves in a semitransitive state. Recall that semitransitivity is characterized by people (teachers, more specifically, in this case) seeing the world as changeable. The flaw, according to Freire and Shor, is that semitransitive teachers see that same changeable world in unrelated segments. What is proposed as a means to get over the hurdle from semitransitivity to critical transitivity are teacher coalitions that seek role identity transformation. Just as semitransitiveness does not go far enough to effect substantive change, so, too, are teacher coalitions themselves impeded if they do not link the coalitions with role identity transformation.

The Foundations School and its teachers illustrate the point. The Foundations School is the first public school in Chicago devised and operated by teachers.[68] Frustrated by positivist mandates, de- skilling expectations, and patronizing hierarchies, the school is comprised of a group of teachers who reject textbook authority and traditional behavior-management techniques. According to Carl Lawson, the principal of Price School (the school that actually houses the Foundations School), the teachers in the Foundations School are like early dissenters of the Protestant Reformation "boldly disputing the authority of the established church."[69] Sutton narrates:

The more one thinks about the history and philosophy of the Foundations School, the more apt Lawson's analogy seems. Unabashed iconoclasts, the Foundations teachers seem to take an almost impish glee in ruffling the feathers of the educational establishment. "We left a trail," Foundations teacher Doris Clark says of their reform efforts at Alexander Dumas School, [the school] where almost all of them worked. "It pissed off [Dumas teachers and administrators] when we made it work. And they didn't like the fact that we weren't docile and didn't allow the children to be docile either." Another teacher, Danielle Norman, says she and her reform-minded colleagues endured heavy-handed intimidation tactics from the more traditional teachers. "If I was out of the building during the day for any reason, this one teacher would have the janitor open my room to [students] roaming the halls. You can imagine what happened; I was vandalized three times. We were a huge threat, empowering ourselves and others."[70]

The Foundations teachers demonstrate critical transitivity by understanding, as Shor notes, that "society is a human creation, which we can know and transform, not a mysterious whirl of events beyond understanding or intervention."[71] Within the Foundations School students study topics that are linked to context, by students and with teachers, as a means *not* to amass or cover material, but to connect content with context and active inquiry with student/teacher/society interests. In this way, Dewey's notion of individualism is not reified. That is, Foundations School teachers are not interested in breaking away from larger society in an attempt to achieve rugged individualism. Instead, they exhibit Dewey's distinction between individual*ism* and individu*ality* when they link both personal and social experiences together with their own intellectual interests.

Furthermore, as McLaren notes, "this critical approach to teaching is based on a social imagination rooted in history and intent on a resurrection of the 'dangerous memory' and 'subjugated knowledges' of oppressed groups such as women and minorities. The task of such an imagination is to build a world in which power relations are contested actively and suffering is finally overcome."[72] With these qualifiers, the faculty is self-governed and democratically oriented. Teachers control policy and set the stage for student involvement in their classes and broader society.

Two points of clarification: (1) the Foundations School is not being highlighted here as any kind of "model." Indeed, if such an idea were offered, it would more closely represent intransitive thought ("It's already been done, so just give over the materials used in that school so it can be replicated.") and/or semitransitive thought ("It's a good idea. Never mind that it happened in Chicago and we're in Atlanta, why don't we try that, too?"); and (2) what actually goes on in the school is significant, but it is of less importance to the present topic because the focus is that teachers formed critical intellectual coalitions to reform the (conveniently intransitive) status quo.

Another example includes, interestingly enough, Milwaukee's Fratney School. Recall from chapter 4 that Milwaukee has been in the midst of "choice" reform supported by a unique coalition of urban poor and wealthy business advocates. The calls have been for "accountable" schools that produce higher test scores and productive workers. The Fratney School is unique.

In 1988, the school was to be closed down and then reopened as a teaching center for less-than-stellar teachers. Students at Fratney were intended to be used as test cases for struggling teachers. But teachers and parents at Fratney had another idea. They wanted "a decent school that children want to attend, based on an integrated neighborhood, teaching children to be bilingual in Spanish and English, using cooperative and innovative methods, governed by a council of parents and teachers."[73]

A team of five teachers put together a curriculum that did *not* include textbooks, but relied on the multiple and varying experiences of both teachers and students. Typical school subjects such as mathematics, social studies, and art were integrated into six themes developed from the diversity of the neighborhood in which Fratney operates: Roots in School and Community; The Native American Experience; The African-American Experience; The Hispanic Experience; The Asian-American/Pacific-American Experience; and We Are a Multicultural Nation.[74] Wood narrates what the themes mean in classroom practice:

> For example, during the African-American theme, Rita Tenorio's students listen to her read *Follow the Drinking Gourd*, a story of slaves escaping to freedom via the Underground Railroad. Finishing the story, Rita pulls out large sheets of newsprint on which she has pasted pictures from the story. Each student takes a turn naming something in the picture, in either Spanish or English, and the words become the class vocabulary list for this theme. During the Hispanic-American theme Becky Trayser's fifth graders have a wide range of choices they can make to explore this element of the curriculum. Activities include an interview with a community member about his or her life in the United States, an art project involving native Spanish style, a mapping exercise, a retelling of a historical event from a Hispanic perspective, or researching a current affairs issue of concern to the Hispanic population. In virtually every classroom the curriculum weaves back and forth through the thematic approach taken by the school.[75]

Note that it is a thematic *approach* that ebbs and flows. It is not rigid, conformist, nor reliant on "proven" (i.e., held to be universally virtuous) "models." It is critically transitive insofar as it demonstrates the connection between personal interests and social concerns. Given that the context of the school is cooperative instead of competitive, personal interests represent Dewey's individu*ality* (not individu*alism*). Further, given the intention of the school to understand numerous perspectives, it represents multiple ways of knowing (both nonpropositionally, propositionally, and other) and is not saddled by corporate-generated textbooks that sterilize history, reduce critique, and (as was illustrated in chapter 1) promote free-market capitalism as the primary object of knowledge.

Central Park East Secondary School in East Harlem, New York, is another example (*not* "model"). Critically transitive teachers connect experiments on nutrition with science, history, and the culture of the students who attend the school. The thrust represents, at the same time, education-oriented schooling (i.e., not limited to "how-to" vocationalism) and multiple ways of knowing (e.g., testing hypotheses, ethnographically understanding generational eating habits, historically narrating conditions that influence nutrition). Nutrition, in other words, is more than a topic to "cover." It is an opportunity for critically transitive teachers and students to link the various connections to academic disciplines with their experiences and interests. Knowing happens more often than simply learning.

There are other examples, as well. The Foxfire program out of Rabun Gap, Georgia, is one.[76] Thayer Junior/Senior High School in Winchester, New Hampshire, is another.[77] Other examples also exist, so the point is that possibility—a necessary condition for critical transitivity—exists. It is not easy to be critically transitive, however, given society's overwhelming (albeit false) assumption that test scores measure what students know and that higher test scores indicate teacher "success." Such an assumption leads to the kinds of consumer-materialist restrictions on teachers and students that the Foundations School, the Fratney School, Central Park East Secondary School, and others, are overcoming. Wood puts it this way:

> Each of these . . . schools is at risk from the reform movement [currently underway]. What the educators in these schools accomplish with the young people in their care goes on unnoticed and often in spite of the reformers who occupy statehouses and sit on blue-ribbon committees. Each of these teachers and administrators has dozens of stories to tell about how state mandates, testing programs, and local bureaucracies work to thwart what they are doing.[78]

State mandates, testing programs, and local bureaucracy are inextricably linked to positivism and consumer materialism. Mandates come from legislatures, testing programs are their litmus tests (the representation of science here should not go unnoticed), and the school bureaucracies in question are, according to Spring, directly traceable to corporate hierarchies.[79]

One way to combat such intimidation is, again, to build teacher coalitions that demonstrate collective autonomy and reveal the inadequacy of science (social or other) as the primary means of evaluating schooling. It is proposed that teacher education programs (not teacher training programs) and colleges of education could help teachers become critically transitive. To do so, colleges of education must be places where teacher roles are questioned, critiqued, and revolutionized.

SUGGESTIONS/IMPLICATIONS: CAN COLLEGES OF EDUCATION HELP?

Changing the roles of teachers requires not only critical transitivity, but a collective autonomy that can best result from teachers-as-intellectuals building teacher-to-teacher coalitions. The contention is that current teacher roles are defined by corporate goals, business attitudes, and Cartesian linearity. Accordingly, each of these rationales privilege businesses, corporations, and consumer materialism; not students, teachers, and critical transitivity. The immediate result is the perpetuation of the teacher's role as semi- or low-skilled clerical worker. Consequently, notions of teachers as critical intellectuals ring strangely in the ears not only of the general population, but are equally strange to practicing and future teachers. One suggestion is that colleges of education offer a viable starting point for practical and substantial reformation of the roles of teachers.

To foster role (re?)-construction and identification, coalition building, and critical transitivity, colleges of education must reform their current function and offer themselves as sites for social transformation. Specifically, colleges of education should limit the extent to which they emphasize minimum certification prescriptions and a discourse of practicality and, instead, broaden the opportunities for students to engage in critical investigations. Such a position denies "privileging practicality as the foundation on which teacher education programs are authorized."[80]

An easier position to take would be to advocate *adding* the aforementioned opportunities for criticality onto what currently exists. This would, however, represent acquiescence to intransitivity. Such a capitulation validates surfaceable ontologies (the way "things" are and have always been) and market demands (levels for certification and certain advanced degrees). Greene suggests that "no longer is there talk of what is not yet, of imagined possibility. Along with this comes a sense of petrification. Publics are asked to accommodate to an objectified 'reality,' marked off and demarcated in cost-benefit terms. It is reified, 'given'; we are all being required to sublimate our private visions and confine ourselves to what Wallace Stevens called 'the plain sense of things.'"[81]

Colleges of education could begin reformation by focusing on furnishing their students with an environment for critical coalition building rather than focusing on providing technorational seminars to meet certification expectations. Even in those instances where methods courses are "useful," the nature of the course must include itself as a part of the inquiry. Investigating the meanings behind behavior management, grading, social conditions of silence, and what McLaren notes as "discursive practices"[82] is vital for teacher role-identity transformation. Since the extent to which intransitivity exists is great, the challenge and task to otherwise complacent cogs (teachers) and machines (colleges of education dedicated as training sites) is equally great. By suggesting teacher coalitions, it is posited that greater advances can be realized as coalitions help take the stigma off of individualization concerns.

Indeed, as with the Foundations School noted earlier, teachers can collectively effect more change than is otherwise typical for singular insurrectionists. The urgency of the call should not be taken lightly. On the cusp of national curriculum and national standards, teachers continue to find themselves in their typical place as receivers of external expectations. What is proposed here, instead, are means for teachers to question histories (the history of teaching/teachers, the history of individual teachers as case studies, the history of the school and its role in society) and assumptions (socializing norms, "basics," etc.) within a site that supports debate, struggle, and critical questioning.[83] Colleges of education are already perched to be such sites. To take flight, they must encourage courses for teacher coalitions and solicit (and support) faculty willing to openly and boldly advocate critical transitivity.

The real point, then, is the problem of praxis; that is, integrating the articulated notion of critical transitivity with the roles of teachers in American schools. To integrate critical transitivity and teachers' roles, the axiological claim is made in favor of critical scholarship, and is the result of a comparative construction set against intransitivity. There is an explicit value claim championing the ethos of criticality. Fine as far as it goes, the problem within and surrounding such a proposal is the possibility of institutionalizing the critical perspective itself such that a critically conscious position becomes intransitive or semitransitive due to a lack of the very criticality that critical transitivity demands.[84] "Empowerment" is one example. The 1990s bear witness to the latest addition to educationese in the form of "teacher empowerment."[85]

Cited by the ideological left *and* right, what is at root a critically transitive conviction easily regresses to technorational chartings and listings of what "empowered teachers" should do and should look like. Part of the problem here is that teachers themselves seek out such information (such as the promise of empowerment contained in concepts such as site-based management)—and in demanding tones. The result is not, however, critical transitivity. What is represented is at best semitransitivity as teachers grasp "empowerment characteristics" on overheads, but fail to link the theoretical underpinnings of "empowerment characteristics" with their students' lives and interests in the classroom. Represented, too, is the problem of the hidden power structure Mikhail Bakhtin calls "authoritative discourse."[86] It is the perpetual problem teachers and teacher educators demonstrate (and, perhaps, reinforce) when they argue for a different "paradigm" but require it to fit conventional practice—arguing for change agency while reifying traditional expectations. Deborah Britzman interprets "authoritative discourse" as "institutionally sanctioned knowledge that demands allegiance to the status quo and authorizes stereotypes as if they were unencumbered by ideological meanings."[87]

What authoritative discourse ultimately connotes is that colleges of education perpetuate corporate-desired, oligopoly-supported consumer materialism by at least two means. First, colleges of education impose upon teacher certification/re-certification students the same power structures that hegemonically reduce the power of the prospective teachers and current teachers in the first place (e.g., passive roles in lectures, segmented curricula rarely if ever linked across disciplines or degrees, little control over or input in the curricula developed and required, NCATE sloganeering, narrow empiricist appeals to individual experiences—again, without link or interrogation or collective meaning built from it). Fine describes the teachers from her study at Comprehensive High School this way:

> They spoke . . . of faculty collaboration, common planning time, the teaming of educators, the sharing of authority, access to information, and redistribution of resources. They advocated critical faculty voice in systemic policy setting. For some it was a rehearsal of what they did anyway—posing critical commentary, whenever possible, of the school's administration and, to a far lesser degree, of the [United Federation of

Teachers] union. For others, this was a novel chance to imagine and dream.[88]

Second, colleges of education may very well arrive at the first position because they are complying with the expectations of the very people (students) colleges wish to attract (intransitive though they may be). Teacher certification/re-certification students are adept at demanding more "tools and methods" courses, and the power of FTEs is often enough to ensure that these demands are promptly met. Roger Simon claims "it is talk exclusively carried out in the language of technique, and usually its purpose is to [seek] doable suggestions that can be tried out in the classroom the next day."[89] The difficulty is that such students are without a language other than one representative of intransitive consciousness. Recall Giroux's earlier concern:

> Most of our students are very comfortable with defining themselves as technicians and clerks. For them to be all of a sudden exposed to a line of critical thinking that both calls their own experience into question and at the same time raises fundamental questions about what teaching should be and what social purposes it might serve [critical consciousness] is very hard for them. They don't have a frame of reference or a vocabulary with which to articulate the centrality of what they do. They are caught up in market logic and a bureaucratic jargon [intransitivity].[90]

This is seen when teachers demand classes through which they can answer the (far from critical) question, "How do I *get* my money's worth, *get* an 'A,' and *get* merit pay via the college course?" Put another way, those teachers who experience little *authentic autonomy* (versus *perceived autonomy* or semitransitive consciousness)—collective or otherwise—in their careers are the very ones who hegemonically reinforce the very postures and roles they have come to lament.

The college of education then finds itself in a bind. On one hand, it represents the problem (status-quo reinforcement via hegemonic power structures and expectations of hierarchical individualism as noted above); on the other hand, it faces a problem (complying with the expectations of students by supplying more courses steeped in the language of technique as also noted above). The point is this: to split the blame between colleges of education and teachers would be a disservice to both entities. Colleges of education may represent a paradoxically bizarre dual problem, because they also represent hope for successful reform.

Knox and Cornell Colleges illustrate the point. With guidance from Landon Beyer, the colleges restructured teacher education in terms of praxis.

The programs are, according to Beyer, "foundationally oriented." Daniel Liston and Kenneth Zeichner note that, "in addition to the introduction of previously excluded areas of the curriculum such as educational philosophy, history, sociology, and curriculum theory (where previously educational foundations was equivalent to educational psychology), Beyer and his colleagues attempted to reconstruct the rest of the educational studies components of the teacher education program so that they would encourage a particular quality of analysis by students."[91] Beyer puts it this way:

> I propose that we regard as foundational any area or course of study that critically examines the underlying ideas, assumptions, and principles of that area, making them a subject for scrutiny; and that considers how the issues in that area relate to broader normative questions and possibilities. The foundations of education regard the nature of schooling, education and teacher preparation as political, moral, and ideological practice, and make such questions a focus of discussion.[92]

Such a position represents praxis because the theory/practice dualism is merged in field experiences that link foundational understandings and questions to the actual practice of teaching. It is more typical for foundations courses to be separated from practice as they are seen as "too theoretical" to have practical importance. What Beyer demonstrates, however, is that unless the practice is consciously informed by theory, the practice risks the very routinization, passive acceptance, and consumer-materialist tendencies that are the present concerns of this work. "In fact, field experiences were seen as key sites for the realization of the program goals because they provided opportunities for students to link their reflections about issues of schooling and society with actions to study, and in some cases, to transform concrete school practices."[93]

Other illustrations exist. Lewis and Clark College has a Master of Arts in Teaching (MAT) program that infuses questions of gender and equity throughout its component courses. Instead of having only one, optional (or required) course on gender politics or multiculturalism, Lewis and Clark focuses students' attention on how gender relates to curriculum development, leadership, foundations, methods, etcetera.[94] Liston and Zeichner detail other examples, such as the one from Deakin University in Australia.

> Here in 1986, a number of staff associated with the three year B.Ed. Teacher education program developed an alternative version of the biosocial-studies block of the course which emphasized the preparation of

teachers to be inquirers into their own teaching practice. The biosocial-studies component consists of three curriculum courses (in science education, physical education, and social-studies education) and a concurrent practicum. The innovative aspects of the revamped courses consisted of placing students in schools for practicum work in pairs (which was consistent with the view of collaborative inquiry underlying the program) and the organization of the methods courses in a way that emphasized understandings that emerged out of students' experiences in testing out propositions about the teaching of the different subjects.[95]

By focusing on colleges of education the argument here is that the sphere of the college is much more closely poised to effect broader and more relevant change than are the parts of public schools, faculties, or individuals alone from within those faculties. Further, the controlled environment of colleges of education provide an excellent opportunity for supportive and (relatively) safe experimentation. Even with eyes focused on certification concerns and bureaucratic mandates, colleges of education are nonetheless better poised to direct and guide innovative practice than any other current sphere.

Importantly, the suggestion(s) offered here are not prescriptive. There is no model to follow, no list to check off. What exists, however, is an ethos of expectancy—on the part of teachers via colleges of education—to grapple with equally challenging problems and decide, themselves, the specific paths to chart. Doing so will, itself, define the very point of this book.

To conclude this effort, for the time being, recall the major stances taken. This work tried to reveal a different narrative regarding the role of teachers and students, the aims of education, and the inordinate influence private corporations have in public schooling matters. Normative philosophical claims were made regarding the nature of schooling, the conceptual distinctions between training, schooling, and education, and differences between propositional and nonpropositional knowledge. Like arguing (only temporarily) in this chapter *for* the anti-Deweyan position of rugged individualism, the point for arguing in favor of propositional knowledge in public schools is to move the reality from the nonpropositional orientation classes currently have to a different point on the continuum. Ultimately, as this chapter illustrated, multiple ways of knowing is a necessary condition for democratic schooling and should be understood as such by teachers, in coalition with other teachers, in order that they might assert their power and effect the kind of change that puts consumer materialism in check.[96]

Also recall that, throughout this text, the claim was made that America does not yet have a democracy, but an oligopoly. The influence and control of corporations cannot be underestimated and the major thrust of this work was to reveal just how pervasive and unacceptable corporate influence is—particularly in relation to schooling. Where business advocates (supporters of privatization, school-business partners, consumer materialists, etc.) want *more* preparation for students in surrogate business training sites (schools), the counter argument was made that publicly funded schools should not be used to further private-sector gain. Indeed, the primary reason public schools are so focused on economistic goals is the widely held assumption that schooling is preparation for future employment and that the best way to achieve preparation is to break knowledge into nonpropositional bits and pieces called "skills." This point was challenged using Dewey's means/ends argument such that schools were considered places for experiential, democratic learning *now* and by offering a tongue-in-cheek assertion to eliminate "skills" from the English language. The point was to highlight the overly instrumentalist approach to schooling teachers are expected to take. While many teachers willingly take such an approach, the linked point was to suggest that critically transitive teachers might still use "skills," but that critically transitive teaching requires connecting questions such as "Whose skills?" and "For what/whose purposes?" with student experiences and interests. In this way, students and teachers—together—are better poised to critique consumer-materialist aspects of schooling (and themselves) and thereby demonstrate democratic citizenship (not prepare for it).

This effort, then, is mainly meant to represent a vision for teacher and prospective teacher consideration. It is one vision among many, but a vision that is only infrequently included in teacher education (training?) and one rarely, if ever, considered in policymaking that impacts teachers and students.

NOTES

1. Maxine Greene, *Teacher as Stranger: Educational Philosophy for the Modern Age* (Belmont, CA: Wadsworth, 1973), 272-273.

2. William Jefferson Clinton, "State of the Union Address," published on the Internet at http://www.whitehouse.gov/white-house-pu . . . 87-02-04-state-of-the-union-address.text, 6.

3. See Henry Giroux, *Schooling and the Struggle for Public Life* (Minneapolis: University of Minnesota Press, 1988), Introduction. Also see Harold Rugg, "The School Curriculum and the Drama of American Life," in *Curriculum Making: Past*

and Present, 22nd Yearbook, ed. Harold Rugg (Chicago: National Society for the Study of Education, 1927).

4. See Joseph Newman, *America's Teachers* (New York: Longman, 1994). The term "profession" is not used here for, as Newman demonstrates in his text, the three qualifiers of a profession (1. it performs a unique, essential service; 2. has a defined, respected knowledge base; and 3. has autonomy [p.102]) currently escape contemporary teachers.

5. Teachers, once behind closed doors, may demonstrate one version of autonomy (or resistance), but this chapter is interested in the larger and broader conceptualizations of autonomy and any implications that come about.

6. Eamonn Callan, *Autonomy and Schooling* (Montreal: McGill-Queen's University Press, 1988), 9.

7. See Deborah Stead, "Corporations, Classrooms, and Commercialism," *New York Times Education Supplement*, section 4A (5 January 1997): 30*ff.*

8. Cheryl Sattler, *Talking about a Revolution: The Politics and Practice of Feminist Teaching* (Hampton, VA: Hampton Press, 1995).

9. Dee Ann Spencer, *Contemporary Women Teachers: Balancing School and Home* (New York: Longman, 1986), 6.

10. On the paradoxical place of teachers in schools, see also John Dewey, *Education Today* (New York: The Macmillan Company, 1940); Seth Kreisberg, *Transforming Power: Domination, Empowerment, and Education* (New York: SUNY Press, 1992); Theodore Sizer, *Horace's Compromise: The Dilemma of the American High School* (Boston: Houghton Mifflin, 1984); and the Carnegie Task Force on Teaching as a Profession.

11. Newman, op. cit, 253*ff.*

12. Michael W. Apple, "National Reports and the Construction of Inequality," *British Journal of Sociology of Education* 7, no. 2 (1986): 171-190.

13. Ibid., 8-24.

14. See Michael W. Apple, *Official Knowledge: Democratic Education in a Conservative Age* (New York: Routledge, 1993); and Kathleen Casey, *I Answer with My Life: Life Histories of Women Teachers Working for Social Change* (New York: Routledge, 1993).

15. Ira Shor, *Empowering Education: Critical Teaching for Social Change* (Chicago: University of Chicago, 1992), 127-28.

16. Cheryl L. Sattler, "Review of Seth Kreisberg, *Transforming Power: Domination, Empowerment, and Education*, (New York: SUNY Press, 1992)," *Educational Studies* 25, no. 4 (Winter 1994): 301-305.

17. Stanley Aronowitz, "Mass Culture and the Eclipse of Reason: The Implications for Pedagogy," *College English* (April 1977), 768.

18. Paulo Freire, *Cultural Action for Freedom* (Baltimore: Penguin, 1975), 29-30.

19. Maxine Greene, *The Dialectic of Freedom* (New York: Teachers College Press, 1988), 26.

20. Casey, op. cit.

21. See Seth Kreisberg, *Transforming Power: Domination, Empowerment, and Education* (Albany: SUNY Press, 1992).

22. Eli Zaretsky, "Identity and Democracy: A Critical Perspective," in *Radical Democracy: Identity, Citizenship, and the State*, David Trend, ed. (New York: Routledge, 1995), 143.

23. George H. Wood, *Schools That Work: America's Most Innovative Public Education Programs* (New York: Plume, 1993), 79.

24. Ibid.

25. Zaretsky, 143.

26. Lord Lindsay, in *Democracy in a World of Tensions*, Richard McKeon, ed. (Chicago: University of Chicago Press, 1951), 174.

27. See Carole Pateman, *Participation and Democratic Theory* (Cambridge: Cambridge University Press, 1970), 18-20.

28. Charles E. Lindblom, *Politics and Markets: The World's Political-Economic Systems* (New York: Basic Books, Inc., 1977).

29. Tony Johnson, *Discipleship or Pilgrimage? The Educator's Quest for Philosophy* (Albany: SUNY Press, 1995), 106-107.

30. Kincheloe, *Toward a Critical Politics of Teacher Thinking: Mapping the Postmodern* (Westport, CT: Bergin & Garvey, 1993), 219.

31. John Dewey, *Experience and Education* (New York: Collier Books, 1938 [1963]), 19. (Italics added.)

32. John Dewey, *Democracy and Education* (New York: The Free Press, 1916 [1944]), 49-50.

33. Adapted from Richard Nelson, "Of Robins' Eggs, Teachers, and Education Reform," *Phi Delta Kappan* (May, 1989), 632-638.

34. This point is directly linked to teachers' schooling and is addressed in the section of this chapter on the role of colleges of education.

35. See, for example, Patti Lather, "Research as Praxis," *Harvard Educational Review* 56, no. 3 (August 1986): 257-277; Henry A. Giroux, *Border Crossings: Cultural Workers and the Politics of Education* (New York: Routledge, 1992); John Dewey, *Experience and Education* (New York: Collier Books, 1938 [1963]); George H. Wood, op. cit., Peter McLaren and Colin Lankshear, eds., *Politics of Liberation: Paths from Freire* (New York: Routledge, 1994); Guy Senese, *Simulation, Spectacle, and the Ironies of Education Reform* (Westport, CT: Bergin & Garvey, 1995); Nancy Fraser, "Equality, Difference, and Radical Democracy: The United States Feminist Debates Revisited," in *Radical Democracy: Identity, Citizenship, and the State*, David Trend, ed. (New York: Routledge, 1996); Tony W. Johnson, *Discipleship or Pilgrimage? The Educator's Quest for Philosophy* (Albany, SUNY, 1995); Maxine Greene, *The Public School and the Private Vision* (New York: Random House, 1965); Maxine Greene, *Landscapes of Learning* (New York: Teachers College Press, 1978); Dennis Carlson, *Teachers and Crisis: Urban School Reform and Teachers' Work Culture* (New York: Routledge, 1992); Henry A. Giroux and Peter McLaren, "Teacher Education and the Politics of Engagement: The Case for Democratic Schooling," *Harvard Educational Review* 56, no. 3

(August 1986): 213-238; Joe L. Kincheloe, *Toward a Critical Politics of Teacher Thinking: Mapping the Postmodern* (Westport, CT: Bergin & Garvey, 1993); and Linda M. McNeil, *Contradictions of Control: School Structure and School Knowledge* (New York: Routledge, 1988).

36. Dewey, *Democracy and Education*, 50*ff.*

37. Henry A. Giroux, *Teachers as Intellectuals: Toward a Critical Pedagogy of Learning* (Westport, CT: Bergin & Garvey, 1988), xxxii.

38. Clinton, op. cit. The teacher, Sue Winski, and her two "top" students, Kristin Tanner and Chris Getsla, were invited to sit with Hillary Clinton during the "State of the Union Address." The current critique does not, to be clear, cast aspersions on either Winski, Tanner, or Getsla. The critique is about what is held in highest regard in a consumerist society "consumed" by the desire to "beat" the world on standardized tests.

39. See, for example, Marilyn DeWall, "Shell Oil Co. Presents $10,000 National Teaching Award to Los Angeles-Area Science Teacher," *Business Wire* (3 March 1992): 1*ff.*

40. See National Education Association, *Status of the American Public School Teacher, 1996- 1997* (Washington, DC: NEA, 1997).

See Paulo Freire, *Pedagogy of the Oppressed* (New York: Seabury Press, 1973).

See Joel Spring, *The Sorting Machine Revisited: National Education Policy Since 1945* (New York: Longman, 1989), 177-185.

43. See the Annenberg/CPB Math and Science Collection resource catalog titled "Building Better Math and Science," 32.

See Giroux, *Schooling and the Struggle for Public Life*.

See, for example, Diane Ravitch and Chester Finn, Jr., "High Expectations and Disciplined Effort," in *Against Mediocrity*, Robert Fancher and Diane Ravitch, eds. (New York: Holmes and Meier, 1984); Thomas Sowell, *Education: Assumptions vs. History* (Stanford: Hoover Press, 1986); and Allan Bloom, *The Closing of the American Mind* (New York: Simon and Schuster, 1987).

46. Clinton, op. cit. Consider the idea that dropout rates and truancy figures indicate the primary problem is the corporate-structured school, not the students.

47. Elbert Hoppenstedt, *A Teacher's Guide to Classroom Management* (Springfield, IL: Charles G. Thomas, 1991).

48. See, for example, John H. Bunzel, ed., *Challenge to American Schools: The Case for Standards and Values* (New York: Oxford University Press, 1985); Dennis Doyle, "Education, Excellence, and the Free Market," in *Education and the American Dream*, Harvey Holtz, et al., eds. (Granby, MA: Bergin & Garvey, 1989), 114-123; and Chester E. Finn, Jr., "The Challenge of Educational Excellence," in *Challenge to the Humanities* (New York: Holmes & Meier, 1985).

49. Hoppenstedt, 48.

50. Chester E. Finn, Jr., *We Must Take Charge: Our Schools and Our Future* (New York: Free Press, 1991).

51. See, for example, John E. Chubb and Terry M. Moe, "America's Public Schools: Choice *Is* a Panacea," *The Brookings Review* (Summer 1991).

52. Giroux, *Schooling and the Struggle for Public Life*, 70.

53. Raymond Callahan, *Education and the Cult of Efficiency* (Chicago: University of Chicago Press, 1962).

54. Kincheloe, *Critical Politics of Teacher Thinking*, 64.

55. Giroux, *Teachers as Intellectuals*, 91.

56. R. W. Connell, "Disruptions: Improper Masculinities and Schooling," in *Beyond Silenced Voices: Class, Race, and Gender in United States Schools*, Lois Weis and Michelle Fine, eds. (Albany: SUNY, 1993), 191-208.

57. McNeil, op. cit.

58. The sample within the text is clearly small. Recall that the purpose of the chapter is not to rehash what is perceived by the author as generally understood truths. Those wishing further sources could read William Bennett, *What Works: Research about Teaching and Learning* (Washington, DC: U.S. Department of Education, 1987) and Jon Moline, "Teachers and Professionalism," in *Against Mediocrity: The Humanities in America's High Schools*, Chester E. Finn, Jr., Diane Ravitch, and Robert T. Fancher, eds. (New York: Holmes & Meier, 1984). Opposing positions can be found in Roger I. Simon, Don Dippo, and Arleen Schenke, *Learning Work* (New York: Bergin & Garvey Press, 1991); Thomas Popkewitz, "Culture, Pedagogy, and Power: Issues in the Production of Values and Colonization," *Journal of Education* 170, no. 2 (1988); and Henry A. Giroux, *Ideology and the Process of Schooling* (Philadelphia: Temple University Press, 1981).

59. See Paulo Freire, *Pedagogy of the Oppressed* (New York: Continuum, 1970 [1990]), 61.

60. Ibid., 101.

61. See Walter Feinberg and Jonas Soltis, *School and Society* (New York: Teachers College Press, 1985), 36-45.

62. Jonathan Kozol, *The Night Is Dark and I Am Far from Home: A Political Indictment of the U.S. Public Schools* (New York: The Continuum Publishing Corp., 1975 [1986]), 100.

63. See Giroux, *Schooling and the Struggle for Public Life.*

64. Barbara Senkowski Stengel, "Pedagogical Knowing: Reconstructing Teachers' Special Knowledge," paper presented at the American Educational Studies Association, Montreal, Quebec, Canada, November 1996, 8.

65. See Plato, *Meno*, in *The Dialogues of Plato, Vol. I*, R.E. Allen, ed. and trans. (New Haven: Yale University Press, 1984), 133-186.

66. Ibid., 8-9.

67. See, also, Barbara Senkowski Stengel, "Moral Knowledge: Moving (Us) to Right Action/Relation in Teaching and Learning," *Philosophical Studies in Education* (1995): 1-28; Henry Giroux, *Teachers as Intellectuals*, op. cit.; Shor, *Empowering Education*, op. cit.; Elizabeth Ellsworth, "Representation, Self-Representation, and the Meanings of Difference: Questions for Educators," in *Inside Out: Contemporary Critical Perspectives in Education*, Rebecca A.

Martusewicz and William M. Reynolds, eds. (New York: St. Martin's Press, 1994); Joe L. Kincheloe, *Toward a Critical Politics of Teacher Thinking: Mapping the Postmodern* op. cit.; Peter McLaren, *Life in Schools*, op. cit.; and John Dewey, *Democracy and Education*, op. cit.

68. See David Sutton, "Woman on a Mission," *Teacher Magazine* IV, 9 (August 1993): 26-31.

69. Ibid., 27.

70. Ibid.

71. Shor, 128.

72. Peter McLaren, *Life in Schools*, 232.

73. George H. Wood, *Schools That Work*, 19.

74. Ibid., 20-21.

75. Ibid., 21.

76. See Eliot Wigginton, *Sometimes a Shining Moment* (New York: Doubleday, 1985); and J. Puckett, *Foxfire Reconsidered* (Champaign, IL: University of Illinois Press, 1989).

77. See Susan Kammeraad-Campbell, *Doc: The Story of Dennis Littky and His Fight for a Better School* (Chicago: Contemporary Books, 1989).

78. Wood, 32.

79. Joel Spring, *Educating the Worker-Citizen* (New York: Longman, 1980).

80. Richard Smith and Anna Zantiotis, "Practical Teacher Education and the Avant-Garde," in *Critical Pedagogy, the State and Cultural Struggle*, Henry A. Giroux and Peter McLaren, eds. (Albany: SUNY Press, 1989), 111.

81. Maxine Greene, "The Art of Being Present: Educating for Aesthetic Encounters," in *What Schools Can Do: Critical Pedagogy and Practice*, Kathleen Weiler and Candace Mitchell, eds. (Albany: SUNY Press, 1992), 203.

82. McLaren, *Life in Schools*, 188. Here McLaren defines "discursive practices" as follows: "the rules by which discourses are formed, rules that govern what can be said and what must remain unsaid, and who can speak with authority and who must listen."

83. See, for example, Giroux, *Teachers as Intellectuals*, 34-42. While Giroux is speaking within the context of secondary social studies, his larger point is easily extrapolated to the present topic.

84. Similarly, arguments for autonomy must be couched in light of the differend. To argue, for instance, that teachers should be autonomous figures, could result in a fragmented relativism (at least theoretically) that denies the social reality of schooling. At the same time, the value of arguing in favor of a specialized version of autonomy (collective autonomy) is in the possibilities it offers, particularly as it is compared to current conditions in American schools.

85. See Michelle Fine, *Framing Dropouts: Notes on the Politics of an Urban Public High School* (Albany, NY: SUNY Press, 1991), 158-159.

86. See Mikhail Bakhtin, *The Dialogic Imagination*, Emerson and Holquist, trans. (Austin, TX: University of Texas Press, 1986).

87. Deborah P. Britzman, "Decentering Discourses in Teacher Education," in *What Schools* Can *Do: Critical Pedagogy and Practice*, Kathleen Weiler and Candace Mitchell, eds. (Albany: SUNY Press, 1992), 152.

88. Fine, 149-50.

89. Roger I. Simon, "Empowerment as a Pedagogy of Possibility," in *Education and the American Dream: Conservatives, Liberals, and Radicals Debate the Future of Schooling*, Harvey Holtz et al., eds. (Granby, MA: Bergin & Garvey, 1989), 135.

90. Henry Giroux, *Border Crossings*, 16.

91. Daniel P. Liston and Kenneth M. Zeichner, *Teacher Education and the Social Conditions of Schooling* (New York: Routledge, 1991), 156-157.

92. Landon Beyer, *Knowing and Acting: Inquiry, Ideology, and Educational Studies* (London: Falmer Press, 1988), 186-187.

93. Liston and Zeichner, 157. See also, Landon Beyer, "Field Experience, Ideology, and the Development of Critical Reflectivity," *Journal of Teacher Education* 35, no. 3 (1984): 36-41.

94. See M.K. Tetreault and J. Braunger, "Improving Mentor Teacher Seminars: Feminist Theory and Practice at Lewis and Clark College," in *Building Bridges for Educational Reform: New Approaches to Teacher Education*, Joseph DeVitis and P. Sola, eds. (Ames, IA: Iowa State University Press, 1989), 63-86.

95. Liston and Zeichner, 161.

96. See Loraine Code, *Epistemic Responsibility* (Hanover, NH: University Press of New England, 1987).

INDEX